Civil Rights Movement

Civil Rights Movement

Jamie J. Wilson

Landmarks of the American Mosaic

AN IMPRINT OF ABC-CLIO, LLC
Santa Barbara, California • Denver, Colorado • Oxford, England

Library of Congress Cataloging-in-Publication Data

Wilson, Jamie Jaywann.
   Civil rights movement / Jamie J. Wilson.
      p. cm.— (Landmarks of the American mosaic)
   Includes bibliographical references and index.
      ISBN 978-1-4408-0426-7 (hardcopy : alk. paper) — ISBN 978-1-4408-0427-4 (ebook)   1. African Americans—Civil rights—History.   2. Civil rights movements—United States—History.   3. United States—Race relations.   I. Title.
   E185.61.W744   2012
   323.1196'073—dc23   2012038013

ISBN: 978-1-4408-0426-7
EISBN: 978-1-4408-0427-4

17   16   15   14   13   1   2   3   4   5

This book is also available on the World Wide Web as an eBook.
Visit www.abc-clio.com for details.

Greenwood
An Imprint of ABC-CLIO, LLC

ABC-CLIO, LLC
130 Cremona Drive, P.O. Box 1911
Santa Barbara, California 93116-1911

This book is printed on acid-free paper ∞

Manufactured in the United States of America

Contents

Series Foreword

THE LANDMARKS OF THE AMERICAN MOSAIC series comprises individual volumes devoted to exploring an event or development central to this country's multicultural heritage. The topics illuminate the struggles and triumphs of American Indians, African Americans, Latinos, and Asian Americans, from European contact through the turbulent last half of the 20th century. The series covers landmark court cases, laws, government programs, civil rights infringements, riots, battles, movements, and more. Written by historians especially for high school students, undergraduates, and general readers, these content-rich references satisfy thorough research needs and provide a deeper understanding of material that students might only be exposed to in a short section of a textbook or a superficial explanation online.

Each book on a particular topic is a one-stop reference source. The series format includes

- Introduction
- Chronology
- Narrative chapters that trace the evolution of the event or topic chronologically
- Biographical profiles of key figures
- Selection of crucial primary documents
- Glossary
- Bibliography
- Index

This landmark series promotes respect for cultural diversity and supports the social studies curriculum by helping students understand multicultural American history.

Introduction

THE CIVIL RIGHTS MOVEMENT is a reference work for students. As one reads, they will note that the Civil Rights Movement includes more than Rosa Parks' refusal to relinquish her seat on a segregated bus. It is also more than Martin Luther King Jr.'s "I Have a Dream" speech. These two events are iconic indeed, and most students know about them even without knowing Parks' contexts or the texts of King's speech. But if we want to understand the extent of the movement, it is necessary to include a discussion of Parks' determination and King's charisma without deifying them and ignoring other important aspects of the struggle for black equality.

What lies ahead in this book is a bird's eye and telescopic view of the black freedom struggle. It is a bird's eye view in that it provides a breadth of discussion and survey of important campaigns and highlights significant contributions by activists. It is telescopic in that it provides a narrative depth that moves beyond the surface discussion and encyclopedic trivia. It is impossible to detail every event that occurred in what historians have often called the second Reconstruction, but this book attempts to provide the reader with a narrative as comprehensive as possible and a point of departure that includes some of the major campaigns waged by African Americans for full citizenship, justice, and equality. In its totality the Civil Rights Movement was the political and social reaction to years of white supremacy in the United States. Interlocking and overlapping attempts to physically, emotionally, spiritually, politically, and economically dominate black people began when the first Africans were traded in the Chesapeake region for goods and supplies from a Dutch Man-of-War in 1619. Though it included white allies, it was a decentralized, mass political movement comprised primarily of African Americans who sought to undermine and overturn the humiliating and oppressive system of segregation, often called Jim Crow, throughout the United States. Efforts were sometimes centralized in one location, but overall the movement included local, state, and nationwide organizations and individuals who at times worked in tandem and at other times in isolation.

As the astute reader will notice, several chapters are titled after an African American gospel or freedom song. I include them for two reasons. The first is to honor the African American musical tradition, which has been, when all else has failed, a salve for those individuals who struggled to maintain their humanity in a society which sought to strip them of it. They are also included to remind the reader that the Civil Rights Movement is both a political movement and a religious movement, as it was based in the church and led largely by clergymen. To invoke black sacred and secular music is to invoke the religious and political heritage of a people who sought to create a little bit of heaven on earth for themselves and their offspring.

Chapter one, "I've been 'buked and I've been scorned," examines the rise of segregation policies and society throughout the South. The enthusiasm and seemingly unlimited opportunities that marked the Reconstruction era were reversed when Reconstruction ended in 1877. Slowly, law by law, in place after place, African American political life entered into what many have called the nadir, or lowest ebb. The chapter notes that customs and laws demanding the separation of whites and blacks in all aspects of life have their roots in the closing decades of the 19th century, and demonstrate that during this era, African Americans were economically, politically, residentially, and educationally circumscribed. "I want to be ready to put on my long white robe," Chapter two, examines the ways African Americans challenged segregation in the 1930s and the 1940s, the decades preceding the zenith of the Civil Rights Movement. The chapter argues that though they may not have been able to dismantle segregation policies and recreate southern society, African Americans joined and created political organizations, challenged federal policies, reversed state laws, and strategized for change. They worked within the political and social limitations of the time. Though they may have imagined a world wherein every individual was protected by basic constitutional rights, the ruling elite did not allow their hegemony to be toppled. In the end, the social and political milieu was not ready and did not allow for fundamental change in the opportunities and life chances of black Americans.

"We Shall Overcome" and "Ain't Gonna Let Nobody Turn Me 'Round," Chapter three and Chapter four, respectively, discuss the major campaigns in Alabama and Mississippi. The Montgomery Bus Boycott in 1955 may not be the start of African Americans' struggle for justice and equality, but it is one of the most important political contestations of the 1950s. The boycott is considered in chapter three, along with other major campaigns in Alabama, including the Birmingham campaign, the march from Selma to Montgomery, and black experimentation with third party politics, with the creation of the Lowndes County Freedom Organization. The state of Mississippi was considered by many to be a closed society and impervious to outside change and influence. Local and state officials were not as open to change as their counterparts in Alabama. Their reluctance, however, did not discourage black activism. Chapter four looks at some of the not-so-successful attempts at creating equality in the state. In so doing, it discusses how local activists, students, and the Student Nonviolent Coordinating Committee worked for civil rights. The highlight of the Mississippi movement was the Freedom Summer of 1964, when white and black college-age activists descended upon Mississippi to work in voter registration drives and create Freedom Schools. In both states, nonviolent direct action, negotiations between black and white elites, and litigation forced the Kennedy and Johnson administrations to side with the black activists.

Chapter five, " 'A Right Denied': Court Decisions' Impacts on the Civil Rights of African Americans" is written by Staci M. Rubin, a public interest attorney and scholar. It uses a legal history approach to discuss the impact of litigation's role in the Civil Rights Movement, how legal challenges brought by African Americans to the courts led to the creation of important civil rights legislation, as well as the implications of these decisions for African Americans. Cases including, but not limited to, *Shelley v. Kramer* (1948), *Sweatt v. Painter* (1950), *Brown v. Board of Education* (1954), and *Boynton v. Virginia* (1960) are discussed.

"We Shall Not be Moved," chapter six, argues that the oppression of African Americans was not limited to the Deep South. Consequently, African American political activity was not limited to this area. If one were driving up and down the eastern seaboard states throughout the 1950s and the 1960s, they would have witnessed a hotbed of activism: sit-ins, boycotts, threats of boycotts, prayer meetings, etc. In places like Greensboro, North Carolina; Cambridge, Maryland; Louisville, Kentucky; and in northern locations like Philadelphia, Pennsylvania, and Brooklyn, New York, African Americans and their white allies fomented change. In southern and border states, they challenged de jure segregation, but in places likes Philadelphia and Brooklyn, they challenged de facto segregation. A discussion of campaigns outside of the Deep South and lesser known individuals highlights the decentralized nature of the movement as well as the scope of African American political activity throughout the country.

Chapter seven, "Power to the People" examines what is often understood as more radical black activity in the mid-to-late 1960s and the early 1970s. During these years, civil rights work was replaced by more militant black power activism. Contrary to the lay persons' and sometimes scholarly rendition that the black power movement was somehow the evil twin of the civil rights movement, wherein violence-prone and angry black youth wanted to destroy America, the chapter argues that black power advocacy paralleled civil rights work. While civil rights activism focused on the removal of boundaries to constitutional rights, black power proponents were more focused on remedying the problems that constrained the life chances of African Americans, including employment, police brutality, and continued black exploitation in the light of civil rights advances. Malcolm X, Huey Newton, Stokely Carmichael, and the ways in which blacks strove to achieve self determination in urban areas are discussed.

The final narrative chapter, "From *Amos 'n' Andy* to *I Spy*" discusses African Americans in television and film. Television was an important ally in the Civil Rights Movement. Civil rights organizations used it to dramatize and show the atrocities meted out to black protestors and black people throughout the country. With television's growing influence in the 1960s, it was no longer possible for many people to ignore what was happening to black people. Equally important, as African Americans struggled to change their political positions in the United States of America, black actors depicted new images of black people on the small and large screens. Particular attention is given to the accomplished actor Sidney Poitier and the comedian Bill Cosby, though other actors are also discussed. The images African Americans portrayed on television were not always a reflection of the lived realities of most black people. Some were criticized while others were praised. However, the actors discussed showed African Americans who were not subservient and offered whites and blacks news ways of thinking about what it means to be black in America.

In addition to the eight narrative chapters, this reference includes biographical profiles of important people and the cultural developments during the Civil Rights Movement. Primary documents follow the biography section. These documents provide the reader with an inside glimpse into specific movement activity, the thinking of policy makers, and the work of people in the movement. Each selection is preceded by an explanatory head note that contextualizes the document and aids in its comprehension. An annotated bibliography section is included, which cites and assesses the most important print, electronic sources, and documentaries that discuss the Civil Rights Movement. A brief glossary in this reference guide explains terms likely to be unfamiliar to high school students and general readers.

Throughout this reference book, the terms African American(s), people of color, black(s), and black American(s) are used interchangeably. For some, this may be obvious. For those unfamiliar with racial nomenclature, however, such terms may be unsettling. Recently, a student of European American ancestry approached me after a class and asked me to explain to her why some people of African descent do not want to be called African American. In another instance, in a class populated by students of European American ancestry, students were shaken when I described myself as black. When I asked why they were so perturbed, a student responded that she was told never to use the word black because black people find it offensive. In yet another class, when discussing people of African descent from the Caribbean, a student classified a Haitian and a Jamaican as African American. It seems that the term African American is used by segments of white America to describe any person of African descent. So as not to confuse the reader, I use the terms African American(s), people of color, black(s), and black American(s) to refer to people of African descent who reside in the United States whose ancestors were the enslaved or subordinate class, and who belong to a specific racial history, culture, or ethnicity throughout most of U.S. history. More to the point, I use them interchangeably because black people use them interchangeably. Despite the re-emergence of "Negro" as a term of classification in the 2010 federal census, I have not, in my research, social interactions, and personal experience, come across someone who self-describes as such. Consequently, Negro is excluded unless used in the context of a direct quote.

I end this introduction with a few words of thanks. Had it not been for others, this book could not have been written. Thank you to my dear wife and partner, Shula. Several of my students deserve my gratitude: Courtney L. Anderson, Emily L. Mercer, Casey L. Castro, Brian A. Kibler, Katherine R. Murphy, and Desiree Sharlee Marquant. Their input helped me clarify the narrative. Kenneth Sterrett and Ashley M. Windsor provided valuable research assistance. Many thanks to the editorial and marketing staff at ABC-CLIO, especially Kim Kennedy-White. They were courteous, responsive, professional, and informative.

Finally, thank you to all those who struggled so that we may all inherit a more just society. We are not where we should be. We are not who we will be. However, as Civil Rights Movement activists have shown through their determination and willingness to challenge the status quo, a better world is possible.

Chronology of the Movement

1954 May 17: *Brown vs. Board of Education of Topeka.* U.S. Supreme Court unanimously agrees that racial segregation in public education is unconstitutional.

June: Malcolm X becomes head minister at the Nation of Islam's Temple No. 7 in Harlem, New York.

July: Mississippi residents convene the first meeting of the White Citizens' Council.

1955 January 7: Marian Anderson, a contralto, is the first African American woman to perform at the New York Metropolitan Opera.

May 7: Reverend George Lee is murdered as a result of his civil rights work in Belzoni, Mississippi.

January 18: President Dwight Eisenhower signs the Executive Order 10590 prohibiting racial discrimination in federal employment.

April 18: Bandung Conference of Afro-Asian States opens in Bandung, Indonesia.

August 28: Emmett Till, a teenager from Chicago, Illinois, is beaten, shot, and dumped in the Tallahatchie River outside of Money, Mississippi, for allegedly whistling at a white woman.

November 25: The Interstate Commerce Commission prohibits segregation in interstate travel.

December 1: Rosa Parks refuses to relinquish her seat to a white passenger on a segregated bus. Her refusal sparks the Montgomery Bus Boycott, which lasts 381 days.

1956 April 4: Jazz singer and pianist Nat King Cole is assaulted after performing for an integrated audience in Birmingham, Alabama.

May 2: Tallahassee Bus Boycott begins. The boycott lasts until March 1958, when the city ended the practice of segregation on public buses throughout the city.

December 17: U.S. Supreme Court upholds a lower court decision in *Gayle vs. Browder*, ending segregation on buses in Montgomery, Alabama.

1957 Malcolm X is named national spokesperson of the Nation of Islam by the organization's leader, Elijah Muhammad.

Stax Records is founded in Memphis, Tennessee. Though the company was founded by two white record producers, it would come to produce some of the most important soul, funk, jazz, and rhythm and blues artists in the late 1950s and the 1960s.

January–February: Reverend Martin Luther King, Reverend Fred Shuttlesworth, Reverend Ralph Abernathy, and other clergy from southern states form the Southern Christian Leadership Conference.

March 6: Ghana achieves independence.

May 17: The Southern Christian Leadership Conference and other civil rights groups stage the Prayer Pilgrimage for Freedom in Washington, D.C., seeking enforcement of the 1954 *Brown* Decision.

September 9: President Dwight Eisenhower signs the Civil Rights Act of 1957 into law. The Act marked the first of such laws since Reconstruction. The law established a Civil Rights Commission and made it illegal to prevent citizens from practicing their right to vote.

September 24: The National Guard descends upon Little Rock, Arkansas, to enforce the integration of Little Rock Arkansas' Central High School.

1958 Bill Russell of the Boston Celtics is named the league's Most Valuable Player.

January 18: William O'Ree integrates the National Hockey League.

June 29: Bethel Baptist Church in Birmingham, Alabama, is bombed by the Ku Klux Klan.

1959 March 11: Lorraine Hansberry's *A Raisin in the Sun* premieres on Broadway in New York City.

June 26: Rather than desegregate its schools, school officials in Prince Edward County, Maryland, dismantle the public school system.

July 13–17: *The Hate That Hate Produced*, an exposé about the Nation of Islam, airs on WNTA-TV in New York City.

December: Berry Gordy founds Motown Records in Detroit, Michigan. Employing some of the best-known rhythm and blues and soul artists of the 1960s and the 1970s, the company helped produce the sound track for the 1960s.

1960 *To Kill a Mockingbird* is published. The fictional work tells the story of a white lawyer who defends a black man accused of raping a white woman.

Eleven African nations achieve independence, providing encouragement for activists involved in the Civil Rights Movement.

February 1: Students from North Carolina Agricultural and Technical College stage a sit-in at a local Woolworth's segregated lunch counter, which begins a wave of sit-ins around the country.

April: The Student Nonviolent Coordinating Committee is founded at Shaw University in Raleigh, North Carolina.

May 6: President Dwight Eisenhower signs the Civil Rights Act of 1960.

August–September: Max Roach records *We Insist! Max Roach's Freedom Jazz Suite* featuring Abbey Lincoln.

September 19: Fidel Castro visits Harlem and stays in the Hotel Theresa.

November 14: Ruby Bridges integrates William Frantz Public School in New Orleans, Louisiana.

1961 Journalist John Howard Griffin's *Black Like Me* is published. The nonfiction work details the travels of a white man who passes as black in the Deep South.

February 16: Black Nationalists take over the United Nations Building in New York City.

March 6: President John F. Kennedy signs Executive Order 10925. The Order establishes the President's Committee on Equal Employment Opportunity. The law prohibits racial discrimination in employment by all government contracting agencies.

May: An interracial group of activists affiliated with the Congress of Racial Equality embarks on Freedom Rides to challenge continued segregation in interstate transit. In Alabama, their bus is attacked by a white mob. In Mississippi, riders are jailed when they attempt to integrate a whites-only rest area.

July–December: The Southern Christian Leadership Conference and Student Nonviolent Coordinating Committee's attempts to desegregate Albany, Georgia, fail.

September 25: Herbert Lee, farmer, father of nine, and member of the Amite County, Mississippi, National Association for the Advancement of Colored people is murdered by E. H. Hurst, a member of the Mississippi state legislature.

December 1961–January 1962: Students at Southern University in Baton Rouge, Louisiana, and the New Orleans branch of the Congress of Racial Equality organize boycotts and protests throughout Baton Rouge to desegregate stores.

1962 June: The Southern Christian Leadership Conference starts Operation Breadbasket—the economic wing of the organization—in an effort to change discriminatory hiring practices and boycott stores that continued to practice segregation.

June 24: James Meredith becomes the first black student to enroll at the University of Mississippi.

1963 January 1: The nation marks the 100th anniversary of the Emancipation Proclamation.

April–May: The Southern Christian Leadership Conference carries out Project Confrontation in Birmingham, Alabama, demanding an end to segregation in downtown department stores and restaurants, the elimination of discriminatory hiring practices in businesses throughout the city, and the creation of an oversight committee that would implement desegregation policies.

April 16: Martin Luther King Jr. writes *Letter from a Birmingham Jail*.

May: James Baldwin's *Fire Next Time* is published in which he offers his commentary on the civil rights struggle.

June 12: Medgar Evers, field secretary for the NAACP branch in Jackson, Mississippi, is murdered by Byron de la Beckwith.

June 23: Organizers, politicians, and activists stage the Great March to Freedom in Detroit, Michigan. Martin Luther King Jr. gives the keynote address at the event and calls it the "greatest demonstration for freedom ever held in this United States."

August 17: W.E.B. Du Bois dies at the age of 95.

August 28: The March on Washington is held with over 250,000 people in attendance. Martin Luther King Jr. delivers his famous "I Have a Dream Speech."

September 15: The Sixteenth Street Baptist Church in Birmingham, Alabama, is bombed.

November 22: President John F. Kennedy is assassinated.

December: Malcolm X is suspended from the Nation of Islam.

1964 January 23: The Twenty-Fourth Amendment to the Constitution is ratified, eliminating the use of poll taxes as a prerequisite for voting.

February 25: Muhammad Ali defeats Sonny Liston to become the world heavyweight champion.

March: Malcolm X officially breaks from the Nation of Islam and establishes the Muslim Mosque Incorporated.

March–June: Southern Christian Leadership Conference stages mass demonstrations in St. Augustine, Florida.

April 12: Malcolm X delivers his address "The Ballot or the Bullet" at the King Solomon Baptist Church in Detroit, Michigan.

April 13: Sidney Poitier is presented with an Academy Award for his portrayal of Homer Smith in the 1963 film *Lilies of the Field.*

June 2: President Lyndon B. Johnson signs the Civil Rights Act of 1964 into law.

June–September: Student Nonviolent Coordinating Committee organizes and commences Freedom Summer in Mississippi.

July 18: Riots erupt in Brooklyn and Harlem, New York.

August 4: The bodies of slain civil rights workers James Chaney, Mickey Schwerner, and Andrew Goodman are recovered.

August 21–26: Mississippi Freedom Democratic Party delegation attempts to unseat the all-white Democratic Party delegation in Atlantic City, New Jersey, at the Democratic National Convention.

December 10: Martin Luther King Jr. is awarded the Nobel Peace Prize in Oslo, Norway.

1965 John Coltrane's *A Love Supreme* is released.

Malcolm X's *Autobiography* is published.

February 21: Malcolm X is assassinated at the Audubon Ballroom in Harlem, New York.

March 7: Scores of protesters are beaten by police while trying to cross the Edmund Pettus Bridge in Selma, Alabama, on their way to the state's capital.

March 11: James Reeb, a white Unitarian minister, dies from head injuries suffered at the hands of white segregationists during a civil rights demonstration in Selma, Alabama.

March 16–25: Martin Luther King Jr. members of the Southern Christian Leadership Conference, and the Student Nonviolent Coordinating Committee lead thousands of activists on a march from Selma to Montgomery to protest the killing of Jimmy Lee Jackson.

August 6: President Lyndon B. Johnson signs the Voting Rights Act, outlawing discriminatory voting practices.

August 11–15: Riots erupt in the Watts section of Los Angeles, California.

September 28: President Lyndon B. Johnson signs Executive Order 11246, prohibiting federal employment discrimination based on "race, creed, color or national origin."

1966   Kwanzaa, the African American cultural heritage celebration, is created by Ron Karenga.

June 6: James Meredith is shot and injured in Hernando, Mississippi, on his March Against Fear.

June: Members of the Southern Christian Leadership Conference, National Association for the Advancement of Colored People, and Student Nonviolence Coordinating Committee continue Meredith's march to Jackson, Mississippi. During the march, Stokely Carmichael popularizes the phrase "Black Power."

September 22: Stokely Carmichael's "What we Want" is published in the *New York Review of Books*.

October: The Black Panther Party is founded in Oakland, California, by Huey P. Newton and Bobby Seale.

November: Edward William Brooke, III, is elected to the U.S. Senate as a Republican from Massachusetts. He is the first African American since the Reconstruction era to be elected to the U.S. Senate. He served until 1979.

1967   *Guess Who's Coming to Dinner*, a film which examines attitudes about interracial marriage, is released, with Sidney Poitier in the lead role.

Eldridge Cleaver's *Soul on Ice* is published.

Martin Luther King Jr.'s *Where Do We Go From Here: Community or Chaos?* is published.

March 25: Martin Luther King Jr. pediatrician Dr. Benjamin Spock, and other activists march in Chicago against the Vietnam War.

April 4: Martin Luther King Jr. delivers his "A Time to Break Silence" speech before the group Clergy and Laity Concerned at the Riverside Church, New York City.

April 28: Muhammad Ali refuses induction into the military, noting that "I ain't got no quarrel with those Vietcong."

June 12: U.S. Supreme Court unanimously decides in *Loving vs. Virginia* that state laws prohibiting interracial marriage are unconstitutional.

July 12–17: Race riots erupt in Newark, New Jersey.

July 17: John Coltrane dies.

July 23–30: Race riots erupt in Detroit, Michigan.

August 30: Thurgood Marshall is confirmed by the U.S. Senate and becomes the first African American Supreme Court Justice.

September 12: Stokely Carmichael publishes *Black Power: The Politics of Liberation,* with sociologist Charles Hamilton

November: Carl Stokes becomes the 51st mayor of Cleveland, Ohio, and the first African American mayor of a major U.S. city.

1968 James Brown's *Say it Loud, I'm Black and I'm Proud* is released.

February 8: Three students die and 27 are wounded after police fire into a crowd on the South Carolina State College campus in Orangeburg, South Carolina.

April 4: Martin Luther King Jr. is assassinated in Memphis, Tennessee, as he stood on the balcony of the Lorraine Motel.

May: Black workers and activists form the Dodge Revolutionary Union Movement in Detroit, Michigan.

June 5: Robert F. Kennedy is assassinated.

July 22: Black Panthers in New York march in protest against Huey Newton's murder trial.

October 16: 200 meter dash sprinters Tommie Smith and John Carlos give the black power salute during the medals ceremony at the Mexico City Olympic Games.

1969 Maya Angelou publishes *I Know Why the Caged Bird Sings.*

December 4: Fred Hampton, leader of the Chicago Black Panther Party, is killed by the Chicago Police Department.

1970 George Jackson's *Soledad Brother* is published.

May 29: California Court of Appeals overturns Huey Newton's voluntary manslaughter conviction.

July: The Federal Bureau of Investigation name the Black Panther Party "the most dangerous and violence prone of all extremist groups."

September 5–7: Revolutionary People's Constitutional Convention meets in Philadelphia, Pennsylvania

October 13: Angela Davis is arrested for allegedly providing a gun used by Jonathan Jackson in a courthouse gun fight during the summer of 1970.

1971 Jesse Jackson organizes People United to Save Humanity.

Toni Morrison publishes *The Bluest Eye.*

August 21: George Jackson is killed in Soledad Prison during an alleged prison break.

1972 Shirley Chisholm becomes the first black woman elected to the U.S. House of Representatives.

March: Black nationalists and elected officials meet in Gary, Indiana, to discuss possibilities for black political power in the 1970s.

May 27: African Liberation Day demonstrations take place around the country.

ONE

"I've Been 'buked and I've Been Scorned": The Rise of Jim Crow and Its Implications for Africans Americans

THE SYSTEM OF RACIAL SEGREGATION in the United States, commonly called Jim Crow, directly affected the lives of generations of African Americans and shaped race relations for millions of whites and blacks in the northern and southern states from the late 19th century to the late 20th century. Jim Crow determined one's residence and educational opportunities, dictated one's behavior and demeanor, and restricted one's employment and political rights. As a system, it was meant to codify white supremacy and politically, socially, and economically subordinate African Americans living in the American South. Historians disagree on the exact period when Jim Crow and segregation became an impregnable system of customs and laws. However, evidence suggests that during the Reconstruction Era, from 1865 to 1877, the policy of segregating African Americans in public accommodations replaced the older, antebellum policy of excluding African Americans from public accommodations in southern states. The Republican Party—the party of the Great Emancipator, Abraham Lincoln—may have freed African Americans from slavery with the Thirteenth Amendment, granted them citizenship and the right to due process with the creation of the Fourteenth Amendment, and bestowed the right to vote upon African American men with the Fifteenth Amendment, but these political rights did not equate to integration, social equality, or unrestricted access to public services. The historian Howard Rabinowitz states it most plainly: "whether because of their own racial prejudice, the need to attract white voters to the party, or the belief that legislated integration was unconstitutional or simply could not succeed, the Negroes' white allies sought to replace exclusion with segregation" (Rabinowitz, 1976, 332).

In the immediate post-emancipation period of the 1860s and 1870s, segregation was instituted and supported by Republican governments throughout the former Confederacy. In 1867, in Richmond, Virginia, the Army and the Freedmen's Bureau sanctioned the creation of separate almshouses for the city's black and white residents. That same year, in Nashville, Tennessee, the city's Board of Education instituted a segregated public school system to cater to white fears of racial equality and racial amalgamation. In Mississippi, republican administrations organized separate wings or buildings in mental health institutions for blacks and whites with disabilities. In Raleigh, North Carolina, blacks' and whites' final resting place in cemeteries were determined on a segregated basis, as African Americans' bodies were interred away from white bodies. During the era, black and white Alabamans who visited traveling circuses by law entered the show tents through separate entrances. In court in Savannah, Georgia, in 1876, blacks and white swore and took oaths on separate Bibles. Perhaps the most glaring example of segregation in public accommodations, that which would be challenged by countless African Americans, was segregation in public transportation. African Americans in North Carolina were provided separate accommodations on trains and steamboats. In Mobile, Alabama, as was the case in many towns and cities throughout the South, street cars either instituted the use of separate cars for blacks and whites or segregated individual cars. In some instances, blacks paid their fare and were forced to ride on the outside of the streetcar on the running board (Rabinowitz 1977).

After 1877, Union troops left the southern states, and the federal government agreed not to interfere in local and statewide race relations throughout the South. At that juncture, redeemers, white former Confederates or Confederate sympathizers, who had argued for the rescue of the South from federal and northern interference, called for the creation of a New South, took control of local and state governments, and expanded the boundaries of Jim Crow. Democratic redeemers openly professed desires to create state governments that subscribed to the tenets of white supremacy and wrote new state constitutions that more clearly circumscribed the boundaries of African American life in the closing decades of the 19th century and the opening decades of the 20th century.

African American men's right to vote was one of the first rights to be curtailed by redeemers. Between 1877 and 1910, legislators from Alabama, Arkansas, Florida, Georgia, Louisiana, Mississippi, North Carolina, South Carolina, Tennessee, Texas, and Virginia inserted voting restrictions into their state constitutions that eliminated, or limited, black participation in electoral politics. Such restrictions appeared race-neutral and, in many cases, eliminated some poor white voters. Through myriad legal maneuvers, however, blacks were disfranchised, and poor white men maintained their suffrage. All of these states used poll taxes to exclude African

Americans from the ballot box. The poll tax was levied by southern governments and due months before an election and were often made due when black farmers were without income during the growing season. For sharecropping families who received credit from the landlord or who were kept in perpetual debt, a poll tax was prohibitive (Bell 1979).

In the post-Reconstruction Era, South Carolina Democrats called a constitutional convention, rewrote the state constitution, and declared it law without statewide discussion and debate. To its arsenal of disfranchising techniques, Mississippi legislators instituted, among other things, the literacy tests and the understanding clause. The literacy tests required voters to be able to read their state constitution, including long paragraphs and legal terminology, to voting registrars. In areas with substandard public schools and large numbers of African Americans who, because of their former enslavement, did not learn to read, black people could not vote (Bell 1979). In many cases when they could read their state constitutions, blacks were still disqualified by registrars for not pausing at periods or for mispronouncing words. Many southern whites could not read their state constitutions, but they were allowed to vote because of the understanding clause. On the surface, the understanding clause required that the registrant demonstrate a "reasonable" understanding of the state constitution in order to vote. In actuality, the understanding clause was a "way to guard the interests of illiterate white democrats, who, while unable to read the state constitution if asked, could presumably provide a 'reasonable' interpretation of it" (Dailey 2008, xxv). "Reasonable" was subjective, of course, and many registrars, often illiterate or semiliterate themselves, merely accepted white voters by posing fraudulent questions (Chafe et al. 2001, 309). One black registrant seeking to register to vote in the Mississippi Delta remembers being asked "how many drops of rain fall in an hour" and "how many bubbles does a bar of soap make" (*The Promised Land*, 1995). Such irrelevant questions were asked by white registrars to prevent African Americans from voting.

Disfranchising laws were promulgated by elected offices and self-proclaimed racists like Ben Tillman, James Vardaman, and Theodore Bilbo. Ben Tillman served in the United States House of Representatives and as North Carolina's senator from 1895 to 1918. James Vardaman was the Governor of Mississippi from 1904 to 1908, while Theodore Bilbo influenced statewide Mississippi politics as governor and national politics as senator for over three decades, from 1916 to 1947. The three represented commonly held beliefs that saw and portrayed black people as inferior to whites and incapable of social, economic, or political development. Because blacks were childlike, given to corruption, and incapable of development, so the arguments went, to provide them with political rights was seen to be a waste of the franchise. Though Tillman and Vardaman may not have openly belonged to the Ku Klux Klan (KKK), many southern politicians like Bilbo openly belonged to the secret society, which as an organization was heavily involved in local, state, and national electoral politics.

The KKK originated in Pulaski, Tennessee, around 1865, but by the end of the 19th century had lost a large portion of its membership from subsequent government prosecution of Klan-related violence. In November 1915, the KKK was reorganized on the outskirts of Atlanta, Georgia, by William Joseph Simmons and, according to some estimates, had as many as 653,000 members from 1915 to 1944. Klansmen were found in more than 100 American cities: from Akron, Ohio, to Atlanta, Georgia; from Dallas, Texas, to Detroit, Michigan; and from Los Angeles, California, to Little Rock, Arkansas (Jackson 1992).

Interestingly, but not coincidentally, the Klan was reorganized during the same year as the release of D. W. Griffin's *A Birth of a Nation*, the world's first full-length feature film. Based on Thomas Dixon's novel *The Clansmen*, the film tells a story of an embattled white democratic South

Members of the Ku Klux Klan (KKK) parade down Pennsylvania Avenue in Washington, D.C., in 1928. (National Archives)

during the Reconstruction Era. It was a South wherein northern, white republicans undermined southern white masculinity, black men lusted after white women, and white women represented the symbol of a virtuous white South. When all seemed lost, gallant, white men of the KKK rescue white women and the South. The film incensed black America and the National Association for the Advancement of Colored People (NAACP), which organized a nationwide campaign against the film. But the film was screened throughout the country, including the White House during Woodrow Wilson's administration, and confirmed the rise of white supremacist politics nationwide. It also emboldened segments of white men throughout the country.

According to historian Kenneth Jackson, who examines the second rise of the KKK from 1915 to 1930, the organization's primary precept was the belief in white supremacy. Klan members "regarded the Negro as a mental pygmy, unable and unwilling to perform any but the most menial tasks" (Jackson 1992, 22). Klan members' social theory and participation in electoral politics and appointments to political positions further undermined black social, economic, and political aspiration in the age of Jim Crow. In 1923, in Atlanta, Georgia, the Klan backed Walter Sims for Atlanta City Council, Walter George for the U.S. Senate, Clifford Walker for governor, and Eugene Thomas as superior court judge. All the candidates won their electoral races. That same year, Clifford Davis, a well-known klansman from Memphis, Tennessee, was elected city judge with KKK support. Concurrently, in the early 1920s in Dallas County, Texas, elected officials responsible for law and order, including the police commissioner, the police chief, sheriff, deputies, and the district attorney, were Klansmen. The same was true of law enforcement officials in Newport News, Virginia, who included among their ranks not only the chief of police, but also the police court judge and the post master (Jackson 1992).

Klan activity was not limited to the South. In Detroit, Michigan, the Klan ran Charles Bowles' write-in campaign for the mayor's position. Bowles lost the 1924 election by a slim margin of less than 15,000 votes, but the turnout for him and grassroots organizing on his behalf demonstrated that the Klan had a foothold in northern urban areas. Klan members won city council positions in Indianapolis, Indiana, in the early 1920s, and in 1925, Klansman John Duvall was mayor of Indianapolis before he was imprisoned on corruption charges (Jackson 1992). As Indianapolis' black population grew as a result of the Great Migration, Klan-backed candidates infiltrated the Citizens' School Committee and instituted segregation policies throughout the city. In 1929, for example, the school committee removed black students from racially mixed elementary schools and relocated them to an all-black school (Thornbrough 1961).

The work of elected officials was bolstered by the judiciary, which repeatedly struck down Civil Rights laws and tendered decisions to support the machinations by which blacks were subordinated. To deal with KKK anti-black violence throughout the South, the U.S. Congress passed the Force Act enacted in 1871. The law made it illegal and punishable in federal court for two or more persons to attempt to deprive an individual of equal protection under the Fourteenth Amendment. In *United States v. Harris* (1882), the Supreme Court invalidated parts of the Force Act when it ruled that the Fourteenth Amendment applied to states and not to individuals, therefore placing the prosecution of such crimes under the jurisdiction of local and state courts. One consequence of the Act was that it allowed white vigilante groups to lynch and violently intimidate blacks who, in turn, had no legal recourse in local and state courts, leaving white anti-black violence largely unchecked. In 1883, the U.S. Supreme Court struck down the 1875 Civil Rights Act. The federal act maintained that "citizens of every race and color, regardless of any previous condition of servitude" were "entitled to the full and equal enjoyment of the accommodations, advantages, facilities, and privileges of inns, public conveyances on land or water, theaters, and other places of public amusement." The U.S. Supreme Court upheld the Louisiana Separate Car Act of 1890, which called for segregation on rail cars in *Plessy v. Ferguson* (1896) and opened the gates to discrimination and "separate but equal" policies in all public accommodations. Two years later, Mississippi's poll taxes and literacy tests were deemed constitutional in *Williams v. Mississippi* (1898). Such decisions were not reversed by the judicial system until the latter half of the 20th century, as we shall see in subsequent chapters.

In subjugating African Americans and maintaining white supremacy during the age of Jim Crow, legislators and the courts were supported by white vigilante justice. In the 53-year period between 1882 and 1935, there were 5,053 reported lynchings, countless incidents of white anti-black violence, and blatant intimidation. Most of the victims were southern-born African Americans (Berry 1979). Whites often argued that black men were lynched for the alleged rape of white women. Activist Ida B. Wells, the stalwart anti-lynching advocate, declared that the major reason for lynching was not rape; rather, lynching was an attempt by whites to maintain their economic and political dominance over African Americans. In 1893, for example, three African Americans—Thomas Moss, Calvin McDowell, and Henry Stewart—owned and operated a grocery store, the People's Grocery, in the Curve, a mixed neighborhood in Memphis, Tennessee. As the popularity

An African American family glances at the Santa Fe Depot segregation sign in Oklahoma City, Oklahoma, after hearing that the
Interstate Commerce Commission had ordered an end to separate
seating on public carriers in 1955. (AP Photo)

of the store grew, local customers stopped patronizing W.H. Barrett's
grocery store, a white-owned establishment, to purchase goods from and
support the People's Grocery. Following an extended period of tensions, including a local street fight among white and black children and a court case
against the families of the children, white residents attacked the People's
Grocery, but were repelled by black riflemen who injured members of the
mob. In coming days, whites pillaged black sections of the Curve, found
and jailed Moss, McDowell, Stewart, and the black rifleman who defended
the People's Grocery. With tempers flaring, the white mob reorganized
and grew increasingly infuriated that black men would have the audacity
to defend themselves and not know their place in Memphis society. They

stormed the jail, captured the black prisoners, took them to the outskirts of town, and lynched them (Bair 1997).

Similar violent acts by whites against blacks occurred elsewhere in the South. On March 3, 1921, Dr. J. L. Cockrell, a dentist in Houston, Texas, was castrated by the local members of the KKK for allegedly associating with white women. About a month later on April 1, Alexander Johnson, an employee at the Adolphus Hotel in downtown, Dallas, Texas, was kidnapped and similarly charged, whipped, and branded with acid on his forehead by the Dallas chapter of the KKK. One African American man was lynched in Canton, Mississippi, because his pet dog trounced a white man's dog. Bobby Hall, a light-skinned African American and son of a locally well-known family, was beaten and shot twice in the head by the sheriff of Baker County, Georgia, during the mid-1940s. When Arthur Searles, a reporter, wrote about the incident in the local black newspaper and threatened to go to the Federal Bureau of Investigation (FBI), his life was threatened by the local chapter of the KKK who, in their white, cone-shaped regalia, marched around his home. Light skin, prominence, and education were no match for the fury of white racism of vigilante violence (Jackson 1992).

One's gender provided no protection, as black women were also beaten and harassed by white men. The South may have been concerned with protecting womanhood, but that included white women only; black womanhood did not matter. Mary Turner, a black woman, along with her husband and two other black sharecroppers, were hanged in May 1918 in Valdosta, Georgia, after a quarrel, physical altercation, and subsequent death of Hampton Smith, a white landowner, over the sharecroppers' account. On June 5, 1946, in Monroe, Georgia, Dorothy Malcolm, a seven months pregnant black mother-to-be, was killed by a lynch mob along with two World War II veterans and another African American woman (Dewan 2005). Since African Americans had no legal recourse, no one was ever charged in any of the cases. In other cases, black women were often abused by the very authorities that were supposed to protect them. Ann Pointer, a black woman of Macon County, Alabama, recalled that during the interwar period, the sheriff, without a warrant, would "just walk in on you and tumble your house up, and don't tell why or how" (Chafe et al. 2001, 50). In 1939, when she was an 11-year-old girl in Fort Worth, Texas, Ferdie Walker, a black woman, was sexually harassed by white police officers, who exposed their genitals to her from their squad car (Chafe et al. 2001). While many of these disappearings, acts of intimidation, and lynchings were ignored by law enforcement officials, white citizens, and the courts, the constant threat of violence was an ever-present reality in the lives of African Americans throughout the South.

Jim Crow was all-encompassing. One's place within it was taught from a very early age and reinforced throughout one's life. By the end of the Reconstruction Era, various states throughout the South—Arkansas (1868), Alabama (1868), Georgia (1870), Mississippi (1870), North Carolina (1868), South Carolina (1868 and 1870), and Texas (1868)—had implemented tax-funded, public schools, many of which were organized by the efforts of recently freed African Americans (Bullock 1967; Anderson 1988). African American former slaves saw education as a way to exercise their freedom, and publicly funded schools, religious-affiliated Sabbath schools, and evening schools provided them with the literacy and intellectual skills to do this.

When the white planter class reasserted their political power in the late 1870s and early 1880s, they maintained publicly funded schools organized by freed persons and Republican coalitions, but created greater restrictions on black education. Many public schools ceased to be places for African Americans to broaden their intellectual horizons; instead, they became places for the elite planter class to train a malleable, agricultural labor force. During the late 19th century and early 20th century, with the ascendance of white supremacist politicians and laws, more segregated schools were established on an unequal basis. During the 1914–1915 school year, for example, Alabama spent $1.14 per black pupil and $9.00 per white pupil. Fifteen years later, the annual per capita expenditure for African American children was $7.16 and $37.50 for white students. Every other southern state, including Arkansas, Florida, Georgia, Kentucky, Louisiana, Mississippi, North and South Carolina, Tennessee, Texas, and Virginia, provided considerably less funding for black education (Bullock 1967). The same states also paid black teachers less. In Alabama, during the 1909–1910 school year, the average monthly salary for an African American teacher was $24.47. The average white teacher received a monthly salary of $53.76. Twenty years later, the average monthly salary for a black teacher and white teacher was $54.46 and $117.18, respectively (Bullock 1967).

Funding for education, of course, is only part of the story; equally important is access to educational facilities. In many cases, African American children were forced to go to school outside of the neighborhood, across town or, in the case of rural areas, miles away from their home. William Coker Jr. of Norfolk, Virginia, was bused ten miles from his Norfolk home to attend a school in Portsmouth, Virginia, because the school board refused to admit blacks to the local high school. Willie Harrell, a black student from Memphis, Tennessee, remembers that the "once or twice out of the year," when he went to school, he "had to walk seven or eight miles" to get there (Chafe et al. 2001, 40). In rural, tenant farming areas, where planters held political sway and when families needed extra labor, especially during harvesting season, African American children like Harrell could not attend school. Ann Pointer attended school from November to the end of April, at which time she had to prioritize her farm work over her education (Chafe et al. 2001). The educational attainment of blacks and whites bears this out. In the American South in 1950, the median educational level of African Americans was 5.9 years while the median for whites was 9.3 years (Bullock 1967, 173).

As primary and secondary schools were segregated, so were state-funded colleges and universities. Many African Americans wishing to obtain baccalaureate, professional, or graduate degrees attended black colleges throughout the South. African Americans were proud graduates of historically black colleges and universities like Fisk University in Tennessee, Tuskegee University in Alabama, Hampton University in Virginia, Howard University in the District of Columbia, Fargo Agricultural School in Arkansas, and Delaware State College in Delaware. Black colleges throughout the South conferred more than 140,000 bachelor degrees between 1939 and 1963 (Bullock 1967, 174). In other cases, black college students attended the predominantly white colleges, universities, and normal schools outside the South. Black students like Doris George of Moultrie, Georgia, left their home state to attend schools in northern areas. Because education officials in Georgia did not integrate the state university until the late 1960s, academically inclined African Americans, like George, utilized the state's policy of sending black students to northern universities. Rather than allowing her to attend the University of Georgia, which was for white students only, state officials paid George's tuition, living expenses, and transportation to a university in the city of Chicago (Chafe et al. 2001).

African Americans not only had to contend with unequal per capita spending for pupils and limited access to educational facilities, they also had to negotiate an education system that promoted intellectual white supremacy and black inferiority. The preeminent black social thinker and educator, Carter G. Woodson, reminds us that during the age of Jim Crow, "the thought of the inferiority of the Negro is drilled into [the black child] in almost every class . . . and in almost every book" (Woodson 1990, 2). The late 19th century and early 20th century witnessed the rise of anti-black white racism in academies and intellectual circles throughout the country.

Thinkers from a variety of disciplines and intellectual traditions, allegedly some of the greatest minds in the United States and the West at the time, participated in the discursive process of making African Americans inferior. Marion Mayo, a psychologist, argued that whites were physically superior to blacks in his 1913 *The Ultimate Solution of the American Negro Problem*. To this notion, Harvard University's well-renowned social psychologist William McDougall agreed. As late as 1923, the naturalist Henry Osborn argued that people of African descent were physically and mentally retarded when compared to their superior European brethren. To this list of Western scientists who espoused racist doctrines, add geographer Ellen Churchill Semple, anthropologist T. T. Waterman, psychologist G. Stanley Hall, anatomist Robert Bennett Bean, economist Joseph Alexander Tillinghast, and pseudo-scientists like horse breeder W.E.D. Stokes (Newby 1965). The professionals wrote texts read by school teachers and administrators who, knowingly or unwittingly, incorporated racist ideologies into school classrooms.

Responding to the political and demographic uncertainty of the early 20th century, some of the nation's leading historians of the era, like Lothrop Stoddard, also adopted and disseminated anti-black social thought. At the dawn of the 20th century, the United States was poised to become one of the world's leading imperialist powers as it gained territory and political influence overseas. Simultaneously, waves of European immigrants continued to arrive in the United States. Both of these realities—the changing ethnic composition of the United States and the shifting national and international political arrangement—caused anxiety and concern among white intellectuals, who promoted histories of world civilization. In their approach, white, Anglo-Saxon men dating back to ancient Greece were responsible for the moral and political development of the earth's people. To ensure that they continued to propel the world forward, it was necessary to maintain their Anglo-Saxon purity, which African Americans, who occupied the lowest rung of world civilizations, threatened (Newby 1965).

Other historians like William Dunning wrote histories of the Reconstruction Era from a southern point of view. From their perspective, the decades following the Civil War were characterized by poorly informed federal policies that attempted to reverse the social system of racial inequality. African Americans were inferior to white people, and any attempt to topple this natural racial order undermined white political power, removed whites from their proper place, and gave African Americans false hope about their potential and ability to be free and equal to whites. White intellectuals theorized blacks as physically inferior, culturally depraved, politically inassimilable, and alien, who offered nothing positive to the nation or the world. Therefore, the type of education a black child or adult received in the South and throughout the nation was, according to Thomas Bailey, Dean of the Department of Education at the University of Mississippi in 1914, one that would "best fit him to serve the white man" and place black people at the bottom of the economic and social hierarchy (Newby 1965).

Large numbers of African Americans worked at the bottom of the economic hierarchy in the South's agricultural system as sharecroppers or tenant farmers. Between 1890 and 1910, according to estimates, 62 percent of African Americans worked in the cultivation of cotton (Mandle 1991). In 1930, 1940, and 1945, African Americans comprised 50.6 percent, 55.3 percent, and 60.5 percent of sharecroppers, respectively, even as the total number of sharecroppers decreased during that period by more than 300,000 (Mandle 1994). Customs and laws restricted the selling of land to black farmers and blacks had little capital to purchase land of their own, so thousands of African American families worked on former slave plantations growing cotton. Under the sharecropping system, families were provided seed, land, and tools for cultivation, limited food stuffs, and rudimentary living quarters to raise cotton in exchange for a monetary share of the cotton crop at the end of the harvesting season. Tenant farmers rented land and were primarily responsible for what they grew and the materials to cultivate their land. When the growing season ended, they owned the crops produced and sold them on the open market rather than working with landowners, as did sharecroppers. In this way, tenant farmers had more freedom to plant what they wanted and negotiate higher prices. The sharecropping system, on the other hand, was one based on a family's indebtedness to the planter. After the cotton was harvested and the planter sold the cotton on the open market, families rarely received their fair share. If they did earn something for the year, blacks often received less for their cotton than white sharecroppers. Frank Perdue, a black former sharecropper on a plantation in Midnight, Mississippi, recalled that when it was time to settle debts for the year, "the white folks got more than the colored. If we got twenty cents per pound, they got thirty or forty" (Gordon 1979, 377). Cheated by the planter and with little to no opportunities for redress, many ended up more in debt than when they began.

Willie Harrell, a black former sharecropper, gives a poignant description:

> They give us so much [farmland] a year, and if we cleared anything, like on the sale of cotton, they would give it. If we didn't, we had to go

over another year if we was going to stay on that plantation, but if we were going to move on another plantation, well, that boss man came to pay for what we owe and move us on their plantation. That's what they did. If you didn't want to stay with them, if you owed them some, this honkie would come over here and buy you from this man, and you go and live with him and work there a year. (Chafe et al. 2001, 38)

Black men and women in southern towns and cities worked a variety of jobs but were constrained by segregation policies, discriminatory hiring practices, and a racial hierarchy that placed white men at the top and black women at the bottom (Stokes 1994). They could be found in all forms of employment: as stevedores on the docks, in tobacco processing plants, in textile and steel mills, and iron mines, and sometimes as skilled laborers. Most black people were employed in the dirtiest, low-level positions because they were largely excluded from white unions in the South and were provided limited opportunities to form all black unions during the age of Jim Crow. To be sure, some African American men and women participated in collective bargaining and organized strikes with whites and others created their own unions, which provided some means of defense against discrimination and coercion. During the 1930s, for example, African American workers joined with the Communist Party to organize the Steel Workers Organizing Committee in Alabama. Similarly, in 1936, the Brotherhood of Captive Miners, Mine Mill—a union comprising white and black iron miners—organized worker demonstrations and a strike throughout the state of Alabama (Kelley 1990). Louise "Mamma" Harris, a tobacco worker in Richmond, Virginia, led a walkout and strike against her employer and helped form the Tobacco Workers Organizing Committee in 1938. In the opening decades of the 20th century, black women domestic servants in Houston, Texas; Norfolk, Virginia; and Washington, D.C., formed unions to fight for higher wages and better treatment, but these attempts failed and their organizations dismantled (Trotter 2001).

Thousands of unskilled or semiskilled black men and women in southern towns and cities found employment in the homes of white families when collective bargaining failed or was not an option and thus were left to the economic and social whims of their employers. Cleaster Mitchell of Blackton, Arkansas, was a domestic servant in the 1930s and 1940s as was her mother, a generation before. In 1943, she worked for one family, ironing and mending clothes, caring for the family's infant, and tending the vegetable garden and livestock for $2.50 per week. During her long work days, she was constantly under the surveillance of her white female employer and frequently sexually harassed by the household's white men. When she worked for the Brown family, the husband of the family "just walked up . . . and put his arms around me." Because she had been taught by her mother how to deal with flirtatious men in the households where they worked, Mitchell asserted herself and told Mr. Brown never to touch her again (Chafe et al. 2001, 215). Uless Carter also worked for a white family in Clarksdale, Mississippi, in the Mississippi Delta region. Arriving to work, he always entered the home through the rear of the house, where he often ate his meals. Ironically, when completing his daily chores, he exited the house through the front door, cleaned the porch, and reentered through the same door. Such a display, while openly contradictory, was to inform everyone that African Americans had to follow whatever customs the whites imposed upon them. One entered the rear of the house in a subordinate social position and only used the front door as a servant, a subordinate social and economic position (*The Promised Land*, 1995).

Customs and laws were inextricably intertwined. Throughout the South, whites called black men "boy" and "uncle," while black women were referred to as "girl" and "auntie." Blacks, on the other hand, always had to refer to whites, even children, with formal title such as "Ms.," "Mrs.," "Mr.," "Sir," or "Ma'am." When walking on sidewalks, African Americans were to move aside to let white pedestrians pass. Segregation statutes were enforced in rural areas, but compared to southern cities and towns, where blacks and whites often interacted, contact between whites and blacks in the rural South was relatively infrequent. It was mostly in densely populated areas throughout the South that spatial segregation was diligently policed and where signs enforcing segregation were ubiquitous. "We Serve Colored, Carry Out Only" and "We Serve Whites Only" told blacks where they could eat. One knew where to get a drink of water by "white" and "colored" signs over water fountains and buckets. The segregated sections in movie theaters were marked with "Colored Balcony" signs. A sign in an apartment building or house announcing "For Rent to Colored" informed the potential renter of availability. Not following social customs and encroaching into white spaces often led to arrests and fines, public ridicule, physical altercations with law enforcement officials or nonofficial protectors of white supremacy, or death. Jim Crow signs were a constant reminder to African Americans that they were not full citizens and were unwanted in the land of their birth and could live only as a docile, subjugated people. For many who found Jim Crow intolerable, leaving the South was seen as the only way out.

During the late 19th and early 20th centuries, a sizable number of African Americans began to exercise their freedom of movement despite, and because of, attempts to keep them politically, physically, and economically tied to the land. Known as the Great Migration, thousands moved to mining towns and homesteads further west, others left for midwestern cities like Indianapolis and Chicago, and still others migrated to towns and cities within the South and to northeastern cities. The black population in large and smaller northern cities saw an exponential increase, beginning in the second decade of the 20th century. New York City's black population grew by 60 percent between 1910 and 1920, while Chicago saw a 148.2 percent increase in the number of African American residents during the same period. Similarly, the African American population in Cleveland grew by 307.8 percent, from 8,448 to 34,451. Pushed out by the boll weevil infestation from Mexico, agricultural mechanization, violence, and second class citizenship throughout the South and pulled by economic opportunities associated with war industry, educational opportunities for their children, and the chance to be free from the laws and customs of segregation, many black migrants left the South during and after the war. During World War I, approximately 400,000 African Americans moved from the South and, during the 1920s, another 800,000 joined the ranks of those who had moved (Laidlaw 1932; Osofsky 1996; Marks 1989).

For many, northern cities offered a new sense of freedom. In his dramatization of a migrant's initial reaction to Harlem, New York, Rudolph Fisher paints a picture of openness and possibility. His main character, Gillis, arrives in Harlem, New York, from North Carolina and sees a black police officer. Fisher writes: "his eyes opened wide; his mouth opened wider . . . For there stood a handsome brass-buttoned giant directing the heaviest traffic Gillis had ever seen . . . with supreme self-assurance" (Fisher 1987, 4). One migrant from Philadelphia wrote that one does not "have to mister every little white boy [who] comes along. I haven't heard a white man call a colored a nigger . . . since I been in the state" (Scott 1919, 461). Writing to family and friends in Hattiesburg, Mississippi, from East Chicago, Indiana, a migrant wrote that his "children are going to the same school with the whites and I don't have to umble to no one. I have registered—Will vote the next election and there isn't any 'yes sir' and 'no sir'—it's all yes and no and Sam and Bill" (Scott 1919, 459). For some migrants, many of whom possessed black Protestant religious sensibilities, the North was as much of the Promised Land for them as Palestine was for the ancient Jews.

Northern cities and town were not immune to racism, and many black migrants found their residential opportunities and economic prospects limited. Local custom, federal and local housing policies, zoning laws, and restrictive covenants kept African Americans segregated in inner cities

(McGrew 2001). African American migrants found more lucrative employment as compared to their southern homes, but African American women found few jobs other than domestic work, and industrial jobs for men often came with white resistance from union members (Grossman 1991). Similarly, the cost of living in northern cities was so high that the cost of rent, food, and basic necessities often left little for saving. But, while they suffered from discrimination in northern cities, African Americans could—and did—seek redress in courts, organized to improve the physical health of their communities, voted and were elected to political offices, joined predominantly white unions or started their own, and participated in grassroots organizing against housing and employment discrimination. Blacks in northern urban areas were members of the Universal Negro Improvement Association in the 1920s, organized "Don't Buy Where You Can't Work" campaigns in Chicago and New York in the 1930s, participated and helped organize socialist and communist groups in the 1930s and 1940s, and organized black workers through the National Negro Labor Council in the 1950s.

The structures of Jim Crow created the economic, political, and social situation wherein black farmers did not own the land they tilled, black teachers did not write the textbooks or control the curricula for their students, and black people survived at the whims and vagaries of whites. But, African Americans were not powerless, and many individually and organizationally challenged the system that made them noncitizens. There were valiant attempts to counter racism and segregation before World War II, as we shall see in Chapter two, when we discuss the political origins of the Civil Rights Movement, but it would take a new crop of activists, leaders, organizations, strategies, and a shift in the national and international political mood and relationships to effectively challenge and destroy Jim Crow.

References

Anderson, James D. *The Education of Blacks in the South, 1860–1935* (Chapel Hill: University of North Carolina Press, 1988).

Bair, Barbara. *Though Justice Sleeps, 1880–1920* (Oxford: Oxford University Press, 1997).

Bell, Derrick. "The Racial Imperative in American Law," in Robert Haws, ed., *The Age of Segregation: Race Relations in the South, 1890–1945* (Jackson, MS: University of Mississippi Press, 1979).

Berry, Mary Frances. "Repression of Blacks in the South 1890–1945: Enforcing the System of Segregation," in Robert Haws, ed., *The Age of Segregation:*

Race Relations in the South, 1890–1945 (Jackson, MS: University of Mississippi Press, 1979).

Bullock, Henry Allen. *A History of Negro Education in the South* (Cambridge: Harvard University Press, 1967).

Chafe, William, H., Raymond Gavins, Robert Korstad, Paul Ortiz, and Robert Parrish, eds. *Remembering Jim Crow: African Americans Tell about Life in the Segregated South* (New York: The New Press, 2001).

Coulthard, Edmund, and Nick Godwin, *The Promised Land*, VHS (Discovery Channel/British Broadcasting Corporation, 1995).

Dailey, Jane. *The Age of Jim Crow* (New York: W. W. Norton, 2008).

Dewan, Shaila. "Group Lynching is Re-created in a 'Call for Justice,' " http://www.nytimes.com/2005/07/26/national/26lynching.html. Accessed July 1, 2010.

Fisher, Rudolph. "City of Refuge," in John McCluskey, Jr., ed., *The City of Refuge: The Collected Stories of Rudolph Fisher* (Columbia, Missouri: University of Missouri Press, 1987), 4.

Gordon, Lawrence. "A Brief Look at Blacks in Depression Mississippi, 1929–1934," *The Journal of Negro History*, Vol. 64, No. 4 (Autumn, 1979), 377–390.

Grossman, James R. "The White Man's Union" in Joe William Trotter, Jr., ed., *The Great Migration in Historical Perspective* (Bloomington: Indiana University Press, 1991), 83–105.

Jackson, Kenneth T. *Ku Klux Klan in the City, 1915–1930* (Lanham, MD: Ivan R. Dee Publisher, 1992).

Kelley, Robin D. G. *Hammer and Hoe: Alabama Community During the Great Depression* (Chapel Hill: University of North Carolina Press, 1990).

Laidlaw, Walter. *Population of the City of New York, 1890–1930* (New York: Cities Census Committee, 1932), 51. Mandle, Jay R. "Continuity and Change: The Use of Black Labor After the Civil War," *Journal of Black Studies*, Vol. 21, No. 4 (June, 1991), 414–427.

Mandle, Jay R. *Not Slave, Not Free: The African American Economic Experience Since the Civil War* (Durham: Duke University Press, 1994).

Marks, Carole. *Farewell, We're Good and Gone* (Bloomington: Indiana University Press, 1989).

McGrew, Teron. "The History of Residential Segregation in the United States and Title VIII," *The Black Scholar*, Vol. 27, No. 2 (2001), 22–30.

Newby, I. A. *Jim Crow's Defense: Anti-Negro Thought in America, 1900–1930* (Baton Rouge: Louisiana University Press, 1965).

Osofsky, Gilbert. *Harlem: The Making of the Ghetto* (Lanham, MD: Ivan R. Dee Publishers, 1996).

Rabinowitz, Howard. "From Exclusion to Segregation: Southern Race Relations, 1865–1900," *The Journal of American History*, Vol. 63, No. 2 (Sep., 1976), 325–350.

Scott, Emmet. "Additional Letters of Negro Migrants of 1916–1918," *Journal of Negro History*, Vol. 4, No. 4, (Oct., 1919), 413, 415, 416, 456–462.

Stokes, Melvyn, and Rick Halpern. *Race and Class in the American South Since 1890* (Oxford: Berg Publisher, 1994).

Thornbrough, Emma Lou. "Segregation in Indiana during the Klan Era of the 1920's," *Mississippi Valley Historical Review*, Vol. 47 (1961), 594–617.

Trotter, Joe William. *The African American Experience* (Boston: Houghton Mifflin, 2001).

U.S. Department of Commerce, *Negroes in the United States 1920*–1932 (Washington, D.C.: Government Printing Office, 1935).

Woodson, Carter G. *The Mis-Education of the Negro* (Trenton, NJ: Africa World Press, 1990).

TWO

"I Want to Be Ready to Put on My Long White Robe": The Political Origins of the Civil Rights Movement

A MIDDLE-CLASS, MIDDLE-AGED black man, an officer of the National Urban League, walks into a car dealership to buy a car in Atlanta, Georgia. He is dapper and sophisticated. The white salesman greets him in a way that white men greeted black men in the early 20th century. "Hey, boy what can I do for you!" The black man tells the salesman his request. They chat about the best car, pricing, etc. Throughout the conversation, the salesman punctuates every sentence with "boy." After successfully haggling for a lower price, the black man tells the salesman that he would have to think about it further. He tells the salesmen that he would return tomorrow. "Alright, boy. But this deal won't last forever," the white salesman says. The next day, the black man returns. When the salesman sees him, he says, "Glad to see you boy. You'll be proud of this car, not another boy in Atlanta will have a better one." The black man calmly, but forcefully responds: "Sorry, but the deal is off. I read the law last night and it says that minors in the state of Georgia cannot purchase cars; and since I am a boy, as you have so frequently reminded me, it would be illegal to buy a car from you" (Burma 1946, 713). In another humorous vignette, two female domestics were discussing their jobs at the market. The first domestic says "At my place I have a terrible time; All day it's 'Yes, Ma'am,' 'Yes, Ma'am.' " The second domestic responds, "It's terrible for me too, but with me it's always 'No, sir,' 'No, Sir,' 'No, Sir' " (Burma 1946, 713).

As the two jokes suggest, African Americans in the northern and southern states made the best of bad situations. They also individually and organizationally resisted racism and segregation decades before the rise of such important leaders as Martin Luther King Jr. the emergence of national organizations like the Student Nonviolent Coordinating Committee, or the passage of Civil Rights legislation—hallmarks of what we call the Civil Rights Movement of the mid-20th century. One such way to contest the status quo was through humor. Black humor allowed African Americans to show the illogicality of racism and discrimination, momentarily escape white hostility, and laugh at themselves—a necessity when nothing else could be done to change a seemingly unchangeable situation. Often, in such a world, "the weak triumphed over the strong through wit, ingenuity, guile, and cunning" (Gilmore 1978, 70). The point, of course, is not that black humor secured better paying jobs, integrated or equalized public facilities, decreased the number of lynchings, improved educational opportunities for black youth, or, in actuality, subverted the system of white oppression. The point is that it provided black folks with a chance to dream and a salve for the open wounds obtained through their daily bouts with life in the United States of America.

Black humor was one of the many weapons available to blacks in their war for citizenship. Whether because of geographic and political isolation, fears of economic reprisal and threats of violence, or personal temperament, overt political activity was unavailable for many. Such individuals negotiated and resisted state-sponsored segregation in whatever ways available to them. At times, African Americans with light skin revealed the fluidity of racial lines by passing off as whites in order to obtain necessary services. Those who could speak Spanish sometimes passed off as Spanish-speaking immigrants. Black domestic workers in the southern urban areas relied on their white employers to shuttle them back and forth to work to avoid the indignities of segregated public transit. Within the limited opportunities and economic constraints, they also exercised their freedom by leaving particularly abusive and exploitative employers to work in other homes. Young and urban black men refusing to be identified with subservience redefined masculinity and fashioned themselves as hipsters, with their distinct clothing, language, and ways of being. Black soldiers returning from World War I (WWI) and World War II (WWII) openly refused to obey segregation laws and boldly attempted to register to vote (Kelley 1996).

Blacks utilized different types of political organizing and agitation in the early 20th century. Ida B. Wells investigated lynchings and published her findings at the turn of the 20th century. The National Association for the Advancement of Colored People (NAACP) lobbied congress to pass anti-lynching laws to allow for the prosecution of lynch mobs in the 1910s and 1920s (Waldrep 2009). The Urban League participated in the politics of art with its *Opportunity* magazine in the 1920s. Marcus Garvey's Universal Negro Improvement Association (UNIA) rallied thousands of African Americans nationwide under the banner of black nationalism, while

A. Phillip Randolph sought to organize white and black workers through grassroots union work and his magazine, the *Messenger.*

In fact, African Americans formed alliances among themselves and with non-blacks, pressured the federal government, boycotted, experimented with radical politics, and used the courts to bring about change. But, it was not until the 1930s and 1940s that civil rights for African Americans became a national issue and it is to these decades that the political origins of the Civil Rights Movement can be traced. During these years, African Americans and their nonblack allies laid the foundation for later civil rights leaders, demonstrating that they would not passively accept the curtailing of their political rights, even before the zenith of the civil rights struggle from 1954 to1965. During these decades, challenges to white racism were not always successful and the national and international stages were not set to allow for long-term political change, but African Americans worked within the social and political constraints of the era to affect small changes, even if full participation in American society was denied them.

Progressive blacks and whites from a variety of political organizations and religious groups worked together throughout the 1930s, demonstrating that an interracial commitment to political equality was important in the inchoate phases of the movement. One such example is the Southern Conference on Human Welfare (SCHW). Deemed a "love feast" by Virginia Durr, a 1930s white southern activist and participant in the conference, the SCHW convened from November 20 to November 24, 1938, in Birmingham, Alabama, and was attended by black and white progressives from throughout the South to discuss the social, political, and economic problems facing the region. Close to 2,000 participants and observers attended the conference—a virtual motley crew of elected officials, academics, activists, clergy, journalists, union representatives, and workers, including Hugo Black, the Supreme Court Justice, historian C. Vann Woodward, black sociologist Charles S. Johnson, the black activist and thinker John P. Davis of the National Negro Conference, social economist and author of *An American Dilemma*, Gunnar Myrdal, Rabbi Jacob Kaplan, whites author and activists W. T. Couch, members of the Southern Tenant Farmers Union and the Congress of Industrial Organizations, and First Lady Eleanor Roosevelt (Egerton 1994).

Participants were in agreement that the politics of the southern states did not live up to the ideals of the Constitution, and while they did not share a common vision of how to improve the South, they were willing to discuss some of the inequities and challenges that faced the region and its people. After days of vociferous debates, speeches, and conversations on how best to resolve racist and discriminatory laws and ameliorate social and political inequities, conferees resolved to condemn the practice of segregated seating during the conference. They also publicly urged the federal government to pass anti-lynching legislation and called for a full pardon for the Scottsboro boys—black teenagers who were falsely accused of raping two white teenagers in Alabama. As the conference participants left Birmingham, they were renewed in their struggle to improve race relations and the South, and affirmed that they were not alone in their struggles. As Virginia Durr reminisced years later, the conference was like crossing "the river together . . . [to] the Promised Land" (Egerton 1994, 189).

Though blacks and whites had a wide river to cross to make it to the Promised Land, metaphorically speaking, Durr's use of religious language should not be easily dismissed because the Civil Rights Movement was both a religious and a political movement. The locus of black political organizing during the height of the movement was the Church and many of its leaders subscribed to a liberationist theology that informed their political stance. Also, religious ethics and faith were also the points of departure for a variety of white and black coalition building during the formative decades of the movement.

Black and white Protestant women joined together to form the Association of Southern Women for the Prevention of Lynching and opposed lynching during the 1930s and the 1940s. With chapters throughout the southern states, the group sought to examine the causes of lynching and use their Christian faith to create local and statewide campaigns against lynching at a time when other Christian organizations remained silent. Their efforts were supplemented by the Commission on Interracial Cooperation (CIC). Founded in 1920 by Will Alexander, a Methodist minister and its executive director, the organization investigated and condemned lynching throughout the 1920s and the early 1930s. The CIC also created the Division of Women's Work, which brought together middle class black and white women from across the South to fight and discuss racial issues that plagued that section of the country (Egerton 1994).

Black Protestants also joined with white Jewish groups to improve their situation. Early black Protestant and white Jewish political alliances were fraught with tensions in ways that black and white Christian alliances were not, especially in regard to real and imagined black anti-Semitism and the economic ties that bound African Americans and white Jews together in black ghettos throughout the country. It was further complicated by the simultaneous racialization of Jews as whites, along with their being perceived as an oppressed minority. During the 1930s, the fear of losing white privilege made an outright attack on anti-black racism politically unfeasible, so the cooperation between African American and Jewish political groups was one of mutual self-interest. Such groups allied when the intolerance affected both ethnic groups. Blacks adopted Jewish causes when such an adoption included a tangential relationship to the issues that they faced. The Jewish groups did the same. Jews were indeed discriminated against throughout the country, and fighting against anti-black intolerance allowed them to voice their concerns about anti-Semitism.

This mutual self-interest, the growing specter of German Nazism and Italian Fascism, and the United States' entry into WWII, led black and Jewish groups to create organizational alliances and local and citywide united fronts. As early as 1935, the National Council of Jewish Women (NJCW) opposed lynching as part of its national platform. By 1943, the NJCW and the National Council of Negro Women (NCNW) formed political ties and worked together to improve race relations (Greenberg 2006). Equally noteworthy is the American Jewish Congress' (AJC) Women's division, which formed an interfaith committee in 1943 to discuss ways to end racism. African Americans called for victory abroad against Nazism and Fascism, and a victory at home against discrimination and racism and such a call included a fight against anti-Semitism, thereby opening the way for African American and Jewish coalition building.

In cities across the country, blacks and Jews joined coalitions. In Chicago, in the early 1940s, the NAACP and the National Urban League (NUL) joined the Chicago Council Against Racial and Religious Discrimination along with Jewish groups, including the AJC, the Anti-Defamation League (ADL), and other political and faith-based groups. In New York City, progressives across the racial, religious, and political spectrum joined together to form the Council Against Intolerance in America. Such a broad, expansive name and concomitant organizational objectives allowed individuals with different constituencies to participate in an effort that would ostensibly benefit all those who participated. Among the ranks of progressives who joined the Council was the NAACP's Walter White, the labor leader and organizer A. Phillip Randolph, Rabbi Stephen Wise, and the Christian theologian Reinhold Niebuhr. Progressives like these attempted to move African American and Jewish groups beyond mutual self-interest to fight for universal causes, and the war years provided opportunities for just that—to confront injustice across racial and religious lines. In Minnesota, for example, the Negro Defense Committee (NDC), an African American organization, received support from the state's Jewish Anti-Defamation Council in their attempt to end the prohibition against blacks serving in the state's militia. San Francisco Bay area Jewish groups supported their black neighbors in protesting local ordinances that institutionalized racism (Greenberg 2006). African Americans alliances with whites did not always bear fruit and overlapping issues of race, class, culture, and geography did not always allow for the execution of the most appropriate and direct strategy to combat the discrimination against blacks, but the creation of such alliances demonstrates a concerted effort by different segments of American society to contest and change the political, social, and economic status quo in the 1930s and the 1940s.

For the NAACP, challenging the status quo meant working through the court system and using the constitution of the United States to dismantle systemic racism. The NAACP was just 20 years old in 1930. Formally founded in 1910 by liberal whites and progressive blacks who founded the Niagara Movement, the organization's primary objective was securing constitutional rights and protections for African Americans. Securing these rights during the 1930s and the 1940s meant attacking segregation and the separate, but equal, policies that undergirded it through litigation. Charles Hamilton Houston was the chief legal strategist for the organization from 1935 to 1940. Born in 1895, Houston was raised in the small black middle class enclave of Washington, D.C., graduated from Amherst College, and received his law degree from Harvard. From 1924 to 1935, as faculty member and later dean of the Howard Law School in Washington, D.C., Houston and his colleagues transformed the school from a part-time night school to a fully accredited three-year law school program (McNeil 1983). By the time he became the NAACP's full time special counsel in July 1935, Houston had not only become committed to using the law to fight discrimination, but had also trained a coterie of black lawyers committed to civil rights

Participants of the 20th annual session of the National Association for the Advancement of Colored People, June 1929. (Library of Congress)

litigation, including Thurgood Marshall, who became the Assistant Special Counsel in 1936.

With Houston's legal mind and strategies, the NAACP directly confronted southern and border states' policies of segregated publicly funded professional and graduate education for whites only. In a 1935 precedent-setting case, *Murray* v. *The University of Maryland*, Houston and the NAACP successfully integrated the University of Maryland Law School when Maryland courts ordered the law school to admit Donald Gaines Murray, a black Amherst College graduate. The victory against the University of Maryland was followed by a 1938 U.S. Supreme Court case, *Missouri ex rel. Gaines* v. *Canada*, wherein it was decided that the University of Missouri Law School denied Lloyd L. Gaines, a qualified African American applicant, equal protection under the law by excluding him from the publicly funded law school because of his race. Coming from the highest court in the country, the victory meant that no state-funded institution of higher education could deny qualified African American applicants unless the state provided equal educational opportunities within the state. No longer was there the option of sending black students outside of the state to be educated using public funds. Equal protection under the law meant that African American students had the right to attend state-funded graduate and professional schools attended by white students or attend a segregated black graduate or professional school and receive the same education in the their home state. Since there were no state-funded black graduate or training programs, southern and border states would have to create them—a price southern state governments and municipalities could not afford, especially during the Great Depression. Houston and the NAACP's strategy not only appealed to constitutional law and the merits of the Fourteenth Amendment of the Constitution, it also appealed to the southern and border states' treasuries and pocketbooks (McNeil 1983).

In addition to fighting discrimination in graduate and professional schools in the 1930s and the 1940s, the NAACP worked with public school teachers in states throughout the South to improve publicly funded education for black children and equalize African American teachers' pay with their white counterparts. Using the 1936 case of William B. Gibbs, an elementary school principal in Montgomery County, Maryland, the NAACP won a case in the state courts against the Montgomery County Board of Education to equalize black and white public school teachers' and administrators' salaries. In 1940, after a series of appeals, the U.S. Supreme Court ruled that unequal teachers' salaries based on race were unconstitutional because they violated the Fourteenth Amendment rights, which called for equal protection and due process under the law (McNeil 1983).

While the NAACP and local groups fought discrimination in education and housing and formulated strategies to make New Deal policies more equitable and responsive to African American needs, the NUL challenged the racial status quo in employment. The organization formed in 1911, when the Committee on Urban Conditions Among Negroes in New York (CUCANNY), the Committee for Improving Conditions Among Negroes in New York, and the National League for the Protection of Colored Women (NLPCW)—three Progressive Era organizations—merged (Moore 1981). Though the NUL was originally concerned with investigating, publicizing, and correcting problems associated with urban life and industrialization, by the 1930s, it began to concern itself with social and political equality between the whites and blacks. In 1934, for example, the League found that African American workers at the Wehr Steel Foundry in Milwaukee, Wisconsin, were dismissed from the plant because the local chapter of the American Federation of Labor (AFL), wanted African American workers removed from the plant. Thereafter, they lobbied the National Labor Relations Board (NLRB) to investigate such allegations. In the end, the NLRB refused, but the NUL's investigation emboldened the group and clearly demonstrates that African American groups did not see workers' rights and civil rights as mutually exclusive issues (Moore 1981).

During the 1930s, African Americans' position in the labor force was a growing concern for black organizations. Though it would continue to challenge unconstitutional laws and segregation throughout the 1930s and the 1940s, the NAACP began to think concretely about an economic program to supplement its litigation work. In its 1935 "Future Plan and Program of the N.A.A.C.P.," a segment of its membership argued that the situation within which African American workers found themselves was one part of a larger system of capitalist exploitation of workers and considered placing the organization at the forefront of getting "Negroes to view their special grievances as a natural part of the larger issues of labor as a whole" (Holt & Brown, 2000, 255). African Americans were excluded from many labor unions that allowed industrial employers to use black workers as scabs, exacerbate tensions between white and black workers, and perpetuate divisions between them. Such divisions, however, were antithetical to white labor's interests because white workers were subject to poor working conditions, low wages, and a weakened ability to contest their exploitation. The NAACP's job, so the argument went, was to help create unified labor movements that did not discriminate according to race, to educate black workers on the necessity of cooperative economics, and to lobby legislative bodies to pass legislation to empower and create a modicum of economic security for the working class, including laws that dealt with issues of child labor, retirement, unemployment, and death benefits. Nationally, the organization was not as successful in implementing such plans as it was in its litigation work, but local branches did help a few Africans Americans gain access to information about unions and working class politics.

In the late 1930s, the National Negro Congress (NNC) also helped African Americans join unions. The NNC emerged one year after a 1935 Howard University conference of black and white political activists and intellectuals who sought to foster a united political front against the nationwide discrimination of black Americans. Members and supporters came from a variety of political perspectives. White politicians—including New York City Mayor Fiorello La Guardia, President Franklin D. Roosevelt, and First Lady Eleanor Roosevelt—joined with communist James Ford, socialist Norman Thomas, United Auto Workers (UAW) leader Walter Reuther, Brotherhood of Sleeping Car Porters' (BSCP) leader A. Philip Randolph, Steel Workers Organizing Committee (SWOC) leader Philip Murray, John L. Lewis of the Congress of Industrial Organizations (CIO), progressive black political activists Walter White of the NAACP and Lester Granger of the National Urban League, Colored Methodist Episcopal (CME) Bishop and educator James A. Bray; and the writer Langston Hughes. The diversity of its membership was reflected at its inaugural meeting on February 14, 1936, wherein 585 local and national organizations sent delegates, including members of the Universal Negro Improvement Association, members of the Baha'i faith, and black fraternities and sororities (Wittner 1970).

In the late 1930s, the NNC boasted 70 local chapters or regional councils throughout the country, all of which challenged discriminatory practices and aided black workers. The Boston council helped build recreational facilities for black children and worked with the city school board to evaluate and change racist school curricula. The Washington, D.C., chapter organized a civilian oversight board to investigate and prosecute abusive policeman in black neighborhoods. In St. Louis, Missouri, the regional council halted discrimination in hiring at a local movie theater. Throughout the country in places like Sparrows Point, Maryland; Baltimore, Maryland; Pittsburgh, Pennsylvania; Chicago, Illinois; and Gary, Indiana; the NNC joined the SWOC to organize over 85,000 black workers, approximately 20 percent of the total 550,000 steelworkers. NNC activists leafleted black neighborhoods, organized rallies, conscripted black ministers in the struggle, and used the black press to successfully appeal to black workers who joined the SWOC to end wage differentials based on race and improve working conditions throughout the industry. The NNC also organized black tobacco workers in Richmond, Virginia, black women in Chicago's garment industry, as well as service sector workers, auto workers, and domestic servants in major cities to improve their working conditions and increase wages. Black peoples' experiences as an oppressed minority were linked with their role as workers. To improve their status and create a program of black progress, African American and white leaders saw the necessity of dealing with the legal challenges that made millions of blacks noncitizens as well as the economic and industrial hurdles that relegated them to the bottom of the economic hierarchy. The NNC's heyday was short-lived and it ceased to be a major political force around 1940, but its regional councils and officers improved the life chances of black families and tens of thousands of black workers throughout the country in the face of seemingly insurmountable odds. It also created spaces for the politicization of black activists, including southern African American youth.

Black southern-born high school students and young adults were in attendance at the 1936 founding conference of the National Negro Congress and were searching for their place in the black struggle among the more seasoned activists and intellectuals. Similar to their grandparents' and parents' generations, they had been denied equal access to quality education, citizenship rights, and likewise wanted to challenge the unjust systems of oppression that were endemic in the South. They wanted to do so as part of an organization wherein their voices could be heard and they could play a prominent part. To respond to and encourage youth participation in restructuring the South and make the southern states more responsive to African Americans' needs, the NNC organized youth councils throughout the country and appointed Edward Strong, a Howard University graduate student, as the national youth chairman. With hopes of uniting black youth throughout the South, Strong organized the first Southern Negro Youth Congress conference in Richmond, Virginia, in February 1937. With 534 delegates from over 20 states, the youth called for the creation of African American history curricula in public schools, the immediate end to black disfranchisement, and improved health facilities and housing options for African Americans (Hughes 1987).

The group had an array of supporters including Angelo Herndon of the Young Communist League (YCL), the black Young Men's Christian Association (YMCA) leader Max Yergan, and Myrtle B. Powell, a white leader in the YMCA movement. They were also assisted by an Adult Advisory Board that included some of the best and brightest minds of the period, including the Howard University scholar Alaine Locke, the inimitable W.E.B. Du Bois, and Charlotte Hawkins Brown, the founder and president of Palmer Memorial Institute, a college for African American women in North Carolina. Their principle advisor was Frederick Patterson, the president of Tuskegee Institute in Tuskegee, Alabama. From its inception in 1936 to its dissolution in 1949, the NYSC was a clarion call for black youth throughout the southern states and the group organized seven major southern conferences in Richmond, Virginia, and Birmingham, Alabama. At each conference, the group made progressive declarations addressing voters' rights, educational initiatives, and workers' rights, demonstrating that the black youth of America were part of the vanguard of social and political change throughout the South. As part of its work with black workers, the NYSC—like the NNC—helped successfully organize black workers in Richmond's tobacco industry. The group also taught African American history classes as part of its worker's education program and organized the Right to Vote Campaign in Alabama (Hughes 1987).

When the United States entered WWII to fight Nazism and Fascism in Europe, the irony of their position was not lost on African Americans, who were discriminated against in the armed services and the defense industries. Unlike African Americans during WWI, when they put their protests against racism and discrimination on hold for the duration of the war, African Americans during WWII called for a double victory: a victory abroad against Nazism and Fascism and a victory at home against racism. Part of that victory at home was to compel the federal government to act on black peoples' behalf and outlaw discrimination in the military, and A. Phillip Randolph was at the forefront.

As a black socialist and president of the Brotherhood of Sleeping Car Porters, Randolph was the chief political strategist behind the March on Washington Movement (MOWM) of the 1940s. The movement was born in March 1941 as an all-black, nationwide protest group, with the primary goal of lobbying and pressuring President Franklin Roosevelt to directly respond to the discrimination African Americans experienced in their support of the war effort. The March on Washington for Jobs and Equal Participation in National Defense was scheduled for July 1, 1941, on which day, Randolph and 100,000 African Americans were to march through the nation's capital and hold a rally at the Lincoln Memorial to bear witness to their treatment and call national and international attention to racial discrimination. Randolph was supported by major black political organizations, including the NAACP and the NUL, black intellectuals, working class activists, and students in New York, Illinois, Michigan, and California.

Throughout the spring of 1941, as plans for demonstration were being made, the Roosevelt administration and the movement organizers entered into negotiations. Roosevelt wanted Randolph to call off the march to prevent a potential surge in racial animosity between the whites and blacks and so that he could maintain the illusion of national unity regarding the war effort. Randolph wanted employers who received federal monies to cease discriminating against African Americans and for the military to allow African Americans to serve in the military without obstacles based on race. After a White House meeting in June 1941 between Roosevelt, Randolph, Walter White of the NAACP, and other government and military officials, the Roosevelt Administration conceded to the MOWM and agreed to issue Executive Order 8802, which banned racial discrimination in the federally funded defense industries and created the Federal Employment Practice Committee (FEPC) to investigate continued discrimination (Kersten 2007). The march was called off, demonstrating that black people could successfully apply political pressure to the White House and change national policies.

When it was created in the summer of 1941, the FEPC was welcomed with open arms by many segments of society. With five members—two blacks and three whites—the committee's job was to hear complaints from individuals who experienced discrimination in industries receiving federal funding and associated with the war effort. However, they were brazenly rebuffed by the very industries they were to investigate, especially those industries located in the South, including railroads and shipyards (Egerton 1984). Despite Randolph's persistent agitation that the committee receive more federal funding and be given more power to actually enforce the non-discrimination clause rather than rely solely on persuasion, the committee only lasted for five years and was dismantled in 1946. African American resistance, it seems, was countered by a restructuring of white political domination.

But, as white political domination reoriented itself, civil rights organizations countered it with its own reorientation. Members of the Congress of Racial Equality (CORE) were experimenting with satyagraha, nonviolent techniques developed by Mahatma Gandhi and applied to anticolonial struggles in India. The founding members of CORE were members of the University of Chicago chapter of the Fellowship of Reconciliation (FOR), a Christian pacifist group. CORE locals around the country challenged discrimination in public accommodations and employment discrimination throughout the city in the 1940s. The Harlem, New York, branch of CORE sponsored a two-week, 240-mile march from New York to

Washington, D.C. in support of anti-lynching and anti-poll tax bills pending in Congress in 1942. In March 1942, Chicago-based members attempted to integrate the White City Roller Rink in Chicago and after a four-year campaign, including pickets, negotiations, and civil disobedience, the rink was integrated n 1946. The group also joined with others in Evanston, Illinois, to conduct a campaign against Wonder Bread Bakers, one of the many companies which benefited from black peoples' patronage but refused to hire black workers. The year-long campaign during 1946 and 1947 resulted in the Chicago-based company hiring five black truck drivers. In Los Angeles, the local CORE chapter succeeded in ending discrimination in restaurants throughout the city by 1947(Meier & Rudwick, 1973).

The most dramatic direct action campaign conducted by CORE in the 1940s was the spring 1947 Journey of Reconciliation. In June 1946, the United States Supreme Court ruled that it was unconstitutional to segregate passengers according to race on interstate passenger vehicles. Despite the ruling, African Americans continued to be victims of Jim Crow seating arrangements throughout the South. To challenge the old practices of segregated seating and to demonstrate the value of nonviolent, political activity, CORE sponsored a two-week-long bus trip through Virginia, North Carolina, and Kentucky on Trailways and Greyhound buses. Sixteen men in total participated in the journey: eight black and eight white. On the Journey, Conrad Lynn, a black New York attorney was arrested for refusing to move to the black section of a Trailways bus in Petersburg, Virginia. Andrew Johnson, a black law student, was arrested along with the black civil rights activist Bayard Rustin and James Peck, the white editor of the Workers Defense League's new bulletin, in Durham, North Carolina, for refusing to abide by illegal segregated seating. In Cargill, North Carolina, Johnson and Rustin were arrested again along with Joe Felmit, a white member of the Workers Defense League, and Igal Roodenko, a white New York printer. After being released from prison on bond, the four were chased out of town by a white lynch mob. In Asheville, North Carolina, Dennis Bank, a black participant and Chicago resident, was arrested along with James Peck. In the end, Rustin, Roodenko, and Felmet were convicted and served 22 days out of a 30-day sentence on a road gang for breaking southern customs, but following federal law. Segregation on interstate vehicles continued, but the Journey of Reconciliation showed activists that interracial, nonviolent political action was a legitimate form of protest—a lesson that would not be lost during the nonviolent demonstrations throughout the South at the height of the Civil Rights Movement in the 1950s (Meier & Rudwick, 1973).

Members of the NAACP Rights March Committee assist in preparing 300 sign-boards for a march in Gary, Indiana, in September 1963. (Courtesy of Indiana University, N.W.)

The political activism and civil rights work performed by the NAACP, the National Urban League, the Southern Negro Youth Congress, CORE, and myriad other groups during the 1930s and the 1940s calls for the re-periodization of the Civil Rights Movement to include their works. Black and white Americans may not have toppled the stronghold of segregation and discrimination throughout the country, but they did fracture the bastions of institutionalized racism for later local and national activists. By extending the chronology of the movement, one is better able to see that the political action of the 1950s and the 1960s was an extension of black activism a generation before (Wittner 1970).

References

Burma, John. "Humor As A Technique in Race Conflict," *American Sociological Review*, Vol. 11, No. 6 (Dec. 1946), 710–715.

Egerton, John. *Speak Now Against the Day: The Generation Before the Civil Rights Movement in the South* (Chapel Hill: The University of North Carolina Press, 1994).

Gilmore, Al-Tony. "Race Relations in the South, 1890–1945," in Edward Hawes' *The Age of Segregation: Race Relations in the South, 1890–1945* (Jackson, MS: University of Mississippi Press, 1978).

Greenberg, Cheryl Lynn. *Troubling the Waters: Black-Jewish Relations in the American Century* (Princeton: Princeton University Press, 2006).

Holt, John, and Elsa Barkley Brown. *Major Problems in African American History* (Boston: Cengage Learning, 2000).

Hughes, C. Alvin. "We Demand Our Rights: The Southern Negro Youth Congress, 1937–1939," *Phylon*, Vol. 48, No. 1 (1st Quarter, 1987), 38–50.

Kelley, Robin D.G. *Race Rebels* (New York: The Free Press, 1996).

Kersten, Andrew A. *Philip Randolph: A Life in the Vanguard* (Lanham, MD: Rowman & Littlefield Publishers, 2007).

McNeil, Genna Rae. *Groundwork: Charles Hamilton Houston and the Struggle for Civil Rights* (Philadelphia: University of Pennsylvania Press, 1983), 63–75.

Meier, August, and Elliott Rudwick, *CORE: A Study in the Civil Rights Movement, 1942–1969* (New York: Oxford University Press, 1973).

Moore, Jesse Thomas, Jr. *A Search for Equality: The National Urban League, 1910–1961* (University Park, PA: The Pennsylvania State University Press, 1981).

Waldrep, Christopher. *African Americans Confront Lynching* (Lanham, MD: Rowan and Littlefield, 2009).

Wittner, Lawrence, S. "The National Negro Congress: A Reassessment," *American Quarterly*, Vol. 22, No. 4 (Winter, 1970), 883–901.

THREE

"We Shall Overcome": The Movement in Alabama

IT WAS IN MONTGOMERY, Alabama, that one of the most popular and iconic civil rights struggles took place. There, a black community of approximately 50,000 people challenged segregation in public transportation by waging a successful boycott of the city's buses for over a year—381 days, from December, 1955 to December, 1956. The segregation policy in the city stipulated that, on any given bus, the seats toward the front of the bus were reserved for whites; however, when the white section was full, the seats immediately behind it and occupied by black customers had to be vacated and given to any white customer on the bus driver's demands. Such was the case on one bus on December 1, 1955. Rosa Parks, a seamstress at the Montgomery Fair Department Store, was returning home on a city bus and sat in the seat immediately behind the all-white reserved section; when that section was fully occupied, the driver demanded that she give her seat to a white male passenger. Parks refused. She had not been the first woman to refuse to vacate her seat. In March of that year, Claudette Colvin, a high school teenager, refused to relinquish her seat for a white passenger and was arrested. In fact, Parks was part of a long history of black women who resisted segregation and humiliation on the buses throughout the city. E.D. Nixon, a local activist, former Alabama state and Montgomery chapter president of the National Association for the Advancement of Colored People (NAACP), and member of A. Philip Randolph's Brotherhood of Sleeping Car Porters, along with attorney Clifford Durr and activist Virginia Durr, arranged for Parks' release from jail and escorted her home. Her trial was set for Monday, December 5, 1955.

Between December 1 and December 5, activists from different sectors of Montgomery's black population met to discuss and organize a one-day boycott of the buses to coincide with Rosa Parks' trial. At the forefront of the boycott preparation was the Women's Political Council (WPC).

Rosa Parks is fingerprinted in Montgomery, Alabama. Parks's arrest for refusing to give up her seat on a bus to a white man on December 1, 1955, inspired the Montgomery Bus Boycott, a prolonged action against the segregated Montgomery, Alabama, bus system by African American riders and their white supporters. (Library of Congress)

Organized in 1946 by Mary Fair Burks, the chairperson of the English department at Alabama State College and 40 other women, the WPC was a political organization comprised of Alabama State College faculty members and the wives of black professional men throughout the city. During the late 1940s and the early 1950s, the WPC sponsored voter registration drives, mentored youth, and met with city officials to challenge segregated public parks and register complaints about abuses meted out to black riders on city buses (Crawford et al. 1993). By the time of the boycott, Jo Anne Robinson, an English professor at Alabama State College, had assumed the presidency of the organization. According to Robinson, the WPC had discussed plans for a citywide bus boycott in early 1955, but it never materialized (Robinson 1987). December 1955, however, offered an ideal moment to capitalize on the growing black dissatisfaction with the buses and the willingness to challenge segregation. On Friday, December 2, WPC members distributed leaflets throughout the black sections of Montgomery. The leaflet requested "every Negro to stay off the buses Monday in protest of the arrest and trial. Don't ride the buses to work, to town, to school, or anywhere on Monday. . . . If you work take a cab or walk" (Robinson 1987, 46). In addition to WPC leaflets, Montgomery's black clergyman urged their congregants to support the planned boycott during sermons delivered on Sunday, December 4.

On Monday morning, December 5, Rosa Parks was found guilty of violating Montgomery's segregation laws and fined $14. Few black Montgomerians were surprised with the verdict. But, what was surprising for many was that the boycott was an overwhelming success. While some African Americans took the bus, over 90 percent of black bus riders refused to ride city buses throughout the day (Sitkoff 1993). Ministers and activists met during the afternoon to discuss the implications of the boycott and possible next steps before the scheduled mass meeting at the Holt Street Baptist Church that evening. Not wanting to lose political momentum generated from the boycott, the Montgomery Improvement Association (MIA) was formed to direct the protest, coordinate transportation for boycotters, garner support from individuals and organizations in and outside of the state, and enter into negotiations with the bus company and city officials. Reverend Martin Luther King Jr. was elected president of the organization. Having recently finished coursework in his doctoral program at Boston University, King moved to Montgomery to assume the pastorate at Dexter Avenue Baptist Church in September 1954. King was the right person for the job and his acceptance of the position was the beginning of his career as a civil rights leader. He was eloquent and well educated, and because he was a newcomer to Montgomery, he was not part of the political infighting among black Montgomerians or the beneficiary of patronage from city fathers, which often had the effect of rendering one innocuous as a political leader.

During the evening meeting on December 5, thousands of black Montgomerians met to celebrate their unity and determination throughout the day and to consider the next steps. When no more weary and eager boycotters could fit in the church, they congregated outside the church, listening to the proceedings on loudspeakers. At the meeting, it was decided that the boycott should continue until the bus company met blacks' three basic demands—more respectful and courteous treatment by bus drivers; seating on a first-come, first-served basis, with black passengers seated from the rear of the vehicle toward the front and whites passengers seated from the front toward the rear; and the hiring of black bus drivers for routes in black neighborhoods (King 1958).

In the closing weeks of 1955 and the opening weeks of 1956, a delegation from the MIA met with city officials, a group of white business owners, and members of the city's social elite to air their grievances and have their demands met. At the time, Montgomery was governed by a mayor, W.A. Gayle, and two city commissioners, Frank Parks and Clyde Sellers. At every turn, city officials and the white delegation rebuffed boycotters and refused to entertain their demands, even when the MIA removed the hiring of black drivers from their demands. According to commissioners, to change bus seating would go against segregation laws and long-held cultural mores.

After several meetings, by late January 1956, it was clear that neither side would relent. The boycotters understood their protest to be a righteous cause and a refusal to cooperate with social evils. To ensure that boycotters could go to and from their jobs, the MIA created a carpool system, with depots and pick up stops across the city. Black churches and scores of black Montgomerians volunteered their cars, station wagons, and time to shuttle people around the city. As the boycott continued, MIA leaders purchased their own vehicles from donations that arrived from individuals around the world. They also held weekly mass meetings to keep protesters abreast of developments and to buoy their spirits. These weekly mass meetings, remembers Martin Luther King Jr., "followed a simple pattern: songs, prayer, Scripture reading, opening remarks by the president, collection, reports from various committees and a 'pep talk'" (King 1958, 73).

The mayor and city officials positioned that the separation of the races was ordained by God and social custom, and white Montgomerians retaliated against the boycotters with harassment, violence, and political deception. At the January meeting of the White Citizens' Council, Clyde Sellers, the commissioner of Montgomery's police force, joined the organization. Several weeks later, Mayor Gayle followed suit. When they were not taunted by white residents with "walk, nigger walk," on their way to and from work, black boycotters were harassed by telephone (Robinson 1987, 125). The movement leaders and the rank and file were called by mysterious voices who threatened violence unless they returned to the buses. Police officers stopped, fined, and arrested carpool drivers on trumped-up charges and imagined violations. The Bell Street Baptist Church, Mount Olive Baptist Church, and the homes of E. D. Nixon, Martin Luther King Jr, Reverend Robert Graetz, and Reverend Ralph Abernathy were all bombed.

Mayor Gayle and Commissioners Sellers and Parks even created an elaborate ruse to trick black residents to end the boycott. The three city fathers summoned three rural black ministers to the city hall under the pretense that they were to discuss issues related to insurance; however, when they arrived, the mayor and commissioners issued a false settlement statement. The news of the settlement was printed in the Sunday, January 22 *Montgomery Advertiser*, the local paper, and informed the readership that blacks would return to the buses on Monday, January 23. King and the MIA executive board were informed of the ruse on Saturday, January 21 and throughout the day and evening they visited black bars, clubs, and juke joints to inform people that there was no settlement. On Sunday, every pastor affiliated with the boycott informed their congregations that the boycott had not ended. On Monday, January 23, African Americans stayed off the buses (Robinson 1987; King 1958).

When violence, harassment, and deception did not work, city officials went to the courts to disrupt the boycott. The MIA was accused of violating Title 14, Section 54 of the state constitution, which prohibits boycotts. In February 1956, Judge Eugene Carter ordered a grand jury to investigate the boycott. On February 21, the jury, comprised of 18 Montgomery residents (17 white and 1 black) indicted and called for the arrest of over 100 black citizens associated with the boycott. The jury identified King as the leader of the boycott. At his trial in late March 1956, he was found guilty of violating the anti-boycotting law. The 89 other defendants were to stand trial, pending King's appeal. Despite the trial and continued harassment, the boycott continued for nine more months, even after November 1956, when a state court-ordered injunction ruled that the carpool that shuttled people throughout the city was illegal.

Throughout 1956, African Americans in Montgomery realized that their demands for better treatment within the confines of segregation would not be met and behind-the-scenes lawyers worked through the courts to outlaw segregation. In May 1956, MIA and NAACP lawyers, including Arthur Shore, Peter Hall, Orzell Billingsley, Fred Gray, Charles Langford, and Robert Carter, presented their case to a three-judge panel in the federal court in Montgomery. Segregation in public transportation, they argued, was unconstitutional because it violated the Fourteenth Amendment. It was a similar argument presented in the *Brown vs. Board of Education of Topeka* in 1954. On June 5, in a two-to-one decision, the panel released its opinion that agreed with the attorneys and ruled that segregation on the city buses was unconstitutional. City officials appealed the decision to the United States Supreme Court, which upheld the decision in November 1956. On December 20, city officials received the Court's order and segregated bus service was eliminated. The boycott ended after 381 days and was a key victory in the Civil Rights Movement (Robinson 1987; Sitkoff

1993; King 1958). Local people, the educated and the uneducated, the affluent and the poor had organized and demonstrated to people around the country and the world, especially African Americans in other southern cities, that they could organize themselves to abolish a system that had oppressed them for decades.

Years later, in 1963 and 1965, African Americans in Birmingham and Selma, Alabama, respectively, mobilized to bring about racial equality under the law in their cities. To do this in Birmingham, black residents, along with the leaders of the Southern Christian Leadership Conference (SCLC) and the Alabama Christian Movement for Human Rights (ACHR), a local affiliate of the SCLC, conducted a direct action campaign and the boycott of local white businesses. The SCLC was founded in January of 1957 in Atlanta, Georgia, by African American ministers mainly from southern states. With Martin Luther King Jr. as its first elected president, the organization used the black church and its members as a political force in cities throughout the South and spread the teachings and strategies of nonviolent protest. The campaign in Birmingham, Alabama, Project C (C for Confrontation) took place in the spring of 1963 during the months of April and May. The SCLC demanded an end to segregation in downtown department stores and restaurants, the elimination of discriminatory hiring practices in businesses throughout the city, and the creation of an oversight committee that would implement desegregation policies (King 2011). It was the SCLC's second major political campaign. The first was in Albany, Georgia, in 1961 and 1962, where the organization failed to change segregation laws and customs in the city. Learning from their failures and determined not to repeat the same mistakes in Birmingham as they did in Albany, the SCLC sought to change a place that many had called the most segregated large city in the South.

On April 3, a small group of black volunteers went to white-owned businesses in the downtown area and conducted a sit-in at lunch counters. The campaign was multifaceted and included the mass jailing of protestors and an economic boycott. While the sit-ins continued, on April 6, Reverend Fred Shuttlesworth, the founder of ACHR, led a march of 50 protestors through the downtown area to the city hall, where they were promptly arrested by the Commissioner of Public Safety, Eugene "Bull" Connor, and Birmingham police officers. Hoping to halt the movement or at least derail it for the time being, city officials obtained an injunction on April 10, which deemed demonstrations and marches illegal. Despite the injunction, Martin Luther King Jr. and Reverend Ralph Abernathy led a march in downtown Birmingham on April 12, Good Friday, and were quickly arrested. King spent over a week in prison, during which time, he wrote his famous *Letter from a Birmingham Jail.*

Throughout the subsequent weeks of the campaign, thousands of protestors were arrested and jailed, as SCLC strategists wanted and predicted. In early May 1963, the SCLC unleashed its most potent weapon against segregation: children. To dramatize the system of segregation and demonstrate to the world their opposition to it, the SCLC enlisted children in the nonviolent movement. Over a period of two days, between May 2 and May 3, thousands of children filled the Sixteenth Street Baptist Church. Many were high school students who left school for the day, but some were as young as six years old.

In the early afternoon of May 2, the city was bracing itself for another day of protests. Officers were posted on street corners throughout the city and downtown businesses were losing money, but the black population was excited as they saw the bastions of segregation crumbling. Around 1 PM, the thousands of students who have arrived at the Sixteenth Street Baptist Church, the Metropolitan African Methodist Episcopal Church, and the Apostolic Overcome Holiness Church of God began to mobilize. Exiting the church two abreast, in groups ranging from as few as 10 to as many as 50, singing, marching students left each building in different directions to descend upon the business district. They were soon intercepted by the police. Singing "We Shall Overcome" and carrying signs, the youth were herded into police vehicles. When the paddy wagons were not enough, school buses were brought to the scene. At the end of the first day of the Children's Crusade, as it has been called, as many as 600 children were in custody. On May 3, the second day of the Children's Crusade, thousands of students filled the churches again. Like the day before, they planned to march on the streets of Birmingham and be arrested. With jails full of adult and children protesters, Bull Connor was running out of space to house the protesters and had other plans. Instead of arresting the protesters, he ordered the police and the fire department to use dogs and fire hoses to disperse the children. High-pressure water knocked children off their feet and dogs lunged at the protesters and spectators, tearing into flesh and ripping off garments.

That Bull Connor would resort to violence was not surprising to the SCLC staff and strategists; they expected the police department to use violent tactics so that the SCLC would demonstrate to the world the viciousness of segregated life in the South. Newspapers and magazines throughout the country and around the world showed pictures of individuals, who had formally pledged their bodies to the nonviolent movement, assaulted by those who promised to serve and protect (King 2011). Violent reprisals also got the attention of the Kennedy administration and forced President John F. Kennedy and Attorney General Robert F. Kennedy to enter into the struggle for justice and use their federal power to persuade the business and political elite of Birmingham to enter into negotiations with the SCLC. They sent Burke Marshall, the assistant attorney for civil rights, to the state to negotiate a deal. During the first week of May 1963, Marshall held closed meetings with white businessmen, civic leaders, and the SCLC. He also mobilized 3,000 soldiers of Alabama's National Guard and deployed them to the outskirts of Birmingham (Wilson 2000). Marshall's negotiations, the SCLC's nonviolent direct actions, local black Birmingham residents' willingness and ability to put their lives on the line, the economic boycott of white businesses, and public pressure wore down white decision makers in Birmingham. On May 10, 1963, a settlement was agreed upon by members of the SCLC and the Senior Citizens Committee, a group of 70 leading private business leaders. It called for:

Desegregation of lunch counters, rest rooms, fitting rooms, and drinking fountains in all downtown stories within ninety days;

Placement of blacks in clerical and sales jobs in stores within sixty days;

Release of protesters in jail and on bail; and

The establishment of permanent communications between white and black leaders. (Garrow 1989, 182)

In late 1964 and early 1965, the SCLC turned its focus to Selma, Alabama, and the passing of federal legislation that would guarantee the enforcement of African Americans' right to vote throughout the American South. In late December 1964, the SCLC was invited to Selma by the Committee of Fifteen, a civic and political organization that represented a cross section of Selma's and Dallas County's (wherein Selma was located) African American population, to help local blacks further their attempts to register to vote. African Americans had been denied the opportunity to register to vote throughout the South by a host of legal and extra legal methods, as discussed in chapter one, but Selma was selected for a nonviolent direct action and voter registration campaign because it was, according to King, "a symbol of bitter-end resistance to the civil rights movement in the Deep South" (Garrow 1980, 39).

The campaign started in earnest on January 4 and lasted until May of 1965. Its primary objective was to dramatize Selma's and other southern locales' blatant and unconstitutional disenfranchisement of thousands of black people to the nation and the federal government. Like the Montgomery campaign, Selma's movement involved mass demonstrations, marches, and mass meetings to enliven and encourage African Americans to fight their generations' long disenfranchisement. In Selma, voter registration occurred on the first and third Monday of each month. It was on those days that black Selma residents mobilized themselves by the hundreds to go downtown to register. On almost every first and third Monday of the month, from January to June, black people went to the registrar and were turned away by Sheriff James G. Clark Jr. Clark was known to be a violent man and the SCLC was counting on his violent behavior and antics to help get the attention of white liberals and the federal government. After an initial nonviolent phase, Clark responded in form. Throughout those six months, hundreds were arrested, including a battalion of nonviolent school children who marched through the downtown area. In one violent episode, Clark was photographed beating Annie Lee Cooper, an African American woman, with his club while police officers pinned her to the ground. The violent confrontation was plastered in the *New York Times* and the *Washington Post* for the world, and particularly, the president, vice, president, senators, and congressmen, to see.

President Lyndon Johnson, Vice President Hubert Humphreys, senators, and congressmen were aware of the need for voting rights legislation. It was well known throughout the ranks of policy makers and political leaders that violence, subterfuge, and intimidation were used to keep blacks from voting throughout the South, despite the passage of the 1964 Civil Rights Act. In fact, in late 1964, Lyndon Johnson was considering a push to pass voting rights legislations. But, while he and other political leaders were considering how such legislation would affect their political careers or the best way to court southern white voters at the expense of black nonvoters, the SCLC and local African Americans took to the streets. The most quixotic and violent confrontation between African American demonstrators and the Selma police force occurred on Bloody Sunday, March 1965. On February 16, black demonstrators participating in a night march were assaulted by Alabama state troopers, who left scores injured in their wake, including Jimmie Lee Jackson, a young black activist who was shot in the back of his head. Jackson eventually died from his injuries eight days later (Garrow 1990). In order to celebrate his life and political convictions as well as the political convictions of Selma's black residents, 500 African Americans and white Americans gathered at Brown's Chapel on March 7 to walk the 54-mile stretch from Selma to Montgomery,

Alabama, the capital of Alabama. With Martin Luther King Jr. absent, 600 marchers were lead by James Bevel, a stalwart SCLC activist, and Reverend Hosea Williams. In the early afternoon, marchers emerged from Brown's Chapel, the headquarters of the SCLC in Selma, and moved toward the Pettus Bridge, the major exit route from Selma to Montgomery.

Governor Charles Wallace had decided the night before that the marchers would not proceed over the bridge and issued an injunction prohibiting the march. They were stopped by the police. Reverend Hosea Williams asked repeatedly if he could speak to the head of the police contingent, Major John Cloud. When the officer on duty refused, the marchers waited. Suddenly, a call went out to the police officers on duty, "officers, march." Tear gas was fired and officers on foot and horseback descended upon the marchers with whips, clubs, and pistols. The incident was chronicled by reporters on the scene—some of whom were assaulted by white bystanders. The officers forced black marchers to retreat to Brown's Chapel or

Flag-bearing demonstrators march from Selma to Montgomery, Alabama, in the historic March 1965 voting rights protest. The march led directly to the 1965 Voting Rights Act, which outlawed the Southern states' attempts to prevent African Americans from voting. (Library of Congress)

to the surrounding black neighborhoods. Hundreds were wounded. The incident was reported in newspapers throughout the country. How was it possible that law-abiding, peaceful protestors could be attacked in such a vicious manner, Martin Luther King Jr., President Johnson, Vice President Humphrey, senators, and congressmen demanded to know? King, upon hearing about Bloody Sunday, as that day had come to be known, called upon hundreds of religious leaders to join him on Tuesday, March 9, 1965, to continue the march.

Despite the Johnson administration's insistence that the march not take place, hundreds of marchers assembled at Brown's Chapel in the early afternoon of March 9. Outside the chapel, they organized themselves into two columns and began their march to the Pettus Bridge. This time, King led the procession of nonviolent activists. When they reached the crest of the bridge, state troopers parted like the Red Sea, providing an open passage for the marchers to proceed. However, rather than march onward to Montgomery, King halted, turned the procession in the direction of Brown's Chapel, and returned to the church, effectively calling off the march. He had made a secret deal with the police to march to the bridge, but not continue over it. For King's approach to march would offend and potentially slight the Johnson administration and federal officials—all of whom the movement needed. Lyndon B. Johnson said that if the march continued, the positive relationship that had existed between the movement leaders and the government would turn sour. Despite angry reactions from other activists, especially the Student Nonviolent Coordinating Committee, King's approach prevailed.

With federal intervention, Governor Wallace's injunction was overturned and the SCLC's march was eventually approved by the Johnson administration, which mobilized close to 2,000 national guardsmen for the marchers' protection (Garrow 1980). On Sunday, March 21, over 3,000 people finally began the long-awaited march from Selma to Montgomery, Alabama. Several days later, on March 25, the tired marchers descended upon Montgomery to join over 20,000 other demonstrators and participated in a rally outside of the Alabama statehouse. The Selma campaign would continue for a couple more months after the successful March 21 march. King, SCLC leaders, and local Selma residents attempted a boycott of stores that practiced discrimination in hiring, but that effort fizzled out with no real successes. They also tried to negotiate with Mayor Joseph Smitherman and create equal hiring practices in public and private sector jobs, to no avail. In the end, the success of the Selma campaign in early

1965 was not an increased number of black registered voters because only 250 African Americans had been registered as a result of the voter registration jobs. Neither can the success of the movement be measured by any real economic indices. Black Selma residents were not hired in large numbers in public and private sector jobs and many were fired from their jobs for participating in the movement, as were blacks elsewhere in the South. The success of the campaign lies in the political mobilization of thousands of black people—adults and children. They no longer suffered from political paralysis and organized themselves to fight injustice. It also revealed to the American public and the world the injustices that black people endured throughout the South, and thereby forced public opinion to the side of black demonstrators and activists. Finally, the Selma campaign forced the hand of the federal government to stand unequivocally with the Civil Rights movement by passing the Voting Rights Act of 1965.

With the passing of the Voting Rights Act, African Americans throughout the South were placed on voter rolls in large numbers. For blacks in Lowndes County, Alabama, the large-scale registration prompted residents to create a third political party, the Lowndes County Freedom Organization (LCFO) in 1965, to challenge the democratic and republican parties at the local level. Lowndes County residents and the Student Nonviolent Coordinating Committee (SNCC) participated in voter registration drives before the passage of the Voting Rights Act. They also boycotted stores that discriminated against black customers, attempted to improve segregated education and integrate publicly funded schools, prayed, marched, and prayed some more. Stokely Carmichael of SNCC was the first to suggest the idea of an independent black political party in Lowndes. The LCFO allowed African Americans the chance to challenge directly the Democratic Party, which for so long, had discriminated against them. There was simply "no room for Negroes in the same party as [George] Wallace" (Jeffries 2009, 147). No one was deluded to believe that the LCFO could affect national policies, but in a county that was majority black, SNCC activists believed that black elected officials could improve daily living conditions on the local level, from the sheriff's department to the board of education.

SNCC began the process of creating the LCFO through political education. In workshops on government and law, SNCC activists taught Lowndes County residents the structure and function of local government. Everyone was invited to attend, including the poor, not just the elite. It was this fact that made the creation of the LCFO truly democratic— the process and the opportunity to run for office were open to both the college-educated elite and those who had limited formal education. Similar to Reconstruction era politics in Richmond, Virginia, about which historian Elsa Barkley Brown writes, leaders and leadership were cultivated from and nurtured by the masses of people—a fundamental belief of SNCC's ideological mother, Ella Baker (Crawford et al. 1993; Brown 1997). In addition to political education workshops, SNCC workers canvassed the county, distributed leaflets, and garnered support for the party through face-to-face interactions. After months of grassroots work, the LCFO was launched on April 2, 1966, with a snarling black panther as the organization's symbol. The president and vice president of the organization, John Hulett and Robert Strickland, respectively, had been known for their work with the Lowndes County Christian Movement for Human Rights, a local, black political group responsible for voter registration drives and other political actions in the county throughout the late 1950s and the early 1960s.

Having determined that there were county seats for which elections would be held in November 1966, a dozen LCFO members declared their candidacy for county positions. In the closing days of April and the opening days of May 1966, each candidate tried to rally support from community members. When the electioneering was over and the May 3, 1966 convention ended, the LCFO members announced its slate of candidates who would challenge the all-white Democratic Party in the fall. The list for the first election bid for the organization was extensive and included the following:

Alice Moore—tax assessor
Frank Miles—tax collector
Emory Ross—coroner
Sidney Logan Jr.—sheriff
Robert Logan—school board
John Hinson—school board
Bernice Kelly—school board
Willie Mae Strickland—school board (Jeffries 2009, 163, 173)

From late spring to late autumn 1966, candidates learned about the duties of their potential positions, rallied support from their constituents, and politicized a population in ways that they had never imagined just a year before. The energy and enthusiasm that marked the preparation for the election, however, was not enough as all of the LCFO candidates were defeated. Debates exist as to why they lost. Some suggest that the plantation owners did not allow black field workers to leave the fields to vote. Others suggest that the whites resorted to the intimidation of black voters. Whatever the reason, LCFO candidates and SNCC activists did not get the black turnout they initially expected. In 1968, with a new name, the Lowndes County Freedom Party, black independent electoral politics was revived and several African Americans ran for county political office again. Like the election of 1966, they were soundly defeated. In 1970, African Americans decided to support the newly reorganized Democratic Party in the state. With the political move, John Hulett, Charles Smith, and other black candidates were elected to several county political offices throughout the 1970s (Carson 1981).

The state of Alabama was a key battleground of the Civil Rights Movement in the 1950s and the 1960s. As a site of political and social contestation, African Americans throughout the state experimented with a host of political strategies, but not without loss of life and some failures. The freedom struggle there was influential in that it dramatized racial oppression in Alabama and throughout the South, mobilized federal support for the Civil Rights Movement in the passing of the Voting Rights Act of 1965, experimented with independent black-supported political parties, and influenced the creation of other independent black organizations, like the National Democratic Party of Alabama and the Black Panther Party in the San Francisco Bay.

References

Brown, Elsa Barkley. "To Catch the Vision of Freedom: Reconstruction Southern Black Women's Political History, 1865–1880," in Ann D. Gordon et al., eds., *African American Women and the Vote, 1837–1965* (Amherst, MA: University of Massachusetts Press, 1997).

Carson, Clayborne. *In Struggle: SNCC and the Black Awakening of the 1960s* (Cambridge, MA: Harvard University Press, 1981).

Crawford, Vicki L., Jacqueline Anne Rouse, and Barbara Woods, eds. *Women in the Civil Rights Movement* (Bloomington: Indiana University Press, 1993).

Garrow, David. *Protest at Selma: Martin Luther King, Jr. and the Voting Rights Act of 1965* (New Haven: Yale University Press, 1980).

Garrow, David. *Birmingham, Alabama, 1956–1963: The Black Struggle for Civil Rights* (Brooklyn: Carlson Publishers, 1989).

Jeffries, Hasan. *Bloody Lowndes: Civil Rights and Black Power in Alabama's Black Belt* (New York: New York University Press, 2009).

King, Martin Luther, Jr. *Stride Toward Freedom: The Montgomery Story* (Boston: Beacon Press, 2010).

King, Martin Luther, Jr. *Why We Can't Wait* (Boston: Beacon Press, 2011).

Robinson, Jo Ann. *The Montgomery Bus Boycott and the Women Who Started It* (Knoxville: University of Tennessee Press, 1987)

Sitkoff, Harvard. *The Struggle for Black Equality, 1954–1992* (New York: Hill and Wang, 1993).

Wilson, Bobby. *Race and Place in Birmingham: The Civil Rights and Neighborhood Movements* (Lanham, MD: Rowman & Littlefield Publishers, 2000).

FOUR

"Ain't Gonna Let Nobody Turn Me 'round": The Movement in Mississippi

FOLLOWING WORLD WAR II (WWII) and well into the 1950s, despite efforts at industrialization, Mississippi was primarily rural and those African Americans who had not migrated out of the state were largely found in the state's western portion and indulged primarily in unskilled labor. As agricultural and service workers, the black Mississippian's median annual income of $601 in 1950 was well short of the white median income of $2,105 (Williams 1985, 23). The agricultural economy allowed economic and political power to remain in the hands of a group of small white elites who, in turn, created an environment where the majority of blacks remained impoverished and uneducated, with poor health, shortened life spans, and limited political options to change their situation. White intransigence provided few options to desegregate public facilities before 1960, but African Americans in Mississippi organized themselves against segregation and discrimination to the extent they could in the immediate post-WWII years. With these limitations in clear view, black activists in the late 1940s and the early 1950s focused their efforts on voter registration, where they thought they would get the best results, rather than focusing on desegregation. Even with voter registration, the black freedom movement in Mississippi was small and mainly the realm of middle class blacks. It was not until the early 1960s, with the Freedom Rides, the black election, the 1964 Freedom Summer, and the organization of the Mississippi Freedom Democratic Party (MFDP) that large-scale civil rights organization and opposition to white supremacy occurred. Mississippi shows that quite often the black people's struggle for equality was decentralized.

Following WWII, there were several organizations that tried to improve black people's lives. The Committee of 100, a group comprised of Mississippi's black middle class, often met with white elected officials and power brokers of the state to increase opportunities for black voter participation and access to educational opportunities. Recognizing the barriers to black achievement and the structures that only allowed black existence within segregated spaces, the organization did not challenge the practice of segregation; instead, they sought to accommodate themselves to, and carve out a space within, the system. The Mississippi Progressive Voters League (MPVL) and the state National Association for the Advancement of Colored People (NAACP) aided blacks attempting to register to vote by providing voter education classes (Williams 1985). Many of the activists working with MPVL and the NAACP were veterans who had recently returned from overseas, two of whom were Earl Brown and Robert Wansley. Both Brown and Wansley traveled throughout the state, meeting other black veterans, gave tips on interpreting the constitution for registrars, and even escorted other veterans to courthouses throughout the state to register to vote. The courage of Brown and Wansley inspired hundreds of returning veterans to register, especially after a 1946 state law was passed, allowing veterans to vote without paying a poll tax. State legislators never intended the law to apply to black veterans since other racist laws disenfranchised them, but black veterans throughout the state persisted, and despite intimidation and violence, some succeeded in voting for the first times in their lives.

Throughout the early 1950s, middle class and working class African Americans began to organize local NAACP chapters throughout the state in Indianola, Clarksdale, Natchez, Meridian, Pike County, and Jones County—places where several years before, organizing a branch was impossible. These chapters, like the MPVL, urged black Mississippians to register to vote and many held voter education classes to assist potential voters in answering the registrar's questions when they registered. But, even with the efforts of newly founded NAACP chapters and the League, by 1954, blacks throughout the state made only limited gains in the voting rolls. In that year, only 22,000 African Americans—about four percent of the eligible number—were registered to vote (Dittmer 1995, 52).

Such political action may have gone unnoticed by the local, white mainstream news agencies or vilified by other white newspapers like the *Daily News* in Jackson, Mississippi, but not by the *Advocate*, a black newspaper, also based in Jackson, Mississippi. The paper was edited by the black journalist Percy Greene, who followed the stories and documented the courage of black activists. Greene would eventually become a supporter of slow, moderate change in the racist status quo in the late 1950s. But during the 1940s and the early 1950s, his *Advocate* was the most popular black newspaper in Mississippi and he used it to speak to the needs of blacks, report anti-black violence, and, as the paper's name indicates, advocate for black people and the political and educational change throughout the state. He was economically independent from whites, unlike the rural and working class blacks, and was less likely to suffer economic reprisals for his political stances. He organized the Mississippi Negro Democratic Association in 1946 to provide a forum and organizational apparatus for black political activity. The *Advocate* promoted voter registration drives conducted by the MPVL (for which he was the state's vice president), advocated for the equalization of black teachers' pay; supported statewide anti-poll tax legislation, anti-lynching legislation, and the creation of the Federal Employment Practices Commission; and reported on blacks' first attempts at desegregating public schools (Williams 1985).

After the May 1954 Supreme Court *Brown v. Board of Education of Topeka* decision, which deemed separate but equal educational policies unconstitutional, black Mississippians were encouraged to try to integrate schools throughout the state. Their attempts failed, but a brief discussion of these unsuccessful efforts demonstrates the optimism of black civil rights activists, the multiple strategies used throughout the movement, as well as the lengths to which white authority would go to maintain the status quo in the state. One strategy was to petition state officials. In June of 1954, a delegation of black educators, academics, political leaders, and clergy met with then Governor Hugh White and urged him to enforce the *Brown* decision throughout the state. White had no plans to integrate schools and wanted the delegation to accept voluntary and better-funded separate education. He went so far as to support the dissolving of state public education to avoid compliance with *Brown*. Such a dismantling never occurred, of course, because the *Brown* decision was not enforced throughout the state in the 1950s and the 1960s. The NAACP urged parents to petition local school boards and also to comply with the Supreme Court decision. Blacks who petitioned school boards were harassed and intimidated as white Mississippians felt as if their entire way of life was under attack.

In their efforts to protect their segregated and racially hierarchical society, the whites formed a Citizens' Council, which sought to neutralize African Americans' attempts for equality, including desegregated education and voting rights. The first Citizens' Council was formed in July of 1954 in Indianola, Mississippi, and had as its primary mission, the maintenance of segregated public education. By October 1954, the organization had over 25,000 dues-paying members throughout the state. One observer correctly noted that the Citizens' Councils "comprises men of stature in the community—businessmen, lawyers, ministers, etc. These are people who have a natural distaste for violence and even at times seriously worry about the effects of brutality by law enforcement officers" (Miller 1985, 291). To thwart black political hopes, the Citizens' Council embarked on what the historian John Dittmer calls, a "campaign of economic intimidation" against Mississippi's black leaders. One prominent example was Emmett Stringer of the NAACP. Stringer was a successful black dentist and his wife, also African American, was a popular teacher. As a result of his civil rights work, he was denied lines of credit from the local bank, had his car insurance canceled, and received threats to his life. Gus Courts, the president of the Belzoni, Mississippi chapter of the NAACP, was forced to resign from his position after receiving a bank notice that his credit rating would be lowered if he continued his political work. In July 1954, in the city of Vicksburg, Mississippi, black parents who petitioned their local board of education to desegregate schools had their names listed in the local newspaper. Shortly thereafter, they were harassed by anxious white citizens (Dittmer 1995).

The Citizens' Council's economic intimidation was supported by a wave of physical violence that marred the state in the mid-1950s, and while such violence may not have been carried out by Council members, they gave it their tacit approval. Virtually no one went on record as opposing the killings and beatings that occurred. In fact, it could be argued that since the Council members were the economic elite and policy makers at the state and local levels and did nothing to counter the wanton killing of black Mississippians, they condoned anti-black violence. In May 1955, the Reverend George Lee was killed after being shot in the face by an unknown assailant. During the same year, in August, Lamar Smith, a black voting rights activist and farmer, was gunned down in front of the courthouse in Brookhaven, Mississippi. Neither Smith's nor Lee's deaths were ever properly investigated by the Federal Bureau of Investigation nor by the state and local authorities and no one was ever charged for their murder (Dittmer 1995).

The most publicized murder was that of Emmett Till in August 1955. Till, a 14-year-old Chicago resident arrived in Money, Mississippi, in the summer of 1955, to spend part of his school vacation with relatives. On August 25, after a day of chores and hanging out with his cousins, he went into the town store. Upon exiting the store after purchasing candy, Till either whistled at the 21-year-old white female clerk, Carolyn Bryant, or said something she took offense to. Some sources say he asked her for a date. Others say that when he exited the store he said "good-bye, baby." Several days later, under the cloak of darkness, Roy Bryant, the husband of the store clerk, and J. W. Milam arrived at Moses Wright's house, Till's uncle's home, seeking revenge for Till's breaking of southern racial norms. Bryant and Milam kidnapped Till, beat him, shot him in the head, and threw his lifeless body in the river. Both were arrested and tried and, despite eyewitness testimony from Moses Wright, Bryant and Milam were acquitted by the all-white male jury. Years later, they sold their story to *Look* magazine, admitting they killed Emmett Till (*The Murder of Emmet Till*, 2003).

In the late 1940s and throughout the 1950s, black challenges to segregation and equality were beaten back by the shifting and overlapping structures of domination. In numerous cases, white economic domination intimidated blacks and prevented them from pursuing their civil rights. White legislative maneuvering removed black voters who were already registered and prohibited unregistered blacks from being placed on the voting rolls. Legislators also passed laws which deemed attempts to desegregate any institution unlawful and subject to fines and/or incarceration. The State Sovereignty Commission, a secret state-sanctioned surveillance group, infiltrated and disrupted civil rights organizations and white vigilante justice enforced the color line with violence. In the 1960s, however, the movement was re-energized and African Americans organized grassroots campaigns in towns and cities to increase black voting and dismantle Mississippi's segregated society. They were not always successful and white Mississippians used tried-and-true tactics to dissuade and disrupt activists, but blacks persevered and continued to try and make Mississippi live up to the American ideals of equality and justice. The movements in McComb and Jackson, Mississippi, offer two vivid examples of political work that African Americans organized and the obstacles they faced in the 1960s.

In the summer of 1961, the Student Nonviolent Coordinating Committee (SNCC), led by Robert "Bob" Moses, began their voter registration drive in McComb, Mississippi, a town in the southwest part of the state with a population of 13,000. Roughly 4,000 residents were black. Activists walked door to door in the black section of town and encouraged the adults to register to vote and the youth to join the organization. To help them pass the registrar's test, SNCC members conducted voter registration classes. In less than a month, several blacks attempted to take the test and passed. Buoyed with enthusiasm and optimism, the local youth formed the Pike County Nonviolent Movement and five members attempted to desegregate a Woolworth's drugstore lunch counter and bus terminals in downtown McComb. They were arrested and subsequently imprisoned for 34 days.

When they were released in September 1961, school officials at Burgland High School would not allow two of the youth activists, Ike Lewis and Brenda Travis, to return. To protest the school administration's policy, over 100 students organized a walkout on October 4, and with SNCC workers, marched throughout the downtown area. The protesters were arrested and charged with offenses ranging from breaching the peace to contributing to juvenile delinquency.

Most were immediately released, but their return to school hinged on the school administration's requirement that each student sign a pledge denouncing public protest. About half the student protesters signed the pledge. The other half refused, organized a second walkout, and refused to return to Burgland High. For those who refused to return, SNCC workers organized Nonviolent High. Bob Moses noted that the school was mostly "a large room" where he and others, like Charles McDew, tried "to break them down with the elements of algebra and geometry, a little English, and even a little French, a little history," before their transfer to Campbell College in Jackson (Dittmer 1995; Carson 1991, 175). SNCC organizers, including Bob Moses, and several student organizers, were eventually convicted. While their several-week stint in county prison may have been their first time behind bars for some, it would not be the last for any of them.

In the early 1960s, McComb was one of the most violent places in Mississippi. The Ku Klux Klan and the Citizens' Council used dynamite to bomb black homes, businesses, and religious institutions. Despite bombings, beatings, arrests, and further threats of violence, in the summer of 1963, members of the Council of Federated Organizations (COFO) organized a Freedom School in McComb. The Federation was an umbrella organization for civil rights groups operating throughout the state and included SNCC, the Southern Christian Leadership Conference, the NAACP, and the Congress of Racial Equality (CORE). The school enrolled high school aged students and taught them academic subjects, literacy, and encouraged them to participate in civil rights activity. COFO members also used the McComb Freedom School to organize the Freedom Day in August 1963, an open air rally that openly called for more blacks to register and vote. Black victims of violence met with federal officials to lobby the federal government to intervene in McComb and help end white anti-black violence. When President Lyndon Johnson and Mississippi Governor Paul Johnson threatened to mobilize the National Guard and send them to McComb in the fall of 1965, violence against black activists decreased. As the year 1965 was coming to a close, black activism continued and the COFO made a breakthrough. In November, the white political elite of McComb met, and after political wrangling and compromise, produced its *Statement of Principles*, which called for an end to violence and demanded equal access to town services for all its citizens. It was also during that month that NAACP officials successful integrated downtown hotels and restaurants (Dittmer 1995).

In Jackson, Mississippi, residents were not as successful as McComb residents. From December 1962 to May 1963, what started as a movement for better treatment in downtown stores by the North Jackson NAACP Youth Council became a fight to desegregate public facilities, integrate the city police force and city crossing guard unit, and obtain equal employment policies. Initially, youth members canvassed black neighborhoods and rallied at community institutions. As the movement gained strength, NAACP strategists began using direct action techniques. One demonstration was a sit-in at the Woolworth's store in the downtown district in late May 1963. Several activist from Tougaloo College—Pearlena Lewis, Memphis Norman, Anna Moody, Joan Trumpauer, Lois Chafee, Walter Williams, George Raymond, John Salter, and Daniel Beittel, Tougaloo College president—sat at a Woolworth's lunch counter that was reserved for white patrons. They were savagely beaten by a white mob before being escorted out of the store by the local police. Several days later, on May 31, high school students marched in downtown Jackson, leading to the arrest of over 450 protesters. NAACP picketeers also demonstrated throughout the downtown area. One such demonstration ended in the arrest of Roy Wilkins, the NAACP executive director. Mass meetings were held in local churches for people to sing freedom songs, vent their frustration with the intransigence of white city officials, and to maintain the momentum of the movement.

With so many demonstrations and arrests, movement strategists, black clergymen, and members of Jackson's black business class formed the Citizens Committee for Human Rights to enter into negotiations with Mayor Allen Thompson. In their first meeting on May 28, Thompson rejected all of their demands in direct opposition to federal law. It was only after President John F. Kennedy called Thompson that he agreed to accept a diluted version of the blacks' demands and keep the city segregated. Several African Americans would be hired to or promoted in the police department, crossing guard unit, and sanitation department, but segregation laws and discriminatory hiring policies would remain, and blacks would not obtain a voice in determining local politics. Without the full support of the Kennedy administration, blacks were left with a few token hires, but they maintained hope that long-term change would come to Jackson (Dittmer 1995).

White youths pour sugar, ketchup, and mustard on the heads of sit-down demonstrators at a restaurant lunch counter in Jackson, Mississippi, on June 12, 1963. (AP Photo)

African Americans' efforts to achieve full citizenship and franchise and white resistance to such attempts in McComb and Jackson were indicative of and paralleled the activists' efforts throughout the state of Mississippi in the early 1960s. African Americans in towns and cities like Hattiesburg, Clarksdale, and Canton challenged political oppression. Their goals may have been the same and different places and campaigns may have included the same activists who were part of national civil rights organizations, but the ways in which political activities were carried out at local and statewide levels were different and determined by municipal and state governmental developments and politics.

Local campaigns in Mississippi bear this out. In Canton, Mississippi, in early 1964, for example, black parents and students organized boycotts of public schools to highlight unequal educational standards and facilities as well as a boycott of white-owned stores in Canton. During the months of

March and May, the small city saw blacks organize three separate days of picketing and demonstrating through the streets. Such efforts were not permissible in Natchez, Mississippi, as Governor Johnson instituted a curfew and brought in the National Guard. The same dynamics determined the nature of statewide campaigns in Mississippi, including the 1964 Freedom Summer and the MFDP's efforts to unseat the Mississippi Democratic Party at the Democratic National Convention in Atlantic City, New Jersey.

In late February 1964, the COFO announced that it was organizing a political project to take place that summer in Mississippi from late June to late August. Appropriately called Freedom Summer, the project was geared to energize and intensify voter registration, create freedom schools and community centers, and organize a predominantly black political party. Approximately 1,000 white students from elite and Ivy League schools participated in the Freedom Summer along with COFO stalwarts. The Freedom Summer project, however, was not the first time large numbers of white students were active in Mississippi. For three weeks in late October and early November of 1963, about 100 students from Yale and Stanford Universities participated in the COFO-led Freedom Ballot Campaign commonly called the Freedom Vote. The Freedom Vote was a mock election wherein disenfranchised black Mississippians cast their votes to demonstrate to local, state, and federal officials that they wanted to participate in the electoral process and would do so when discriminatory and racist policies and obstacles were removed. During the election, black Mississippians could vote for the Democratic or Republican candidates or for the "Freedom Ticket," a grassroots movement affiliated with the Freedom Vote, which slated Dr. Aaron Henry for governor and Ed King for lieutenant governor. Henry was African American and the state NAACP president while King was a white chaplain at Tougaloo College, who had been active in the states' Civil Rights Movement for many years. The Freedom candidates, unlike the Democratic or Republican candidates, endorsed an end to segregation, state enforcement of the *Brown v. Board of Education* decision, a state minimum wage of $1.25 per hour, and an end to discriminatory hiring practices throughout Mississippi. White college students were important to the Freedom Vote due to their canvassing in black neighborhoods, informing people of the issues, encouraging potential voters, working at polling places, and donating resources. Over 80,000 people voted with the overwhelming majority, close to 99 percent, voting for the "Freedom Ticket" (Sinsheimer, 1989, 231–232, 240).

But, while the Freedom Vote campaign was only three weeks in duration and included 100 white volunteers, Freedom Summer was two months and even longer for some and would entail many more volunteers, so the

A volunteer worker urges Southern African Americans to register to vote in 1964. (National Archives)

decision to bring middle class white students into the Mississippi struggle was not an easy one to make, for several reasons. First, COFO organizers, especially SNCC members, went to great lengths to engage local, black Mississippians in their own struggle against racial inequality. Field hands, farmers, businessmen, clergyman, housewives, domestic workers, college students, and high school students had become involved in the civil rights struggle, and in some cases, at a great expense to their lives and careers. So to bring in white students, who would only be in the state for the summer during their summer vacations, had the potential to offend and set back grassroots organizing. Second, black activists were not at all comfortable with the idea of recruiting white students. Some feared that the white students' paternalism would create fissures throughout the organization as they would seek to take over movement activities and lead the organizers who were responsible for bringing them to Mississippi, and the black Mississippians they were supposed to be helping. Third, black southern activists, growing up in a racist society, had anger toward and misgivings about white student participation and white students had little, if any, personal or professional contact with black people (Mills 1992).

However, COFO needed a new strategy and a new perspective. Despite efforts since the late 1940s, by 1964, only 28,500 African Americans were registered to vote. The number of those eligible to vote exceeded 422,000 (Mills 1992, 21). In addition, the black struggle against inequality in Mississippi had been largely ignored by the outside press and the closed society of Mississippi had thwarted most all-black challenges to segregation throughout the state. Blacks had been maimed, killed, and arrested and their deaths, while mourned by black communities, had not lead to meaningful intervention by the federal government. The participation of white students was critical, COFO strategist and Freedom Summer director Bob Moses reasoned. White participation was needed philosophically and politically because the Civil Rights Movement had to become a multiracial movement in order to further its goals of integration. They were also needed practically and strategically because the federal government and the mainstream press would not stand by idly as white students suffered brutality and violence. On the contrary, their participation would not only open the state to outside scrutiny, but also lead to federal intervention (Rachal 1999).

Around 600 volunteers participated in Freedom Summer. Ninety percent were white and about one-third were women. The average volunteer was a white male in his early 20s from an affluent background and enrolled at an elite or Ivy League school. In June 1964, volunteers attended orientation at Western College for Women in Oxford, Ohio. There, they were taught Mississippi history and politics, instructed in the philosophy of nonviolence, and participated in role playing. A host of movement stalwarts, including Bayard Rustin, Stokely Carmichael, and Bob Moses also addressed the volunteers throughout the training to help them better understand the mission and goals of the summer project and its place in the larger Civil Rights Movement. One of the most discussed issues during the training was that of violence. Movement activists continuously warned volunteers that the culture of Mississippi was one of violence and that federal authorities would not provide protection from state-sanctioned authorities or vigilante groups. On June 21, 250 volunteers, the first wave, descended upon the state of Mississippi. Among them were Andrew Goodman, James Chaney, and Michael Schwerner (Dittmer 1995, 244).

Michael Schwerner was a graduate of Cornell University. He and his wife Rita joined CORE in January of 1964 and moved from New York State to Meridian, Mississippi, leaving his job as a social worker for the city. Between January and March 1964, the couple helped build a community center in the black section of Meridian, where they met James Chaney. In 1964, James Chaney was a 21-year-old high school dropout-turned-activist. He joined CORE in Fall 1963. A native of Meridian, Mississippi, he had seen his share of violence and discrimination, and no doubt joined CORE to change the politics and culture of Mississippi. In Oxford, Ohio, Schwerner and Chaney met Andrew Goodman, a 20-year-old sophomore and anthropology major at Queens College in New York City. Like most of the other white volunteers at the orientation, Goodman had liberal viewpoints and was eager to participate, though he had had limited experience in the movement. Having completed the orientation, the three, along with other volunteers, left Oxford, Ohio, on Saturday, June 20. On June 21, Goodman, Chaney, and Schwerner went to investigate the burning of a black church in Neshoba County. Around 3pm on June 21, the three were stopped by Deputy Sherriff Cecil Price, who accused Chaney of speeding and took all three activists to the jailhouse in Philadelphia, Mississippi. Around 10 PM, seven hours later, the three were released after paying a $20 bond. At approximately 11 PM, the three were arrested again, given to a mob, and were shot at point blank range. Their bodies were buried in a construction site and not found until over a month later, on August 4. The deaths of Goodman, Chaney, and Schwerner were clear examples to other volunteers of the extent to which white Mississippians would go to protect the racial hierarchies and oppression so important to their society. Their deaths also brought extensive media coverage to Mississippi and encouraged President Lyndon Johnson to move forward with civil rights legislation.

The Freedom Summer project continued despite the deaths of Goodman, Chaney, and Schwerner. White volunteers fanned out across Mississippi, stayed in black Mississippians' homes, attempted to register black voters, and created freedom schools. Steve Bingham, a volunteer from Connecticut, worked on the voter registration campaign during the summer of 1964. In a letter he wrote after the project, Hingham noted that "each morning until late afternoon we would find ourselves trudging from house to house in the broad expanse of the Mississippi countryside, fighting off the heat, the dust, the discouragement, the fear, going from one dingy shack to the next" (Miller 1985, 301). Les Johnson, another white volunteer, wrote that "canvassing is very trying. You walk down a little dusty street, with incredibly broken down shacks. The people sitting on porches staring away into nowhere.... I almost feel guilty, like I'm playing for numbers only" (Mills 1992, 132). In addition to canvassing black communities, COFO staff and volunteers held voter education classes to help potential registrants interpret sections of the state constitution, answer questions that may be asked of them by registrars, and to encourage them as they opposed social and political customs by attempting to vote. It was difficult work. Black Mississippians knew well the cost of attempting to register.

In the recalcitrant political climate of Mississippi, for an African American to register, it sometimes meant job loss, being thrown off rented land, and sometimes even death. In the end, Freedom Summer did not register as many blacks as they planned. By the end of the project, COFO was successful in getting 1,600 blacks registered out of 17,000 who attempted (Carson 1981, 117).

The Freedom Summer campaign was more successful in creating freedom schools. Charlie Cobb, SNCC's field secretary, developed the concept of the freedom school in 1963. The goal of the freedom school was "to fill an intellectual and creative vacuum" left by Mississippi's educational system and help young people "articulate their own desires, demands, and needs" (Dittmer 1995, 258). White northern college students, mostly young white women, were teachers and freedom schools were intended for high school-aged students. Eventually, as the popularity of the schools increased throughout the state, the attendees ranged from nursery school-aged children to adults who wanted to learn to read. The curriculum included basic high school courses, including reading, mathematics, social studies, and even foreign languages. These subjects were supplemented with arts and crafts, poetry, and the study of contemporary political and cultural developments facing black Mississippians and African Americans nationwide. Howard Zinn, a contemporary observer of freedom schools in Mississippi, notes that "the object of the Freedom School was not to cram a prescribed amount of factual material into young minds, but to give them that first look into new worlds" (Zinn 2002, 248).

The curriculum for Mississippi's freedom schools was created by educators and activists and was deeply influenced by curricula developed in schools in Boston, Chicago, and New York. It was mostly organized around case studies of contemporary issues that related to the lived experiences of the students, African American history, and issues and ideas surrounding citizenship. In the Gulfport freedom school, for example, teachers played baseball with students and asked them why white youth have a baseball field on which to play, but black youth did not. From the game, students were made "to think from a base of their own everyday personal and community experiences, to examine what was represented by these experiences, and ultimately to consider why and how their society needed to be changed" (Chilcoat & Ligon 1999, 113). Local circumstances and needs determined the extent to which and how much the curriculum was followed. In Clarksdale, students investigated local discrimination and published their findings and ideas in their own newspaper, the *Clarksdale Freedom Press*. In Ruleville, students used role-playing to learn the techniques of picketing. In other schools, teachers taught basic literacy (Mill 1992; Perlstein 1990;

Chilcoat, Ligon 1999). While some continued to operate into the fall, most freedom schools ended in early August, with a statewide student convention from August 8 to 10. Representatives were elected from each school and they, in turn, converged on Meridian, Mississippi, to discuss their experiences and challenges facing black youth throughout the state. The convention ended with students writing and passing a political platform that included progressive issues ranging from concerns about state voting rights to apartheid in South Africa. From late June to early August 1964, 41 freedom schools served as many as 3,000 students.

Through voter registration drives and freedom schools, the Freedom Summer made important strides to change local and statewide electoral politics and educational initiatives throughout the state of Mississippi. The MFDP's attempt to unseat the Mississippi Democratic Party at the 1964 Democratic Convention in Atlantic City, New Jersey, was an attempt to influence national politics. The MFDP was organized in April 1964 in Jackson, Mississippi, to provide African Americans who had been excluded from the state democratic party with an independent political voice. In June of that year, the MFDP conducted its own democratic primary and put forward candidates for the U.S. Senate and the House of Representatives. Though they did not expect to win the seats, the primary object, like the 1963 Freedom Vote, was to demonstrate African Americans willingness to participate in the electoral process if given a chance and to build independent, local political power (Burner 1994). Mississippi's statewide exclusion of the majority of African Americans from voting meant that the Mississippi delegation to the convention was not a democratically chosen group or reflective of the state's population and was, therefore, illegitimate. Most of the 68 members of the MFDP were black and represented a cross section of black Mississippians—sharecroppers, farmers, domestics, teachers, and clergy. Four delegates were white. They arrived in Atlantic City on August 21. No one expected to displace the all-white delegation and be seated on the convention floor. Instead, the purpose was to dramatize to the nation the disfranchisement of millions of African Americans throughout the nation during a presidential election.

MFDP delegates lobbied congressmen and delegates from other states. For fear of losing southern support, as early as June 1964, President Lyndon Johnson decided that the MFDP would not be seated. He even sent a letter to the governor of Mississippi stating as much. However, in a stunning turn of events after political wrangling by Civil Rights Movement activist Bayard Rustin of CORE, Roy Wilkins of the NAACP, SCLC president and Nobel Peace Prize winner Martin Luther King Jr. MFDP legal counsel

Al Lowenstein, MFDP delegate and attorney Joseph Rauh, President and Democratic Party presidential candidate Lyndon Johnson, and high ranking members of the Democratic Party, a compromise was brokered. The compromise stipulated that Aaron Henry and Ed King of the Mississippi Freedom Democratic Party would fill two seats with the all-white delegation who would be required to take a loyalty oath, pledge allegiance to the National Democratic Party, and support Johnson as the party's presidential candidate. All other MFDP delegates would be designated convention guests (Mills 1992, 153). After debate, the MFDP delegates rejected the offer, noting that they did not go to Atlantic City to participate in a racist, discriminatory state delegation, but to replace it. Many of the MFDP delegates felt that an acceptance of the compromise was tantamount with political jockeying rather than receiving justice for the thousands of black Mississippians who had been excluded from the political apparatus for generations.

The MFDP's attempt to be seated at the Democratic Convention is insightful because it demonstrates how civil rights workers and organizations in Mississippi, considered the most politically isolated state, experimented with different political strategies to gain black freedom since the early post-WWII era. It was also a culmination of experimental efforts in many ways. On the local level, civil rights workers tried to register blacks to vote, conduct direct action campaigns, educate and politicize black youth, and integrate public spaces. On the state level, they ran candidates for political office. On the national level, they tried to influence a party that quietly accepted the discrimination of blacks for sake of expediency. Their work and courage was mirrored by other local and national civil rights workers in other states, and despite the violence, intimidation, and a constant shifting reorientation of white economic and political power, and political setbacks, the work of black Mississippians embodied the ethos of the freedom song "Ain't Gonna Let Nobody Turn Me 'round":

Ain't gonna let nobody turn me 'round
I'm gonna keep on a walkin', keep on a-talkin',
Marching up to freedom land.

References

Burner, Eric. *And Gently He Shall Lead Them: Robert Parris Moses and Civil Rights in Mississippi* (New York: New York University Press, 1994).

Carson, Clayborne. *In Struggle: SNCC and the Black Awakening of the 1960s* (Cambridge: Harvard University Press, 1981).

Chilcoat, George, and Jerry Ligon, "Developing Democratic Citizens: The Mississippi Freedom Schools," in Susie Ehrencrich, ed., *Freedom is a Constant Struggle: An Anthology of the Mississippi Civil Rights Movement* (Washington, DC: The Cultural Center for Social Change, 1999), 113–115.

Dittmer, John. *Local People: The Struggle for Civil Rights in Mississippi* (Urbana: University of Illinois Press, 1995).

Miller, Char. "The Mississippi Summer Project Remembered: The Stephen Mitchell Bingham Letter," *Journal of Mississippi History*, Vol. 47, No. 4 (Nov., 1985), 284–307.

Mills, Nicolaus. *Like a Holy Crusade: Mississippi 1964—The Turning of the Civil Rights Movement in America* (Chicago: Ivan R. Dee, 1992).

Moses, Robert. "Mississippi: 1961–1962," in Clayborn Carson et al., eds. *The Eyes on the Prize Civil Rights Reader* (New York: Penguin Books, 1991).

The Murder of Emmet Till. DVD. Directed by Stanley Nelson Boston, MA: Public Broadcasting System, 2003.

Perlstein, Daniel. "Teaching Freedom: SNCC and the Creation of Mississippi Freedom Schools," *History of Education Quarterly*, Vol. 30, No. 3 (Autumn, 1990), 297–324.

Rachal, John. "The Long Hot Summer: The Mississippi Response to Freedom Summer, 1964," *The Journal of Negro History*, Vol 84, No.4 (Autumn, 1999), 315–339.

Sinsheimer, Joseph. "The Freedom Vote of 1963: New Strategies of Racial Protest in Mississippi," *The Journal of Southern History*, Vol. 55, No. 2 (May, 1989), 217–244.

Williams, Kenneth H. "Mississippi and the Civil Rights Movement, 1945–1954." (Ph.D. Dissertation, Mississippi State University, 1985).

Zinn, Howard. *SNCC: The New Abolitionists* (Cambridge: South End Press, 2002).

FIVE

"A Right Denied": Court Decisions and the Civil Rights Movement

Staci M. Rubin
Staff Attorney, Roxbury, Massachusetts

AFRICAN AMERICANS' ATTEMPTS to dismantle white supremacy and segregation through grassroots organizing, lobbying the federal government, and non-violent direct actions were bolstered by coordinated tactics that sought to transform American social and legal structures from ones wrought with racism to systems based on equality. Organizations, especially the National Association for the Advancement of Colored People (NAACP), challenged the legality of racism through impact litigation, lawsuits that aim to make legal arguments that apply to a large number of people, get a decision in favor of that group, and result in a new law that is fundamentally different and just. Civil rights attorneys argued that state and municipal laws and practices that stripped blacks of their social and economic rights violated the U.S. Constitution under the Fourth and Fourteenth Amendments. The Fourth Amendment provides protection against unreasonable searches and seizures. It states that "[t]he right of the people to be secure in their persons, houses, papers, and effects, against unreasonable searches and seizures, shall not be violated, and no Warrants shall issue, but upon probable cause, supported by Oath or affirmation, and particularly describing the place to be searched, and the persons or things to be seized." The Fourteenth Amendment allows citizens the right to due process and equal protection declaring that "[n]o state shall make or enforce any law which shall abridge the privileges or immunities of citizens of the United States; nor shall any State deprive any person of life, liberty, or property, without due process of the laws." What follows is a discussion of several major U.S. Supreme Court cases and their implications for the movement between 1932 and 1968.

United States v. Powell (1932)

On March 25, 1931, during the early days of the Great Depression, nine poor and functionally illiterate black youth were traveling on a freight train through Alabama seeking adventure and employment. Collectively, they have come to be remembered as the Scottsboro Boys. Other passengers on the train included several young white men and two young white women. After a fight erupted between the white and black men, most of the whites were ejected from the train leaving the black men and two white women alone in one train car. The women claimed that the black men sexually assaulted them, and by the time the train reached Scottsboro, Alabama, the young men were greeted by a hostile white crowd.

Following the incident, the young men were placed in jail and denied opportunities to communicate with their families in other states. At the time of trial, just two weeks after the alleged assault, the trial judge decided not to designate an attorney licensed to practice law in the state of Alabama to defend the men. Instead, the defense was coordinated by a Tennessee lawyer, who was not licensed to practice in Alabama, had not spent much time preparing the case, and had little knowledge of Alabama law. He had volunteered to be the primary attorney for the Scottsboro Boys in partnership with other attorneys knowledgeable of Alabama law. Eight of the nine men were found guilty because the all-white jury members relied on the word of the two white women on the train—the only evidence presented in the cases. On appeal to the Alabama Supreme Court, seven of the eight men were deemed to be correctly convicted and the judgment against the eighth man was reversed. The cases reached the Supreme Court of the

The Scottsboro boys with activist Juanita E. Jackson, January 1937. (Library of Congress)

United States because the men argued that by being denied the right to an attorney of his own choice, each was denied due process and equal protection of the laws in violation of the Fourteenth Amendment.

As per the Sixth Amendment to the U.S. Constitution, the right to assistance of counsel includes the right to counsel of choice, the right to court-appointed counsel, the right to conflict-free counsel, the effective assistance of counsel, and the right to represent oneself without an attorney. In hearing the case, the Supreme Court of the United States was deciding whether the Sixth Amendment's Assistance of Counsel clause included the right to the appointment of counsel in certain capital cases, and whether this right is incorporated by the Fourteenth Amendment. It decided that the young men were denied the constitutional requirement of due process of law because they were not awarded a fair trial and denied adequate representation by an attorney knowledgeable of the state criminal laws. There were several facts that helped the Court reach their conclusion. The first was that the young men were functionally illiterate. The second was that their Tennessee attorney was not versed in the laws of Alabama and had little time to prepare an effective defense. Additionally, the residents of Scottsboro and the surrounding towns were hostile to the men. Further, the young men's families were located in different states. Finally, if convicted, the young men would be sentenced to death, a sentence that "would be little short of judicial murder." The Supreme Court's decision did not prove or disprove the young Scottsboro Boys' innocence, though all of the men were eventually released. It did prove, however, that the arrest and trial process used to convict them was inherently flawed by institutional racism.

Missouri ex el Gaines v. Canada (1938)

In 1936, Lloyd L. Gaines, an African American college graduate, applied for admission to the University of Missouri School of Law. After the school denied him admission due to his race, Gaines collaborated with the NAACP to establish a legal precedent. Gaines was encouraged by a then-recent case, *University of Maryland v. Murray* (1936), in which Charles Hamilton Houston and Thurgood Marshall, two young African American lawyers, argued that the University of Maryland School of Law could not meet its constitutional burden of equal treatment by offering to reimburse a black man, Donald Murray, for tuition at an out-of-state school instead of permitting him admittance to the university, from which he was barred due to his race. In Murray's situation, the Maryland Court of Appeals agreed with the Maryland trial court and ordered the University of Maryland to admit

Murray. While this was successful, Marshall and Houston sought a clear ruling that state-segregated higher education was unconstitutional. Thus, Marshall agreed to work with Gaines.

Upon filing his application for admission to the law school, the registrar advised Gaines to communicate with the President of Lincoln University and to read Section 9622 of the Revised Statutes of Missouri, which stated:

> Pending the full development of Lincoln University, the board of curators shall have the authority to arrange for the attendance of negro residents of the state of Missouri at the university of any adjacent state to take any course or to study any subjects provided for at the state university of Missouri, and which are not taught at the Lincoln University and to pay the reasonable tuition fees for such attendance; provided that whenever the board of curators deem it advisable they shall have the power to open any necessary school or department.

The law school registrar, Sy Woodson Canada, denied Gaines admission to the law school on the ground that it was "contrary to the constitution, laws and public policy of [Missouri] to admit a negro [sic] as a student in the University of Missouri." There were four schools of law in connection with state universities of adjacent states (Kansas, Nebraska, Iowa, and Illinois) where nonresident blacks would be admitted. The trial court determined that because state law required there be separate public high schools for whites and children of African descent and specified that Lincoln University, a historically black college, should pay tuition fees for courses at universities in adjacent states not offered at Lincoln, the University of Missouri School of Law could deny admission to Gaines because of his race.

During the litigation, the state of Missouri recognized its obligation to provide blacks with advantages of higher education substantially equal to the advantages offered to white students. It argued that it did so by furnishing equal facilities in separate schools and that such provisions were legal based upon the U.S. Supreme Court ruling in *Plessy v. Ferguson* (1896) as well as in other cases. However, it remained true that the state of Missouri provided only one law school, the University of Missouri, and that school did not afford admission privileges to blacks. While law schools in other states may have accepted blacks, the real issue was that the state of Missouri granted the opportunity of attending its law school to whites, but denied that opportunity to blacks. Houston and Marshall argued that such an exclusion was a violation of equal protection of the law, a legal argument agreed upon by the Supreme Court when they ruled that the state

On October 8, 1962, James Meredith, the first African American to attend the University of Mississippi, leaves class during his second week at the school. (Library of Congress)

curators' action of denying admission to Gaines constituted a denial of equal protection of law.

This case was the beginning of the NAACP Legal Defense Fund's effort to chip away at the separate but equal doctrine. The *Gaines* case articulated an important rule of law in the sequence of NAACP cases, leading to the eventual desegregation order: that any academic program that a state provided to whites had to have an equivalent available to blacks. The *Gaines* case laid the foundation for the landmark ruling in *Brown v. Board of Education* (1954), which ordered all public schools desegregated and overturned *Plessy* by holding that separate facilities were inherently unequal.

Smith v. Allwright (1944)

In July 1940, Lonnie Smith, a black resident of Harris County, Texas, attempted to cast a ballot in a state primary election, but was denied a ballot solely because he was African American. His circumstances presented just the case that Thurgood Marshall and other lawyers were interested in taking to the courts. Marshall, on behalf of Smith, brought a suit against S. E. Allwright, the election judge, and James Liuzza, associate election judge, arguing that they deprived Smith of his rights under the Fourteenth, Fifteenth, and Seventeenth Amendments. The Fifteenth Amendment avows that "[t]he right of citizens of the United States to vote shall not be denied or abridged by the United States or by any State on account of race, color, or previous condition of servitude." The Seventeenth Amendment maintains that "[t]he Senate of the United States shall be composed of two Senators from each State, elected by the people thereof, for six years; and each senator shall have one vote."

When the Supreme Court was considering which actions were found to be a violation of the Fourteenth Amendment, the primary consideration was whether the activity constituted an action by the state. In *Smith*, justices considered whether the exclusionary action of the Democratic Party in Texas was an action of the state. In its ruling, the Supreme Court decided in the affirmative. The Democratic Party of Texas was, indeed, an action of the state. Texas law required the election of county officers of a party, which once elected, became the county executive committee. The county executive committee then chose a chairman for the district. Primary elections were conducted by the party under the authority of the state statute. The Texas courts had the authority to review the contested elections and compel the party officers to perform their legal duties. Since the state required a certain electoral procedure, regulated ballot requirements, and limited the choices of the voting public in elections for state officers, such actions amounted to the political party acting as a state agency. Further, if a party adopted and enforced any discrimination against blacks, which was entrusted by Texas law to determine the qualifications of voters in a primary, this, too, was state action under the Fifteenth Amendment. In the end, the Court decided that "[t]he United States is a constitutional democracy. Its organic law grants to all citizens a right to participate in the choice of elected officials without restriction by any state because of race. This . . . choice is not to be nullified by a state through casting its electoral process in a form which permits . . . racial discrimination in the election." This decision helped remove the legal barriers that black Americans faced at polling stations.

Shelley v. Kraemer (1948)

Thurgood Marshall continued his work to bring change for African Americans in the 1940s when he forced the U.S. Supreme Court to consider the validity of racially restrictive covenants, private agreements between whites that expressly excluded blacks from owning or occupying property in certain predominantly white locations. On February 16, 1911, 30 white property owners on Labadie Avenue, between Taylor and Cora Avenues in St. Louis, Missouri, signed a restrictive covenant which stated that "people of the Negro or Mongolian Race," could not reside on their property for at least 50 years. At the time of signature, there were a total of 47 properties and several were occupied by black families, many of whom had lived there for years before the agreement was signed.

On August 11, 1945, the Shelleys, a black family, signed a contract granting them ownership of a property within the district. One of their neighbors, Louis Kraemer and his wife, signatories of the 1911 covenant, brought the lawsuit and asked a judge to prevent the Shelley family from occupying the property. The Supreme Court of Missouri decided that the restrictive covenant did not violate the federal Constitution and that the Shelley family should not occupy the property. However, by the time the state court granted its decision, the Shelley family had already moved into the home.

A similar situation occurred in Detroit, Michigan, when in June 1934, the Fergusons, a white family, signed a contract regarding a home in a subdivision on Seebaldt Avenue, which prohibited persons who were not white from using or occupying the property until 1960. Eighty percent of the owners on the block signed the restrictive covenant. On November 30, 1944, the McGhee family, an African American family, purchased and moved into a property on the block. The Fergusons brought a suit, and the state trial court found that the McGhee family was violating the restrictive covenant and had to move out within 90 days. Thurgood Marshall represented the McGhee family and argued that the residential restriction on people of color was unjust.

In both cases, the black families argued that the states were violating their equal protection rights guaranteed by the Fourteenth Amendment because the courts had acted to enforce the covenants and ordered the families to move out. The Supreme Court determined that in both "cases the States . . . acted to deny petitioners the equal protection of the laws guaranteed by the Fourteenth Amendment." The decision stated that racially restrictive provisions, agreements, and terms or obligations in property deeds that limited property rights to Caucasians and excluded members of other races are unenforceable.

What made *Shelley v. Kraemer* particularly useful in advancing the Civil Rights Movement was that the Supreme Court was willing to extend the rights granted by the Fourteenth Amendment to situations involving a contract between private individuals. The legal theory in *Shelley v. Kraemer* was that there was, indeed, state action by the mere fact that a court enforced the contract. Consequently, the court involvement, which amounted to state action, ran afoul of the Fourteenth Amendment. The decision legally barred the practice that prevented blacks from purchasing homes in white neighborhoods. There is little doubt that racially restrictive covenants barring black ownership of property had the effect of segregating blacks to certain sections of cities prior to 1948. Despite this important Court ruling, there was a high degree of residential segregation in virtually all American cities in the 1950s. Blacks were excluded from newer suburbs because of private and institutional discrimination, racial biases of white real estate brokers and landlords, and by discriminatory practices of the Federal Housing Administration loans. In the closing decades of the 20th century, residential segregation declined throughout the nation, but blacks remained overwhelmingly concentrated in central cities.

Sweatt v. Painter & McLaurin v. Oklahoma State Regents (1950)

Heman Marion Sweatt applied for admission to the University of Texas Law School for the February 1946 term. His application was rejected by the Board of Regents, including Theophilis Shickel Painter, solely because Sweatt was black. At that time, no law school in Texas admitted black students. A Texas constitutional provision and statute restricted admission to the University of Texas to white students. Thurgood Marshall represented Sweatt and brought a suit in the state court, seeking an order that the University admit him. The state court ruled that the state University's denial of Sweatt's application denied him the equal protection of the law guaranteed by the Fourteenth Amendment. The state court required that the state of Texas supply substantially equal facilities for black students in six months' time. At the expiration of the six months, in December 1946, the court failed to order that the University admit Sweatt because University officials called for the opening of a law school for black students in February 1947. Sweatt refused to register for the new law school.

Marshall argued that the new law school was not equal to the University of Texas Law School. The trial court disagreed and found that the two law schools were substantially equivalent. The state appeals court agreed with the trial court. The case reached the U.S. Supreme Court, which compared the two law schools. The University of Texas Law School had 16 full-time faculty, a library with 65,000 volumes, scholarship funds, and it was considered to be one of the nation's top-ranking law schools. The other law school for black students had no independent faculty, four law school professors who also taught at the University of Texas, a library with fewer than 10,000 volumes, no librarian, and was not accredited. The Supreme Court decided that the two schools were not equal and declared that the "Equal Protection Clause of the Fourteenth Amendment requires that [Mr. Sweatt] be admitted to the University of Texas Law School."

G. W. McLaurin was a black resident of Oklahoma with a master's degree who applied for admission to the University of Oklahoma to pursue a Doctorate of Education. His application was denied solely on the basis that he was black. The admissions staff was required to exclude him by Oklahoma law, which declared it a "misdemeanor to maintain or operate, teach or attend a school at which both whites and blacks are enrolled or taught." McLaurin filed a suit against the Board of Regents for denying him equal protection of the law. A district court decided that the state had a constitutional duty to provide McLaurin with the education he sought so long as that education was offered to whites. Following the district court decision, the Oklahoma legislature amended the laws to permit the admission of blacks to institutions of higher learning attended by white students in cases where such institutions offered courses not available in the black schools. This legal amendment stated that the courses should be given at institutions of higher learning on a segregated basis. Following this amendment, McLaurin was admitted to the University of Oklahoma Graduate School, but was required to follow certain rules. He was required to sit apart at a designated desk in a room adjoining the classroom next to a sign that read "Reserved for Colored." Additionally, he was forced to sit at a designated desk on the mezzanine of the library that was separate from the desks in the regular reading room. McLaurin also had to sit at a designated table in the school cafeteria and eat at a different time than the white students.

McLaurin sought to modify the order of the district court and remove the conditions of his enrollment by arguing that the conditions violated the Fourteenth Amendment. The case reached the Supreme Court, which decided that McLaurin was handicapped in his pursuit of effective graduate instruction. His education, the Supreme Court stated, "will necessarily suffer to the extent that [McLaurin's] training is unequal to that of his classmates. State imposed restrictions which produce such inequalities cannot be sustained." The Supreme Court found that the university conditions denied McLaurin the equal protection of the law under the Fourteenth Amendment and that he must be able to attend the university and receive the same treatment as students of other races.

Both the *Sweatt v. Painter* and *McLaurin v. Oklahoma State Regents* cases were argued at the Supreme Court on the same day and struck down the segregation of African American students in law and graduate schools throughout the nation. The Justice Department, in its brief to the Court, said it believed *Plessy v. Ferguson* was unconstitutional and should be overturned. However, the *Sweatt* and *McLaurin* opinions did not overturn *Plessy*. As a result, NAACP Legal Defense Fund lawyers, led by Thurgood Marshall, began to devise a strategy that would force the Supreme Court to re-examine the constitutionality of the separate but equal doctrine.

Brown v. Board of Education I (1954)

The aforementioned Supreme Court decisions were delivered by justices who were generally willing to admit that the social, political, and educational opportunities available for black Americans were different from those available to white Americans. They were also willing to admit that these differences put blacks at a disadvantage. However, justices prior to 1954 were not ethically, intellectually, or politically prepared to rule that these disparities were unconstitutional, unjustified, and untenable. The *Brown* case of 1954 was the first time the Supreme Court was willing to rule that the legal infrastructure and associated systems used to preserve African Americans' second class status were no longer welcome. Class action lawsuits in Delaware, Kansas, South Carolina, and Virginia focused on whether black children could attend public schools on a nonsegregated basis.

The Kansas case involved black children enrolled in a Topeka, Kansas, elementary school who challenged the legality of a state statute that required cities with a population greater than 15,000 to maintain separate schools for black and white children. To comply with the state law, the Topeka Board of Education established segregated elementary schools. A district court decided that school segregation has a detrimental effect on black children, but ultimately upheld school segregation because black and white schools were substantially equal with respect to buildings, transportation, curricula, and teacher qualifications.

The South Carolina case involved black children enrolled in elementary and high schools residing in Clarendon County. The state constitution required the segregation of blacks and whites in public schools. A district court in South Carolina decided that black schools were inferior to white schools and ordered the Board of Trustees of Clarendon County to improve the black schools. The district court, however, denied black students admission to white schools.

The Virginia case involved high school students residing in Prince Edward County. The state constitution and law required the segregation of blacks and whites in public schools. A district court decided that black schools were inferior, based on the building, curricula, and transportation, and ordered the County School Board to provide equal curricula and transportation and improve the building. Despite this finding, the district court refused to order the admission of the black students to white schools.

The Delaware case involved black children—elementary and high school students residing in New Castle County. State law required the segregation of blacks and whites in public schools. A judge ruled that the children should be immediately admitted to schools previously attended only by white children because the black schools were found to be inferior with respect to the student-teacher ratio, extracurricular activities, building infrastructure, teacher training, and distance traveled to the school. In all four cases, black children sought the aid of the courts in obtaining admission to integrated public schools. In three of the four cases, a federal district court ruled that the children were not permitted to attend public schools attended by white children due to laws requiring segregation by race. The argument in the cases, once consolidated and heard by the U.S. Supreme Court, was that the separate but equal doctrine announced by the Supreme Court in *Plessy v. Ferguson* was not equal and was a violation of the Fourteenth Amendment.

The Supreme Court chose to question public education and its place in American life throughout the country. "In these days, it is doubtful that any child may reasonably be expected to succeed in life if he is denied the opportunity of an education," the Court stated. "Such an opportunity, where the state has undertaken to provide it, is a right which must be made available to all on equal terms." When separation is legally enforced on the theory of racial superiority and inferiority, as Jim Crow segregation plainly was, then separate must necessarily mean unequal, even if the physical facilities were somehow comparable, which they never were. Chief Justice Warren, a newly appointed justice, held that segregation of children in public schools solely on the basis of race, even though the physical facilities may be equal, deprives children of color equal educational opportunities in violation of the Equal Protection Clause of the Fourteenth Amendment.

This case presents a great illustration of community organizing and legal strategy and was years in the making. Often, cases are litigated, but do not reach the nation's highest court. Many lawyers seek to appeal cases from lower courts to the U.S. Supreme Court, but are often denied approval for review by the Supreme Court. A case has a better chance of reaching the Supreme Court if there are multiple federal circuit courts that have considered the same issue, but decided that issue differently. Knowing this reality, civil rights lawyers around the county sought people willing to serve as plaintiffs in cases that challenged the constitutionality of educational apartheid. Because three federal appeals courts decided the cases in favor of segregation, and the fourth court decided in favor of racial justice, the civil rights attorneys had the opportunity for review at the Supreme Court (Dershowitz 2004).

NAACP v. Alabama, Patterson (1958)

Marshall argued many of the cases at the Supreme Court for the NAACP and his lawyering furthered the NAACP's mission. The Alabama Secretary of State took aim at the NAACP by alleging a violation of a state law that required organizations operating solely within the state to file paperwork with the state, including a list of the organization's members. The NAACP felt it had not violated a law since it was a national organization operating within and outside the state of Alabama. The organization was willing to complete the paperwork with the state solicitor, with the exception of turning over the organization's membership list. Relinquishing the list would lead to economic reprisals, loss of employment, threats of physical coercion, and public hostility toward its members. The NAACP stated its refusal to turn over the membership list and argued that if the state were to compel the organization to provide the lists, it would be a violation of the Due Process Clause of the Fourteenth Amendment.

Prior to Alabama's attorney general bringing suit against the NAACP, the organization provided financial support and legal assistance to black students seeking admission to the state university, and helped organize the Montgomery Bus Boycott. The organization's work to challenge racial injustice was a threat to many, including government officials. Alabama's attorney general sought to halt the organization's work by arguing that it did not comply with state law, especially by not providing a list of its members. The Supreme Court, however, decided that disclosure of the membership list would likely impair members' collective effort to foster beliefs, which they admittedly have the right to advocate, induce withdrawal from the organization, and dissuade people from joining for fear of exposure of their beliefs through association with the NAACP. It maintained that "[e]ffective advocacy of both public and private points of view, particularly controversial ones, is undeniably enhanced by group association."

Boynton v. Virginia (1960)

Boynton v. Virginia, another case challenging racial segregation in public places reached the Supreme Court in 1960 and was argued by Thurgood Marshall. A black law student, Bruce Boynton, purchased a bus ticket to travel from Washington, D.C., to Montgomery, Alabama. When the bus reached Richmond, Virginia, the bus driver stopped at the bus terminal and announced a 40-minute break. Bruce Boynton exited the bus, entered the restaurant inside the bus terminal, and sat on a stool in the section specifically designated for white customers. Boynton refused to move when a waitress and assistant manager asked him to sit in the area designated for blacks. He was arrested and convicted for violating a Virginia law requiring people to be found guilty if they remain on one's land after being forbidden by the person in charge of such land. Marshall argued that the restaurant staff's refusal to serve Boynton while he was sitting in the section for white customers was a violation of the Fourteenth Amendment. The Supreme Court did not consider the constitutional question and instead decided whether Boynton's conviction for trespass violated the Interstate Commerce Act. The Interstate Commerce Act made it unlawful for a common carrier engaged in interstate commerce to give unreasonable preference to any particular person or to subject one to unjust discrimination. The Supreme Court ruled that this particular restaurant operated as an integral part of the bus service, a common carrier engaged in transporting people across state lines, and should not have discriminated against Boynton under the Interstate Commerce Act.

Heart of Atlanta Motel, Inc. v. United States (1964)

Not long after the passage of the Civil Rights Act of 1964, its prohibition against discrimination in public accommodations was challenged in the courts. The issue that reached the Supreme Court involved a motel located in Atlanta, Georgia, called the Heart of Atlanta Motel. Prior to 1964, the 216-room motel routinely refused to rent rooms to black visitors. Despite the Act's clear statements against racial discrimination, the Heart of Atlanta Motel stated that it would continue its practice of refusing to rent rooms to black visitors. The public accommodation language in the 1964 Act that was challenged read: "All persons shall be entitled to the full and equal enjoyment of the goods, services, facilities, privileges, advantages, and accommodations of any place of public accommodation, as defined in this section, without discrimination or segregation on the ground of race, color, religion, or national origin." Justices ruled that the motel had no right to select its guests as it sees fit, free from governmental regulation. While nearly all the civil rights cases that reached the Supreme Court were decided under the Fourteenth Amendment, this case upheld the constitutionality of the Civil Rights Act of 1964 under the Commerce Clause of the Constitution. Black travelers argued that the unavailability of motel rooms for them interferes significantly with interstate travel and that Congress, under the Commerce Clause, had the authority to prohibit discrimination by passing the Civil Rights Act of 1964. As a result of this ruling, the Civil Rights Act of 1964 remained intact and thereby reduced many of the social and economic barriers facing African Americans at the time.

Loving v. Virginia (1967)

In June 1958, two Virginia residents, Mildred Jeter, a black woman, and Richard Loving, a white man, married in the District of Columbia. Shortly after their wedding, Mildred and Richard returned to Caroline County, Virginia, where a Virginia law prohibited interracial marriages. The Lovings were charged with violating the state law, "An Act to Preserve Racial Integrity." That act stipulated that "[i]f any white person and colored person shall go out of this State, for the purpose of being married, and with the intention of returning, and be married out of it, and afterwards return to and reside in it, cohabitating as man and wife, they shall be punished. . . ." At the time, the case was litigated, 15 other states had laws which prohibited individuals belonging to different racial groups from marrying, including Alabama, Arkansas, Delaware, Florida, Georgia, Kentucky, Louisiana, Mississippi, Missouri, North Carolina, Oklahoma, South Carolina, Tennessee, Texas, Virginia, West Virginia. To be sure, 14 states outside of the South had laws similar to Virginia's "An Act to Preserve Racial Integrity," but during the years leading to the *Loving* case, repealed their laws outlawing interracial marriages. While many couples of different races were deeply disturbed by the blatant racism enveloped in such laws and those who enforced them, it took a couple courageous enough to endure the litigation and associated public oppression to serve as plaintiffs.

On January 6, 1959, the Lovings pleaded guilty to the charge and were sentenced to one year in jail. The trial judge suspended the sentence for 25 years on the condition that the Lovings leave Virginia and not return for 25 years. He stated in his opinion: "Almighty God created the races white, black, yellow, malay and red, and he placed them on separate continents.

And but for the interference with his arrangement there would be no cause for such marriages. The fact that he separated the races shows that he did not intend for the races to mix." The Lovings moved to Washington DC and asked a state trial court to set aside the Virginia trial court sentence because it violated the Fourteenth Amendment. When the case reached the Supreme Court, justices had to determine whether or not anti-miscegenation laws, which equally punished white and black individuals in interracial marriages, constituted invidious discrimination based upon race. The justices also were asked to decide whether the Virginia law that prevented marriages between two people solely on the basis of racial classifications violates the Fourteenth Amendment. The justices decided that state laws prohibiting interracial marriage were unconstitutional. They noted that "[t]he fact that Virginia prohibits only interracial marriages involving white persons demonstrates that the racial classifications must stand on their own justification, as measures designed to maintain White Supremacy. . . . Marriage is one of the 'basic civil rights of man,' fundamental to our very existence and survival. . . . To deny this fundamental freedom on so unstoppable a basis as the racial classifications embodied in these statutes, classifications so directly subversive of the principle of equality at the heart of the Fourteenth Amendment, is surely to deprive all the State's citizens of liberty without due process of law." Following the Court decision, the Lovings were free to return to Virginia and interracial and multiracial couples were recognized by all 50 states. Despite this significant court case, discrimination against interracial and multiracial marriages endured in many places, but such discrimination was no longer government-sanctioned.

Jones v. Alfred H. Mayer Co. (1968)

Joseph Lee Jones, a black man, sought to purchase a home in the Paddock Woods neighborhood of St. Louis County, Missouri. The Alfred H. Mayer Company, a white-owned and operated company, refused to sell Jones the home for the sole reason that Jones was black. Jones' attorneys argued that the Thirteenth Amendment states that "[n]either slavery nor involuntary servitude, except as punishment for crime whereof the party shall have been duly convicted, shall exist within the United States, or any place subject to their jurisdiction." The federal law enacted pursuant to the Thirteenth Amendment is 42 U.S.C. § 1982, which grants to all citizens, without regard to race or color, the same right to purchase and lease property as is enjoyed by white citizens. The Supreme Court decided that the Thirteenth Amendment and federal law bars all racial discrimination, private as well as public, in the sale or rental of property. When "racial discrimination herds men into ghettos and makes their ability to buy property turn on the color of their skin," the Court maintained, "then it too is a relic of slavery." The Supreme Court decided in this case that federal law bars all racial discrimination (private or public), in the sale or rental of property.

In the course of the opinion, Justice Stewart refers to multiple other cases that involved housing discrimination against black families by white property owners. Justice Douglas wrote a concurring opinion in which he noted that some badges of slavery remained even in 1968. He noted that while the institution of slavery had been outlawed, it remained in the minds and hearts of many white men. "Cases which have come to this Court depict a spectacle of slavery unwilling to die." He proceeds to list a series of cases detailing challenges to situations in which white men actively worked to restrict blacks from voting, serving on juries, sitting with whites in courtrooms, attending superior schools, entering colleges and graduate schools, marrying whites, living in integrated residential neighborhoods, eating in certain restaurants, sitting in certain rail cars, visiting certain public beaches, visiting certain golf courses and amusement parks and libraries, and sitting in the front of public buses. The case reiterated the need for the Supreme Court to continue to hear cases of specific stories of oppression and decide in favor of equality for blacks and whites. While the case had important implications for the freedom of black families to purchase and sell property, it also affirmed the innumerable occurrences of blatant oppression by whites against blacks in many aspects of social life.

In their attempts to obtain their constitutionally granted civil rights, black community organizers and political organizations worked in partnership with attorneys who used litigation to erode the separate but equal doctrine. Thurgood Marshall and other attorneys at the NAACP who brought cases before the Supreme Court were strategic in their approach. The Fourteenth Amendment was the leading constitutional provision used to convince the Supreme Court to conclude that states could not allow circumstances for white Americans that were different than those permissible for African Americans. The Fourteenth Amendment, in their opinion, epitomized the very basis of American citizenship and the stories that became the subjects of Supreme Court cases between 1932 and 1968 were clear examples of the rampant discrimination black Americans endured that stripped them of their citizenship. By challenging state laws and policies that kept African Americans segregated, civil rights court case plaintiffs and their attorneys overcame legal barriers to equality and achieved legal justice for African Americans.

References

Darden, Joe T. "Black Residential Segregation Since the 1948 Shelley V. Kraemer Decision," *Journal of Black Studies*, Vol. 25, No. 6 (July, 1995), 680–691.

Dershowitz, Alan M. *America on Trial: Inside the Legal Battles That Transformed Our Nation* (Warner Books: New York, 2004.)

James, Rawn. *Root and Branch: Charles Hamilton Houston, Thurgood Marshall, and the Struggle to End Segregation* (Bloomsbury Publishing: New York, 2010.)

Boynton v. Virginia, 364 U.S. 454 (1960).

Brown v. Board of Education, 347 U.S. 483 (1954).

Heart of Atlanta Motel, Inc. v. United States, 379 U.S. 241 (1964).

Jones v. Alfred H. Mayer Co,. 392 U.S. 409 (1968).

Loving v. Virginia. 388 U.S. 1 (1967).

McLaurin v. Oklahoma State Regents for Higher Ed., 339 U.S. 637 (1950).

Missouri ex. rel. Gaines v. Canada et al., 305 U.S. 337 (1938).

National Association for the Advancement of Colored People v. State of Alabama ex rel. John Patterson 357 U.S. 449 (1958).

Plessy v. Ferguson, 163 U.S. 537 (1896).

Shelley v. Kraemer, 334 U.S. 1 (1948).

Smith v. Allwright, Election Judge et al., 321 U.S. 649 (1944).

Sweatt v. Painter, 339 U.S. 629 (1950).

University of Maryland v. Murray, 169 Md. 478 (1936).

United States v. Powell, 287 U.S. 45 (1932)

SIX

"We Shall Not Be Moved": The Quest for Civil Rights outside the Deep South

DISCRIMINATION AGAINST African Americans and African Americans' response to it was not limited to cities, towns, and states in the Deep South. Black people also suffered from white racism and oppression in southeastern seaboard and Mid-Atlantic states like North Carolina, South Carolina, Virginia, Maryland, and Delaware. Even northern urban areas like Philadelphia, Pennsylvania, New York City, and Midwestern cities like Milwaukee, Wisconsin, were sites of civil rights struggles. They are not as well known, but were nonetheless dramatic and important in securing justice, equality, and a sense of self-worth for Americans who resided there. These campaigns did not follow the same patterns as those in Mississippi and Alabama. But, like activists in those states, participants developed strategies and tactics that responded to the political and cultural realities of their location.

In Monroe, North Carolina, a city less than 20 miles from the South Carolina border, African Americans organized to challenge de jure segregation. Their efforts were largely led by the local chapter of the National Association for the Advancement of Colored People (NAACP), under the leadership of Robert F. Williams. Williams was an Army and Marine Corps veteran and like many other veterans during the late 1940s and the 1950s, his military experiences led him to expect more of his country. After being dismissed from the Marine Corps for challenging the racial status quo, Williams became the president of the local chapter of the NAACP, one of the few NAACP chapters with a working class political base and working-class sensibilities. In 1957, the group used picketing and public demonstrations to desegregate the town's public library, which black Monroe residents helped pay for and maintain with their taxes, but were legally unable to use. After they desegregated the library, black Monroe residents mounted efforts to challenge school disparities, segregation in publicly funded accommodations, mistreatment and discrimination in the criminal justice system, and racist violence and intimidation (Barksdale 1984).

The height of the campaign occurred in 1961, when activists challenged a law which prohibited blacks from using the publicly supported swimming pool. Initially, like the opening stages of the Montgomery Bus Boycott, black Monroe residents did not want to eliminate segregation. They did not demand equal access to the pool; instead, they asked that the pool be available to blacks one or two days per week with the whites using the pool on the remaining days. City leaders, however, refused blacks' accommodation to segregation and when African Americans' protest continued into the summer of 1961, the pool was closed to both whites and blacks. Despite the pool closing, picketing continued into late June 1961. White economic intimidation and physical attacks on black Monroe residents was commonplace, but unlike African American communities in other locations throughout the South, many black residents in Monroe did not subscribe to the strategy of nonviolence. A large segment subscribed to a philosophy of self defense. They would not, like Martin Luther King Jr., turn the other cheek. When members of the Ku Klux Klan marched in black neighborhoods and fired shots into their homes during the summer of 1961, blacks returned fire with shotguns, rifle, and pistols. In spite of white violence, the black freedom struggle in Monroe, North Carolina, continued when on August 15, 1961, Robert Williams and Dr. Albert Perry, the vice president of the NAACP chapter, sent a 10-point petition for equal rights and justice to the city council of Monroe, in which they demanded fair employment practices in the private and public sectors, an end to segregation in municipal facilities and schools, and the prohibition of the use of segregation signs "designating one area for colored and another for whites" (Williams 1962,76).

To agitate and make their demands known and felt by white townspeople, a group of black Monroe residents joined with Student Nonviolence Coordinating Committee (SNCC) members from across the country to form the Monroe Nonviolent Action Committee (MNAC). Throughout August 1961, the MNAC picketed Monroe's courthouse, integrated local churches, and boycotted businesses (Barksdale 1984). White elected officials ignored blacks' calls for equal treatment and local white residents, fearing the end of white supremacy, responded violently. On a Saturday, August 26, 1961, protest demonstrators were assaulted by white Monroe residents and then arrested on trumped up charges by the sheriff's deputies. Later that day, two activists were assaulted and chased out of a popular restaurant in nearby Mecklenburg County. As the lynch mob gathered, the two activists were separated, with one speeding away in his car and the other scurrying into a nearby wooded area. Miraculously, neither was injured, and both found their way back to the black section of Monroe.

On Sunday afternoon, August 27, black demonstrations resumed and angry white mobs of approximately 3,000 people milled around the town to intimidate and heckle the protestors. In the confusion, an unknown gunman fired off shots and hostile exchanges between blacks and whites ensued. During the evening, those blacks who were not arrested made their way back to the black section of town, New Town, and began stockpiling weapons and reinforcing barricades for the arrival of gun-toting white vigilantes and the police. The white mob never materialized as state troopers were called in by the governor to quell the riot, but Robert Williams was forced to flee Monroe. After his departure, blacks' protests fell into disarray. Unable to change local and state laws, the movement's black Monroe residents only saw improved conditions in the mid-1960s, with the passage of civil rights legislation (Barksdale 1984).

On February 1, 1960, Ezell Blair Jr., Franklin McCain, Joseph McNeil, and David Richmond, students at North Carolina Agricultural and Technical College in Greensboro, North Carolina, ignored local custom and mores and sat down at the lunch counter at the local Woolworth's Department store, and asked for coffee and a doughnut. While few Woolworth's stores exist today, in the 1950s and the 1960s, the apogee of the Civil Rights Movement, the store was located in most major southern cities and towns. African Americans could shop in stores and be served at other counters, but in most stores, the lunch counters were either off limits or had seats reserved for blacks at the end of the counter. In stores throughout the country, black customers had suffered the humiliation of having to wait until a white customer was served before they were taken care of. Nonetheless, Woolworth's provided black customers with some of their basic necessities and sundries. In 1960, in Greensboro, North Carolina, students were impatient with the pace of racial progress and the intransigence of white racism in the city and used sit-ins and non-violent mass demonstrations to change the situation.

Blair, McCain, McNeil, and Richmond's requests were denied, as they had been before and as they had expected. Unlike times before, however, the four refused to move from the counter until they were served and on that cold February afternoon, they sat at the counter without being served until the store closed at 5:30PM. On February 2, they returned to the store

Four young African American college students stage a historic sit-in at the Woolworth's Department Store "whites-only" lunch counter. Shown here on February 2, 1960, are (left to right) Joseph McNeil, Franklin McCain, Billy Smith, and Clarence Henderson. (Library of Congress)

with other students, sat down at the lunch counter, and asked to be served. Again, the students were rebuffed by the waitress and the store manager. Word about the sit-ins, as they have been called, spread throughout the campus and the surrounding community, so that by Friday, February 5, over 300 black and white students from local colleges and universities not only descended upon the Woolworth's store, but spread the sit-in campaign to other department stores that observed the same discriminatory policies. Throughout that spring semester, students demonstrated and many were jailed. By the end of the semester, the white business elite of Greensboro grew weary with the energetic students who were supported by their parents, churches, and civic organizations and detrimentally affected their profit margin. The cracks of segregation were revealed and undaunted, the sit-in movement continued.

By the end of the summer of 1960, the business elite of Greensboro desegregated lunch counters and the sit-in movement had expanded to other towns in the state, including Winston-Salem, Charlotte, Raleigh, and Wilmington, North Carolina, and around the country to other southern states (Sitkoff 1993). In Richmond, Virginia, students at Virginia Union

University organized a sit-in at Talheimer's department store in late February 1960 (Hall 2007). Motivated by what was happening on other campuses, 1,000 students at South Carolina State College, a historically black college in Orangeburg, South Carolina, marched to the downtown business district with hopes of organizing sit-ins, but were repelled by police wielding tear gas and high-pressure fire hoses (Hine 1996). According to some estimates, in the 17 months following the initial Greensboro sit-in, approximately 75,000 people participated in hundreds of similar demonstrations. Martin Luther King Jr. declared in his speech at the Great March on Detroit in June 1963 that the sit-in movement throughout the country desegregated lunch counters in 285 cities and towns. The issue was not that students wanted to eat next to white people. The issue was "bigger than a hamburger." Desegregating restaurants and lunch counters was a way of showing the world that African Americans would no longer accept inferior positions to which they were subjugated by the larger white society (Carson 1991).

Wilmington, North Carolina's youth and adult activists received their cue from the mass demonstrations and sit-ins that had began several years earlier in Greensboro, North Carolina, and spread throughout the state. In Wilmington, North Carolina, too, along the eastern seacoast, African Americans organized themselves against racism. As early as 1948, black residents organized to equalize the pay of African American teachers and principals with their white counterparts. In the 1950s, black political leaders started a political education campaign to help African Americans understand the workings of local government and the maneuverings of politicians. Using black schools, churches, social organizations, and the African American-owned *Wilmington Journal*, black activists, including physician Hubert Eaton, Reverend Edwin Kirton of St. Mark's Episcopal Church, Reverend J. Ray Butler of Ebenezer Baptist Church, and newspaper editor Tom Jervay attempted to mobilize black support around civil rights issues and encourage African Americans of voting age to register to vote and inform the African American community of municipal political developments and practices (Godwin 1992). Ebenezer Baptist Church was the organizing center. NAACP youth activists used the church to organize nonviolent mass demonstrations throughout the downtown business district of Wilmington in the summer of 1963. Their campaign forced the city's mayor and the city council to foster change in racial relations and policies in the city.

Blacks in Cambridge, Maryland, had similar sentiments and the desire for full citizenship rights, but their political struggle was not as successful

Civil rights activist and leader Martin Luther King Jr.
(Library of Congress)

as the sit-in movement in North Carolina. During the spring and summer
of 1963, the Cambridge Nonviolent Action Committee (CNAC), was the
foremost African American grassroots organization and represented the
interests of a cross section of African Americans and led a movement to
desegregate downtown facilities. Gloria Richardson was the organization's
leader. Their demands included the desegregation of public places and
schools; the creation of equal employment opportunities; the construction of affordable housing for black Cambridge residents, and "an end
to all forms of police brutality and appointments of a Negro deputy
sheriff" (Brock 1993, 129). Local activists picketed, boycotted, and demonstrated at the local movie theater, downtown restaurants, the county
courthouse, and the jail. Mass arrests shortly followed and Richardson and
others were charged with disorderly conduct. In one instance, Dinez White,

a black teenager, was arrested, jailed, and held without bond for conducting a pray-in outside the local bowling alley.

Black activists were not asking for anything outlandish. Statewide, Maryland lawmakers passed the Public Accommodations Law in June 1963, which prohibited discrimination based on race, but Dorchester County lawmakers (the county wherein Cambridge is located) decided that the law did not apply to their county. By mid-June 1963, peaceful demonstrations by blacks were met with violence by the white vigilantes. White anti-black violence and black self-defense prompted the governor of Maryland, J. Millard Tawes, to mobilize the National Guard and state police to halt mob rule. For two weeks, martial law was declared and political demonstrations ceased. Eventually, violence subsided and the guardsmen and troops were removed on July 8 and demonstrations resumed, but so did the violence. The whites had decided that they were unwilling to relinquish any of their power and privilege over blacks, and again enforced the color line with guns and bombs. Tired of being pushed, blacks responded in kind. Again, on July 11, the National Guard took control of Cambridge and remained there until early 1964 (Brock 1993).

In late July and throughout August 1963, Richardson and other CNAC leaders met with city and county officials and members of the federal government, including Attorney General Robert F. Kennedy to desegregate Cambridge and institute a fair public accommodation ordinance. However, like the white electorate, local white officials were unwilling to cede power. It was decided after weeks of negotiations that the public accommodation amendment addressing the desegregation of publicly funded institutions, affordable housing, and employment discrimination—basic citizenship rights in Cambridge and Dorchester county—would be left to a public referendum. After all the votes were tallied in the October referendum, the amendment was defeated by 274 votes (Brock 1993, 134–136). Neither CNAC's widespread, nonviolent direct action nor electoral politics led to change in segregation laws throughout the city in the early 1960s. It was only after the passage of federal civil rights laws in the mid-1960s that black Cambridge residents received some relief from political and economic discrimination in that city.

Like white legislators in Cambridge, Maryland, it was not uncommon for white lawmakers and segments of white communities in other Atlantic seaboard states to effectively ignore state and federal legislation or U.S. Supreme Court decisions on civil rights for African Americans. Just as Dorchester County, Maryland, lawmakers and political elites decided that Maryland's Public Accommodations Law did not apply to their county, white residents of Milford, Delaware, a small town in southern Delaware, argued that the 1954 *Brown v. Board of Education* did not apply to their southern Delaware town.

During the summer of 1954 the Milford, Delaware, board of education had discussed and made plans for beginning the process of desegregating their school system. On September 8, 11 black 10th-graders, who would have had to travel to nearby towns to go to all black high schools, were to be the first black students to enter the all-white Lakeview Avenue School. The process proceeded smoothly until white parents became anxious that black and white students would interact socially. Like other towns throughout the South and border states, the whites feared the prospect of black boys and white girls becoming romantically involved. During a September 17 meeting white residents turned out by the thousands to a local meeting, which resulted in a petition sent to the board of education announcing their resistance to integration. In response, the school board closed all public schools in the district on September 20, with the hope of hearing Milford's white residents' concerns and to restate its position on integration. The board intended to reopen school on Tuesday, September 21, but received numerous threats of violence against the 11 black children and decided to close the district schools indefinitely.

With no clear leadership, white Milford residents were looking for someone for a voice and direction. They found both in Bryant Bowles, a failed businessman with a questionable past and founder and president of the National Association for the Advancement of White People (NAAWP). Bowles had recently arrived in the area in early September just as the process of desegregation was underway. On Sunday, September 26, in a hastily organized meeting of several thousand people, Bowles introduced the organization to local residents and appointed Manean Warrington, a local preacher, to be president of the Delaware chapter. Schools reopened on September 27, but in the days and weeks to come, Bowles helped organize pickets in front of the Lakeview Avenue School and, along with followers, mounted a campaign of veiled threats of violence and economic pressure against the whites who did not subscribe to the NAAWP platform of complete "separation of the races of mankind" and a boycott of the school system (Kee 1997/1998, 221). Ultimately, the boycott was successful. White parents kept their children out of the Milford schools in large numbers and surrounding towns that were not involved in any desegregation process removed their children from these schools in sympathy. By October 1, after school board members' resigned and were replaced by segregationists, the new Milford school board removed the 11 black students and reinstituted segregation at the Lakeview Avenue School. Fears of toppling the racial status quo led the whites to openly oppose federal law and it was not until 1962 that black students started to attend Milford schools on a desegregated basis (Kee 1997/1998).

The small black population and their dependence on the local whites for resources and their livelihood meant that they could not mobilize in ways that blacks in deep southern states could. Blacks in Milford, Delaware, comprised roughly 16 percent of the local population in the 1950s, and while they received some political support from members of the Wilmington, Delaware, NAACP chapter, the closest chapter with political connections, Wilmington was over 50 miles away and worlds apart. Situated in a border state with both a sizable white moderate population and a large contingent of segregationists, African Americans' political rights and educational opportunities in places like southern Delaware were ephemeral and meted out or refused, depending on who the white electorate voted for.

This was the case in Virginia in the late 1950s and the early 1960s, but challenges to segregation in education were made in the courts under the aegis of the NAACP. Shortly after the 1954 *Brown* decision, state officials lead by U.S. Senator Harry F. Byrd, state governor Thomas B. Stanley, and state senator Garland Gray organized a statewide and legislative resistance to the Supreme Courts' decision called "massive resistance." The crux of the resistance was convincing the white electorate that school integration would not only deteriorate schools and would also diminish educational opportunities for white children, but it would also destroy the purity of white Virginian racial stock and usher in a decline of a cherished way of life that kept "the Negro" in his place. Rather than seeing the issue in terms of universal civil rights for all Americans, Byrd and his followers framed the discussion in terms of the state's rights. Accordingly, an individual state, not the federal government, possessed the authority to dictate the educational policy within its boundaries. Since Section 140 of Virginia's state constitution forbade African American and white students to attend the same school anywhere in the state, *Brown* was in direct contradiction to Virginia state law (Pratt 1992). For their part, the Stanleys and Byrds of Virginia were successful. Whites across the state from Richmond to Norfolk agreed to have their schools closed if any black children were transferred in by local school boards. School boards were dismantled and whites who could afford it sent their children to private schools. In Prince Edward County, the whites dismantled the entire public school system in the fall of 1959, only to reopen it by order of the U.S. Supreme Court in 1964. In the interim, politicos throughout the state passed the Pupil Placement Act in the fall of 1956, which created Pupil Placement Boards throughout the state and gave each the responsibility for placing every student in area. Complex criterion was allegedly used to place the children, but in the end, only racial classification mattered. Black students continued to go to inferior segregated schools and whites to better-funded white schools (Bly 1999).

For many African Americans in parts of Virginia, mass protest was not an option. However, many refused to consent to the authority of the whites and did not submit their child's school application form. In September 1957, when their children were removed from schools for not having the form complete, black parents like Chester Hampton of Richmond, Virginia, used the social and political networks of the black community to organize childcare centers in African American churches. Other black parents turned to the courts. With black attorney Oliver Hill of the NAACP representing them, local activist Alice Calloway and others challenged the Pupil Placement Act in the federal court, which ordered the expelled students to be reinstated (Pratt 1992).

Calloway's legal challenge was not the last for black Richmonders or blacks in other Virginia towns and cities. In September 1958, attorney Martin A. Martin appeared before the U.S. District Court on behalf of the parents of six black Richmond students, who were denied admission to a nearby all-white school, on the grounds that the local Pupil Placement Board illegally used the students' race as the sole criterion for denial. The case was not settled until 1961. In the end, the court decided that Renee Warden, after whom the case was named, should be transferred to the nearest all-white school. It would not be the harbinger for policy change as attorney Martin had hoped for. The court also decided that Warden did not represent all black students and therefore sweeping change in the school assignment policy was not necessary. In 1961, 11 black families successfully integrated the local white school when their children entered a local white school in Fall 1962. In *Bradley v. Richmond School Board*, it was successfully argued before the Court of Appeals that the Pupil Placement Board used differing criteria when they placed black and white students, an act tantamount to racial discrimination (Pratt 1992). African Americans in Arlington and Norfolk also filed court cases and won. By the early 1960s, some black children in all three cities attended all-white schools in the 1960s.

Complete school integration in Richmond never happened because of residential segregation patterns and it continues to be elusive, with post civil rights era demographic changes in urban residency and the defunding of urban education. In sum, in the closing decades of the 20th century, white people left Richmond for the suburbs, leaving black people behind to attend the schools they fought to desegregate. African Americans never constituted a sizable population in Arlington, Virginia, which remained predominately white. As of this writing, the city is close to 80 percent white. Norfolk, Virginia, suffers from the same white flight as Richmond; however, it was and is influenced by the country's military (which had integrated housing and schools since the 1960s) and has had a more successful history of desegregation. Nonmilitary residents still suffer from segregated housing patterns and segregated schools exist, but not to the extent of Richmond and Arlington. Late-20th century developments, of course, were unforeseen in the 1960s and such shifts do not detract from the real legal struggles that African American parents participated in or from the hard work and legal action of local black attorneys and NAACP lawyers. The same can be said of the efforts by Reverend Milton Galamison and the Parents' Workshop For Equality in New York City Schools in Brooklyn, New York; Cecil B. Moore in Philadelphia, Pennsylvania; and the Detroit Revolutionary Union Movement in Detroit, Michigan.

By the late 1950s and the early 1960s, New York City Public Schools had a history of poor and underperforming schools that served communities of color. In 1959, Reverend Milton Galamison, the pastor at Siloam Presbyterian Church in Brooklyn, New York, founded the Parents' Workshop for Equality, whose aim was to end discrimination against African Americans and Puerto Ricans in New York City public schools and improve instruction in city schools. The organization was primarily comprised of working-class and working poor black and Puerto Rican women and a few men of color. It was headquartered in Brooklyn, though meetings were held on satellite sites throughout the boroughs of Manhattan, Queens, and the Bronx. The Parents' Workshop saw the full integration of New York City's schools as the primary vehicle through which all children could achieve their full potential. They used nonviolent, direct action to force the New York City Board of Education to develop and support a plan to bring integration to fruition. In April 1960, hundreds of parents of school-age children rallied at the Board of Education to demonstrate their concerns to the city's superintendent. Despite the April 1960 demonstration, no concrete steps were created by the Board to meet parents' demand. Consequently, the Parents' Workshop organized rallies and demonstrations throughout the summer of 1960 to force the hand of school officials. Parents held workshops to inform communities around the city of their

goals, recruited clergymen and congregations to their cause, and continued to pressure and dialogue with school officials to create a meaningful
process of integration.

The result of such activism and pressure was the Open Enrollment plan.
Open Enrollment selected a handful of primary and junior high schools in
predominantly white areas and areas with high concentrations of people
of color and gave parents the option of voluntarily transferring their children to schools outside their neighborhoods or enrolling their children in
schools in their community. The Parents' Workshops supported the plan
and helped families interested in participating complete the necessary
paperwork. Galamison kept the idea of citywide integration a subject at
Board of Education meetings and the mayor's office, so as to not have
the plan lose momentum and interest by elected and appointed representatives. After its initial trial during the 1960–1961 academic year, Open
Enrollment became a citywide initiative in 1961 and remained in operation
until 1963, when it was abandoned. Its failure was the result of a lack of
imagination and support by school board members and New Yorkers' and
black community members' misgivings about the scope and unintended
consequences of the program.

White parents argued that the black students' attendance in their children's school would lower the educational achievement of their children.
In most cases, the issue was less about educational attainment and more
a fear of social relationships that could possibly emerge between white
and black students. In this way, the whites' fears were similar to southern
whites who resisted school integration for fear that their very whiteness
and social status were in jeopardy. For black and Puerto Rican parents,
Open Enrollment was a double-edged sword. On the one hand, it gave
opportunities for the most motivated and gifted African American and
Puerto Rican students. But, on other the hand, the program was a tacit
admission that their schools and other schools in heavily minority communities were not good enough or equipped enough to educate community children. Rather than send the strongest students elsewhere, many
reasoned, such students should remain in their neighborhoods and be
role models to struggling students. Additionally, parents and the Board of
Education should commit to improving schools that serve their children.
Such ideas were indicative of more militant notions of community control
popular in the black power era, which will be discussed in the next chapter
(Waller 2011).

Like Galamison, Cecil B. Moore was a civil rights maverick in Philadelphia, Pennsylvania. In the 1960s, Philadelphia had a population of approx-

imately one million residents. Roughly 30 percent were black. Moore moved to the City of Brotherly Love in the late 1940s and studied law at Temple University after a stint in the Marine Corps. In 1963, in what many believed to be an upset, he won the presidency of the local chapter of the NAACP, the city's most well respected civil rights organizations. In 1964, Moore and the NAACP challenged the use of blackface painting and racially demeaning behavior by white participants in the Mummer's Parade, an annual tradition celebrating the New Year. The parade was held throughout the 19th century, but the first official city-sponsored parade occurred in 1901. Groups of individuals organize themselves into clubs and create a theme-based performance, practice their parade performance throughout the year, and perform for crowds of thousands in costume on New Year's Day. Throughout the history of the parade, white men dressed in blackface, the practice of painting one's face with dark paint or burnt cork and acting in stereotypically "black" ways—ways many white Americans imagined African Americans to act. By the 1960s, the parade was a city institution and financed by contributions from individuals, local businesses, and tax payer dollars. In late 1963, Moore and the NAACP threatened nonviolent mass boycotts to prevent the January 1964 parade from occurring. Moore argued that since black Philadelphians paid taxes and the citizens' tax dollars were used for the winning cash prize, the use of racist caricatures during the parade was unethical. The group won an injunction filed at the court and blackface minstrelsy was prohibited that year, and in coming years, the mayor and city officials instituted measures to prevent the practice in future parades (Early 2003). Moore's and the NAACP's political activity may not have dismantled racism and segregation in the city, but their actions revealed the obstacles African Americans faced in northern cities and the mounting political power that communities of color were developing in the post-war era.

The same can be said about Midwestern cities, where African Americans demonstrated the interconnection between discrimination, segregation, and economic inequality in the industrial Midwest. Calvin Sherard and other working class black men formed the Crusaders in Milwaukee, Wisconsin, in the late 1950s, to fill what they saw as a gap in black political leadership in the city. Shortly after its founding, the group changed its name to the Milwaukee Negro American Labor Council (MNALC) and affiliated with the national body of the Negro American Labor Council, a black working class organization whose aim was to increase African American representation in nationwide unions like the American Federation of Labor-Congress of Industrial Organizations (AFL-CIO). Throughout the early 1960s, the MNALC combined nonviolent direct protests in the form of picketing and boycotting with closed door negotiations to secure jobs for black people in white-owned stores located in predominantly black neighborhoods. Their efforts resulted in a change in discriminatory hiring policies in small businesses and chain grocery stores alike (Jones, 2010). Similarly, in 1963 and 1964, the St. Louis, Missouri, chapter of the Congress of Racial Equality boycotted the city administration, business, and local institutions as well as the Jefferson Bank and Trust Company for its discriminatory hiring practices against blacks and forced the financial institution to change its policies.

Black political activism in areas outside the deep southern states highlights the extent of inequality throughout the United States as well as the varieties of political struggle and resistance that African Americans organized. Tactics available in one place were not readily accessible in another, and in some cases were not successful. But even if these movements did not have the powerful, national leadership of Martin Luther King Jr. receive contemporary media attention, or achieve their goals, the participants' political activities were important. They require our attention and further research. Their heroic work also demonstrates the depth and breadth of the Civil Rights Movement and how everyday people were willing to risk their livelihoods, and sometimes their lives, to improve African Americans' opportunities throughout the country.

References

Baker, Ella. "Bigger than a Hamburger," in Clayborn Carson et al., eds. *The Eyes on the Prize Civil Rights Reader* (New York: Penguin Books, 1991), 120–122.

Barksdale, Marcellus. "Robert F. Williams and the Indigenous Civil Rights Movement in Monroe, North Carolina, 1961," *Journal of Negro History*, Vol. 69, No. 2 (Spring, 1984), 73–89.

Bly, Antonio. "The Thunder During the Storm—School Desegregation in Norfolk, Virginia, 1957–1959: A Local History," *The Journal of Negro Education*, Vol. 67, No. 2 (1999), 106–114.

Brock, Annette. "Gloria Richardson and the Cambridge Movement," in Vicki Crawford et al., eds., *Women in the Civil Rights Movement* (Bloomington: Indiana University Press, 1993), 121–144.

Carson, Clayborne, David J. Garrow, Gerald Gill, Vincent Harding, and Darlene Clark Hine, eds. "Interview with Franklin McCain" in *The Eyes on the Prize Civil Rights Reader* (New York: Penguin Books, 1991), 114–116.

Early, Gerald. *This is Where I Came In: Black America in the 1960s* (Lincoln: University of Nebraska Press, 2003).

Godwin, John L. "Taming a Whirlwind: Black Civil Rights Leadership in the Community Setting, Wilmington, North Carolina, 1950–1972," Proceedings of the South Carolina Historical Association (1992), 67–75.

Hall, Simon. "Civil Rights Activism in 1960s Virginia," *Journal of Black Studies*, Vol. 38, No. 2 (November 2007), 251–267.

Hine, William. "Civil Rights and Campus Wrongs: South Carolina State College Students Protest, 1955–1968," *South Carolina Historical Magazine*, Vol. 97, No. 4 (Oct., 1996), 310–331.

Jones, Patrick D. "'Get Up Off of Your Knees!': Competing Visions of Black Empowerment in Milwaukee during the Early Civil Rights Era," in Peniel Joseph, ed., *Neighborhood Rebels: Black Power at the Local Level* (New York: Palgrave MacMillan, 2010), 45–65.

Kee, Ed. "The Brown Decision and Milford, Delaware, 1954–1965," *Delaware History* Vol. 27 (1997/1998), 205–244.

Pratt, Robert. *The Color of Their Skin: Education and Race in Richmond, Virginia, 1954–1989* (Charlottesville: University of Virginia Press, 1992).

Sitkoff, Harvard. *The Struggle for Black Equality, 1954–1992* (New York: Hill and Wang, 1993).

Waller, Lisa Yvette, "The Pressures of the People: Milton A. Galamison, the Parents; Workshop, and Resistance to School Integration in New York City, 1960-63,"in Manning Marable and Elizabeth Kai Hinton, eds., *The New Black History: Revisiting The Second Reconstruction* (New York: Palgrave MacMillan, 2011), 35–52.

Williams, Robert F. *Negroes with Guns* (New York: Marzani & Munsell, 1962).

SEVEN

"All Power to the People": Black Power Politics during and after the Civil Rights Movement

THE PHRASE BLACK POWER was popularized in 1966 by Stokely Carmichael during a march in Mississippi. Since its first utterance, black power has become an amorphous term and was conceptualized differently by many of its most vocal adherents and activists. However, for the purposes of this chapter and discussion, black power is defined as African Americans' experimentation with democratic processes to bring about social, cultural, and political self-determination to the communities they lived in and served (Joseph 2010, 11). As the years between 1954 and 1966 represent the classical period of the modern Civil Rights Movement, the years between 1966 and 1974 is the era commonly understood to be the zenith of black power politics. To be sure, African Americans' search for self determination paralleled, overlapped, informed, and was informed by the civil rights activists' attempts to achieve school integration, equal access in public accommodations, and voting rights. In fact, it was the Civil Rights Movement's reforms that gave black power activists the courage to challenge persistent and growing economic and political inequalities. Historian Clarence Lang's comments about black power activism in St. Louis, Missouri, can be applied to activists nationwide. He notes that "bitter experiences of arrests, beatings, church bombings, and assassinations" of John F. Kennedy, Medgar Evers, Malcolm X, Martin Luther King Jr., Robert F. Kennedy, and countless other grassroots activists "helped to sour younger activists on the idea that they could end racism, poverty, and militarism through American liberalism" (Lang 2010, 75).

Throughout the nation, though mainly focused in northeastern, Midwestern, and western cities, black power advocates attempted to improve their communities which, by the late 1960s, were all-black enclaves. In so doing, they exposed the contradictions between equal rights and equality of opportunity on the one hand, and continued racism and poverty on the other. The movement radicalized civil rights groups like the Congress of Racial Equality (CORE) and the Student Nonviolent Coordinating Committee (SNCC), spurred the creation of new black political organizations like the Black Panther Party, and encouraged organizational coordination. It also led to rivalries among and between organizations and conflicts between the activists and law enforcement. Historians are just beginning to understand and reconceptualize the complexities and the extent of the black power movement, so to discuss the extent of it would be impossible here. However, the notion that it was "consistent with preceding" black political efforts and reflected "continuity and change in the African American experience" in the decades following WWII is common knowledge among historians of the African American experience and merits our attention in any discussion of the Civil Rights Movement (Lang 2010, 68). What follows is a discussion of how black power political activists dreamed of black political freedom, strategized, and worked to make that dream a reality. It discusses the influential theorists, some of the most important black power organizations, and major campaigns.

Black power advocates and activists were unanimously influenced by Malcolm X. Born Malcolm Little on May 19, 1925, to Earl and Louisa Little in Omaha, Nebraska, during his early years he was taught the black nationalist teachings of Marcus Garvey and the Universal Negro Improvement Association (UNIA). With its headquarters in Harlem, New York, and branches in towns and cities across the United States and throughout the world, the UNIA was the largest black mass movement in U.S. history. Garvey taught race pride, pan-Africanism, black cooperative economics, and an anti-colonial message that would provide the basic ideological tenets of Malcolm's life work as a Muslim minister. When Malcolm was six years old, his father died under mysterious circumstances when he was hit by a street car. Officially, his death was ruled an accident, but the Little family believed that Earl's death was the result of violence meted out by local white men, who had repeatedly intimidated and assaulted the Little family. With his father gone, his mother struggled to keep her family together, but with too many mouths to feed, Malcolm was placed in foster care. Eventually, poverty and stress took its toll on his mother. In 1939, she was committed to the Kalamazoo State Hospital, where she stayed for over two decades.

In 1941, Malcolm moved to the Roxbury section of Boston, Massachusetts, to live with his half sister Ella Collins (Earl's daughter from a previous marriage). In Boston, Malcolm became acquainted with jazz (a love of his for his entire adult life) and petty crime. At the age of 16, he obtained employment as a cook and later as a waiter on the railroad. Through his travels between Washington, D.C., and Boston, he frequented Harlem, New York, the black cultural capital of the United States. In the mid-to-late 1940s, Malcolm made frequent trips between Boston and New York City and became more involved in crime burglarizing homes in Boston's affluent suburbs. In January 1946, he and his friend in crime, Shorty Jarvis, were arrested, charged with firearm possession, larceny, and breaking and entering, and were sentenced to four concurrent sentences of eight-to-ten years each. During his time in prison, he converted to the Nation of Islam (NOI). The NOI is a heterodox, American Islamic movement in the United States founded in Detroit, Michigan, during the Great Depression by W. Fard Muhammad, a traveling peddler who declared he was the messiah for black people. Throughout the 1940s, despite internal disputes and turmoil, the organization remained afloat under the leadership of Elijah Muhammad—a position he would hold until his death in 1975. In the spirit of Marcus Garvey, the Nation created black owned businesses and taught black racial pride. It also restricted adherents from participating in partisan politics. More importantly, it offered its members—many of whom were ex-convicts and recovering drug addicts—a regimented life.

Malcolm was released from prison in 1952. After his parole ended in 1953, he traveled the country teaching the ideas and doctrines of Elijah Muhammad. In 1957, after several tireless years of work as the head minister of Temple No. 7 in Harlem and principle organizer of temples throughout the eastern seaboard, his charisma and work brought him to the attention of Elijah Muhammad, who promoted him to the position of national spokesman for the organization. In 1958, he married Betty Shabazz (née Sanders), a nurse and health instructor for the Nation's Muslim Girl's Training General Civilization Class. During the late 1950s and the early 1960s, Betty would give birth to six girls. It was also during these years that Malcolm continued to seek converts for the organization, hold rallies, speak at colleges and universities, travel to the Middle East to prepare the way for Elijah Muhammad's pilgrimage, write columns for black newspapers, and frame himself as a burgeoning civil rights leader. In 1959, he was featured in Mike Wallace's *The Hate That Hate Produced*, a documentary which unflatteringly introduced white Americans to the Nation of Islam's politics and leaders. By 1960, Malcolm was one of the most popular and hated black leaders in the nation.

Malcolm's affiliation with the Nation changed on November 22, 1963, when John F. Kennedy was assassinated. Elijah Muhammad ordered that

Portrait of Malcolm X, spokesman for the Nation of
Islam during the Civil Rights Movement. (Library
of Congress)

no minister or member of the organization was to make a public statement
about the death of the president. Despite this, when asked by a reporter
what he thought about the Kennedy's death, Malcolm commented that it
was a case of "chickens coming home to roost," a statement for which
he was suspended (Marable 2011, 270). Knowing that he would not be reinstated to his position, on March 8, 1964, Malcolm announced that he would
leave the Nation. Throughout the spring of 1964, he made plans to organize the Muslim Mosque Incorporated (MMI), for which he was the head
minister.

1964, the final year of Malcolm's short life, was a busy one. Shortly after
organizing the MMI, he made a pilgrimage to Mecca, converted to Sunni

Islam, and changed his name to El Hajj Malik el Shabazz. Upon his return to the United States he denounced the heterodox views of his mentor Elijah Muhammad, exposed Muhammad's adulterous activity with secretaries in the organization, and organized the Organization of Afro American Unity (OAAU), as a secular political wing for his civil rights works. In the fall of 1964, he set out on a tour of Africa to gain support from African heads of state and dignitaries for a United Nations resolution condemning institutional racism and segregation in the United States. His work during this year was a major shift in his approach. He was now willing to work with whites and blacks in the Civil Rights Movement and place black people's fight against oppression on a world stage.

Malcolm X's fiery speaking style, his willingness to engage the most educated and uneducated listeners and debaters, his ability to distill complex ideas to their very essence, and his linking African Americans' political struggle against racism with the anti-colonial struggles around the African Diaspora are what so many black power activists found attractive and influential. For people who were victims of police brutality in urban areas, his call for self defense was appealing. To the impoverished, his assessment of the causes of their poverty rang true. For young people looking for someone who could speak the language of the street, who was from the street, understood the complexities of urban living, and could offer an ideological and political alternative to Martin Luther King Jr., Malcolm was an obvious choice. His work, however, was cut short when he was assassinated on February 21, 1965, while speaking at an OAAU rally at the Audubon Ballroom in Harlem, New York. His *Autobiography* was published posthumously in 1965 and, along with his speeches, was considered required reading by activists.

Stokely Carmichael, Huey Newton, and the Black Panther Party were Malcolm X's ideological offspring. Stokely Standiford Churchill Carmichael was born in Port of Spain, Trinidad, to May and Adolph Carmichael on June 29, 1941. In 1952, he moved to New York City and from 1956 to 1960, he attended the Bronx High School of Science. There, he would meet leftists of all persuasions, including socialist and communist. In 1960, he attended Howard University in Washington, D.C., where he majored in philosophy. At Howard, Carmichael joined the Nonviolent Action Group, a student group interested in desegregating downtown Washington's establishments. In 1961, he joined the Freedom Riders in their attempt to challenge segregation on interstate transit in Mississippi. When he and his fellow activists tried to integrate a whites-only waiting room in Jackson,

Mississippi, Carmichael was arrested and sent to the notorious Parchman Farm, where he spent five weeks.

Over the next three years, he managed to balance his activism and school work, and in 1964, he was awarded his bachelor's degree in philosophy. Determined to make a lasting change in race relations, Carmichael returned to Mississippi. In the summer of 1964, shortly after receiving his degree, he, along with Bob Moses, Bayard Rustin, and more seasoned activists, helped train white college students participating in the Freedom Summer. During that hot Mississippi summer, Carmichael was a project director and helped white college student volunteers organize voter registration drives and create freedom schools. Known by his overalls and for his gregarious nature, Carmichael motivated volunteers when they were weary and empowered blacks to attempt to register to vote.

In 1966, Carmichael was elected chair of SNCC and steered the organization away from its previous integration aims toward black nationalism. SNCC's 1966 position paper declared that the organization "rejecte[ed] the American dream as defined by white people and must work to construct an American reality defined by Afro-Americans" (Van Deburg 1997, 124). That year, when James Meredith was gunned down in Mississippi during his one-man March Against Fear, Carmichael joined Martin Luther King Jr. and hundreds of other activists to finish the march. It was there on his way to Jackson, Mississippi, that he declared that "the only way we gonna stop them white men from whuppin' us is to take over. What we gonna start sayin' now is Black Power!" (Joseph 2011, 175). Carmichael's notion of black power included a cultural return to African heritage and mass political participation by black people. The idea of using black voting power and forming black political parties was something he had witnessed and participated in during his work in Lowndes, Alabama, with the Lowndes County Freedom Organization, which challenged the democratic and republican parties at the local level. If blacks could organize in Alabama, Carmichael saw no reason why they could not do so in Mississippi or anywhere else in the country. With clear influences from Malcolm X, he elaborated on the concept in *Black Power: The Politics of Liberation*, which he co-authored with sociologist Charles Hamilton. In it, he writes that "Black Power is full participation in the decision making processes affecting the lives of black people, and recognition of the virtues in themselves as black people" (Carmichael & Hamilton 1992, 47).

Throughout 1967, he toured black colleges in the United States discussing his ideas and further explaining his position. In the summer of 1967, he embarked on a five-month worldwide tour, speaking with leftist groups in Europe and met with African dignitaries and political leaders. By this time, he had made his anti-Vietnam war stance known in the United States, and as part of his tour, he met with Ho Chi Minh in Vietnam. Upon his return, Carmichael toured the United States as a much sought-after speaker. In 1968, he was approached by the Black Panther Party and was given the nominal title of Prime Minister, a position he only held for a little over a year.

By late 1968, his ties with SNCC were severed. Dismayed by the assassination of Martin Luther King Jr. black nationalism and black power no longer seemed to fit Carmichael as a political ideology. For seven years, he grappled with American race relations, but his and others' efforts had not yielded the political fruits they had deserved and desired. In September 1968, he left the United States with his recent wife, the South African singing sensation Miriam Makeba, and took up residence in Conakry, Guinea, in West Africa. The two divorced in 1978. During the 1970s, he was a prominent member of the All African People's Revolutionary Party and changed his name to Kwame Ture after his two major Pan Africanist influences, Kwame Nkrumah of Ghana and Sekou Toure of Guinea. In 1996, Ture was diagnosed with advanced stage prostate cancer. Two years later, despite treatment in the United States, Cuba, and Honduras, he died on November 15, 1998, in his home in Conakry, Guinea.

That Carmichael affiliated with the Black Panther Party is not surprising. The Black Panther Party (BPP) was founded in 1966 in Oakland, California, as an armed community police patrol by Huey Newton and Bobby Seale. Bobby Seale was the organization's chairman. Newton was the Minister for Self Defense and the group's chief political philosopher. In 1967, Eldridge Cleaver, the left-leaning author of *Soul on Ice*, joined the organization and became the organization's Minister of Information. The Panthers were influenced by Malcolm X's internationalist approach, the Martinican psychologist and author Franz Fanon who argued that armed violence used by the colonized is necessary and can be cathartic, Marxist ideologies, Mao Zedong, as well as local, national, and international radical politics, including anti-colonial struggles in Latin America, Africa, and Asia. Newton guided the Black Panthers toward Black Nationalism in its opening years and argued that black people possessed the right to control the politics, culture, and economies of their communities. Throughout its lifetime, the organization shifted its ideological position to socialism, then intercommunalism. As intercommunalists, "the Panthers saw their struggle in the United States as not only necessary for the liberation of blacks

Huey P. Newton poses for a Black Panther poster.
(Library of Congress)

and other oppressed people in America but as a struggle whose success
was critical for the liberation of nations worldwide" (Jeffries 2002,74). Intercommunalism as a political approach wed the complexities of empire
building, western neo-imperialist projects, and international grassroots
mobilizations that were not limited by political geography.

Carmichael's, Newton's, and the Black Panther Party's activism demonstrate that the black power movement was concerned with the domestic
political situation affecting African Americans and saw their plight within
a larger anti-colonial assault against empire taking place across the world.
Such an international perspective harkens back to W.E.B. Du Bois' pan-
African Conferences between WWI and WWII, Marcus Garvey's UNIA of
the 1920s, and the Council of African Affairs, which sought to cultivate

political ties across the African diaspora in the immediate post-WWII decade. With the emergence of the nonaligned movement in Bandung, Indonesia, in 1955 and as Asian, Latin American, and African nations broke the yoke of colonialism, black activists built on previous ideas of internationalism and individually, collectively, creatively, and strategically made political connections with and were inspired by people of color in other nations.

The Black Panthers portrayed themselves as young revolutionaries known for their bellicose rhetoric and style. On May 2, 1967, a group of armed Panthers demonstrated on the Capitol Building in Sacramento, California, to decry legislation being considered that would criminalize the carrying of weapons. The demonstration gave the Panthers media attention throughout the country and brought the organization to the attention of both urban blacks seeking a political outlet and the Federal Bureau of Investigation. In early 1968, the Party launched its weekly newspaper, *The Black Panther*, which had a circulation of over 100,000 at the height of its popularity. By 1970, four years after its creation and to the surprise of its founders, the Party grew to over 5,000 members divided into 40 chapters nationwide.

Its growth is partially the result of the group's brief merger with SNCC in 1968. Both SNCC and the Panthers sought to use the other to extend the reach of their work into new area. SNCC wanted to reach out to blacks in urban locations and the Panthers wanted to help mobilize African Americans in the South. With SNCC's Stokely Carmichael as Prime Minister of the Party, James Forman and H. Rap Brown became the Minister of Foreign Affairs and Minister of Justice, respectively. The union failed not only because of mutual distrust, leadership difference, and FBI subterfuge, but also because both organizations were moving in opposing political directions, SNCC toward black nationalism and the Panthers closer to socialism.

As they emerged on the national scene, the Black Panther Party became one of the targets of the FBI's Counter Intelligence Program (COINTEL-PRO). In conjunction with local police agencies, the Bureau used a variety of techniques to destroy the organization, including, but not limited to, spreading misinformation in media outlets, raiding local headquarters, and creating a culture of harassment. During an October 28, 1967, traffic stop, an altercation ensued between Officer John Frey, Officer Herbert Heanes, and Newton that left Frey dead, Heanes hurt, and Newton's body riddled with bullets. The state accused Newton of murder and several other charges. At his trial on September 8, 1968, the court found him guilty of manslaughter and sentenced him to two-to-fifteen-years at the California

Men's Colony in San Luis Obispo, California. After a series of retrials, New-ton was exonerated and was released from prison in August 1970.

Around the country, local branches started running survival programs. Survival programs had three purposes. The first was the empowerment of African Americans, especially young people living in urban areas, through political education. The second purpose was to ensure the health and safety of poor, urban black communities within which the Panthers worked. The third was more far reaching. Through such initiatives, the Panthers sought to break down exploitative economic relationships that made urban black people poor in the first place. Not all of the chapters ran the same pro-grams and different names were used, depending on the location. Despite differences in names, chapters throughout the country ran survival pro-grams that included free breakfast programs for children, before and after school education programs, Free Busing to Prisons program, Sickle Cell Anemia Research program, Seniors Against Fearful Environment, as well as household maintenance services.

By 1974, state chapters throughout the nation closed and nationwide membership dwindled to around 500. During that year, Newton fled to Cuba to avoid imprisonment for the alleged murder of a prostitute. During this period, Elaine Brown became the party's chairwoman, reversed many of Newton's policies, and tried to save the crippled organization. As head of the party and with the leadership of a cadre of black women who she appointed, Brown opened and operated the Oakland Community School. Newton returned in 1977 to be cleared of all charges. From 1977 to 1982, he assumed leadership of the party. But with just close to 200 members, the Party was a shadow of its former self. *The Black Panther* ceased publica-tion in 1980 and the Oakland Community School closed its doors in 1982, the same year the party disbanded.

The Panthers' national profile and community programs often made them models for other organizations around the country. The Liberators was one such group. A short-lived, male dominated group of young activ-ists in St. Louis, Missouri, the Liberators was founded in 1968 by Charles Koen, a former member of SNCC who recruited members from rival gangs in the city. The Liberators organized a free breakfast program, donned berets and leather jackets like the San Francisco Bay Area Pan-thers, worked to end police brutality, and openly protested the drafting of black men into the military (Lang 2010). It was the Panthers' willing-ness to experiment with the concept of black power that inspired other black power activists like those in Louisville, Kentucky's West End Com-munity Council (WECC). In 1968, the WECC examined school conditions and urged the city of Louisville to address over-enrollment in the city's black schools. One year later, after applying political pressure, they forced white-owned stores in black neighborhoods to hire black employees. According to historian Tracy K'Meyer, the WECC's founding of the Black Unity League of Kentucky (BULK) in 1967 was one of its most important achievements as an organization. With black adolescents in leadership positions, BULK was an educational, cultural, and political group. The youth met with the city's education officials to include African American history as part of the curriculum. They also worked with community residents to organize celebrations of African American arts and culture. When several members of the WECC and BULK were arrested on charges of conspiracy for causing a riot in May 1968 in Louisville, the WECC was instrumental in organizing a broad interracial united front of political organizations to rally in support of the arrested. The front critiqued the racially motivated arrests by the police department, organized and raised monies for a team of lawyers for their defense, and eventually obtained their release (K'Meyer 2010).

The multiplicity of interpretations of black power in the late 1960s led to a multifaceted grassroots approach that sought to improve employment opportunities, end segregated housing policies, and integrate public accommodations in Baltimore, Maryland. Black power activists in Baltimore also applied a variety of meanings to the term. "Black power meant shoring up black manhood, advocating self-defense, seeking self determination, exercising political power, attacking discrimination in education, employment, housing, and welfare, challenging entrenched white and black leaders, and mobilizing poor black people to transform society" (Williams 2010, 216). By 1966, the Congress of Racial Equality, like SNCC, had embraced black power, and during that year, the organization set its sights on Baltimore. In February 1966, the group held its national convention in the city at the Knox Presbyterian Church. There they decided that one of their major goals for the coming two years was to bring sustained attention to citywide segregation policies and confront continued racial discrimination there. One of its first actions was to have rallies and demonstrations throughout the city in front of luxury apartment buildings that were only rented to white tenants. Despite counter rallies and intimidation by white racist groups in the city, CORE successfully persuaded city officials to establish the Task Force on Civil Rights to deal with black residents' concerns and complaints and broker an agreement between landlords and the city to rent to black Baltimore residents. In attempts to improve educational opportunities for African American children throughout the city, CORE established Freedom Schools in low income areas and, like those organized in Mississippi during the Freedom Summer, taught courses in math, literacy, social studies, and African American history (Williams 2010). Additionally, CORE organizers secured a U.S. Department of Labor grant to establish a work training program for young black men in 1967.

Other grassroots groups embracing black power emerged during and after CORE's activism including the Civil Interest Group (CIG), the Maryland Freedom Union (MFU), and Union for Jobs or Income Now (U-JOIN). CIG was founded at Morgan State College, a historically black college, in Baltimore in 1960. By 1966, it changed its political activities away from what was then typical civil rights activism (i.e., challenging racial discrimination in public accommodations) to organizing the black underclass into a voting political bloc in an attempt to influence electoral politics. Black women health care workers organized the Maryland Freedom Union in early 1966 to fight for a fair and livable wage for themselves and for the black poor throughout the city. Together with CORE and CIG, MFU activists picketed white-owned stores to secure an increase in wages. Like the MFU, the Union for Jobs or Income Now was concerned with economic issues in Baltimore's poorest black neighborhoods. But, while the MFU focused on businesses, U-JOIN focused on public assistance. U-JOIN linked the idea of black power with women's rights and economic empowerment mainly by helping African American women organize a welfare rights group to pressure the city's officials to reform the welfare system (Williams 2010).

Throughout the classical black power era, activists came together in several conferences and assemblies to discuss the meaning of black power in their communities and brainstorm about the future of black activism on a nationwide level. Black students and intellectuals met on college campuses, black radicals gathered in smoke-filled rooms and bars, and black bohemians assembled in cafes to discuss issues prior to the conference, but these meetings were often clandestine and held in isolation. What is significant about the conferences and assemblies which met in Newark, New Jersey (1967), Philadelphia, Pennsylvania (1970), and Gary, Indiana, (1972) is that they brought together a diverse set of activists, intellectuals, and community organizers from around the country.

Nathan Wright, the executive director of the Department of Urban Work at the Episcopal Diocese of Newark and author of *Black Power and Urban Unrest*, served as chairman of the July 1967 Black Power Conference in Newark, New Jersey. Close to 200 organizations were represented at the downtown Newark meeting with 1,300 people in attendance. Discussions were focused on the economic, political, and educational empowerment of black America. In general assemblies and plenary sessions, conferees resolved to support the economic development of black urban communities nationwide through the creation and expansion of boycotts, small business, and black-owned financial institutions. They also agreed to create a lobbying group and a think tank in the nation's capital to influence policy making. Educationally, participants called for more community input and community control of public schools found in predominantly black areas. The conference elucidated the concept of reform nationalism, according to Robert Allen, a scholar of the black power movement and the author of *Black Awakening in Capitalist America.*

Ron Karenga and Amiri Baraka were the most vociferous proponents of reform nationalism. Karenga was the founder and member of Us, later known as United Slaves, in southern California and would be later credited for founding Kwanzaa, an African American cultural holiday held in the closing days of December. Baraka was a Newark-based poet, activist, and founded the Council of African Peoples. The take away was that African Americans constituted a particular and unique ethnic group in the United States and as such, should work together to reform and integrate themselves into the American body politic and economy.

The Black Panther Party and its affiliates organized the two-day conference of the Revolutionary People's Constitutional Convention, which began on September 5, 1970, in Philadelphia, Pennsylvania. There are discrepancies over the official number of people in attendance. But, conservative estimates suggest that over 10,000 participants attended, many of whom were residents in the City of Brotherly Love. Workshop reports produced at the meeting show an internationalist approach that sought to reconfigure U.S. foreign policy, challenge exploitative economic systems on the domestic front, and change social and personal relationships between individuals and groups within the nation itself. Workshops included discussions on a variety of topics, including Internationalism and Relations with Liberation Struggles Around the World, Self Determination of Street People, Self-Determination of Women, The Family and the Rights of Children, Control and Use of Military and Police, Health[care], and Revolutionary Art, and Gay Liberation. While some of the ideas and demands expressed in the reports are naïve and an indication of youthful exuberance, together, they are robust and offer an insight into the revolutionary aims and principles of the conference.

Space here does not allow for discussion of all of the workshops, but several warrant our attention. The session on Internationalism called for the liberation of Palestine wherein "Palestinians, Jews, Christians and Moslems are equal" (Cleaver & Katsiaficas 2001, 289). Besides calling for a socialist system free from sexism, racism, and classism, the Self Determination for Women session argued that every women has the right to determine her sexual orientation and that family planning information, materials, and services, including abortion, should be free and "available upon demand" (Cleaver & Katsiaficas 2001, 292). Representatives of the Gay Liberation Movement declared that "all modes of human sexual self-expression deserve protection of the law and social sanction" (Cleaver & Katsiaficas 2001, 294). Health care was deemed a right that should be provided freely by the state, run by community boards at medical facilities, and include health education, preventative care, and mental health services. The 1970 Revolutionary People's Constitutional Conference moved away from reform nationalism and black nationalist principles of the Newark conference to address what has been called a rainbow coalition of ideas.

The third important conference of the classical black power era was the National Black Political Assembly held in Gary, Indiana, in March 1972. Unlike the two aforementioned conferences, the Gary conference had the full support of Gary's mayor, Richard Hatcher, who also addressed the assembly. Touting his motto, "Unity without Uniformity," the conference brought together celebrities including Sidney Poitier, Harry Belafonte, soul singer Isaac Hayes, politicians, and over 9,000 representatives from major civil rights groups, including the Southern Christian Leadership Conference, black nationalist groups including the Congress of Racial Equality, Jesse Jackson's newly formed, reform-oriented organization, People to Save Humanity, the intercommunalist Black Panther Party, and separatists groups—the Nation of Islam and the Republic of New Afrika, as well as a motley crew of grassroots activists and unaffiliated black power adherents (Joseph 2006). Amiri Baraka, one of three co-conveners (the other two were House of Representative Charles Diggs of Michigan and Richard Hatcher), recalls in his autobiography that the Assembly was patterned after the United States House of Representatives, including proportional representation from states.

The conference did not produce the progressive platforms and resolutions on par with the 1970 Philadelphia Revolutionary People's Constitution Convention. But two resolutions echoed the Philadelphia conference in sentiment, if not in specifics. The first called for an end to busing school-age children as a form for education equalization. Rather than transport children out of their community, schools in communities of color should be provided adequate funding to educate their children in ways similar to predominantly white neighborhoods and suburbs. The second resolution presented an international sentiment as it called for peace in Israel and offered support for the Palestinian cause. The Assembly also produced what has become known as the Gary Declaration.

The Declaration is essentially a call to arms for the participants at the conference. It criticizes the contemporary economic and political environment that created a crisis for segments of the African American population. The crisis of poor educational and housing opportunities and high unemployment and underemployment, they argue, are the result of economic policies that bolster corporate power and prioritize profit motives over citizens' wellbeing. In no uncertain terms, it denounces the status quo in politics and race relations. The assembly exclaims that "the American system does not work for the masses of our people, and it cannot be made to work without radical fundamental change" (Van Deburg 1997, 140). Accordingly, one of the major shortcomings of the Civil Rights Movement was that its activists and ideologues attempted to integrate into a flawed system. Since the country was marked by "social degradation," black people had no recourse but to be the vanguard of a movement "that places community before individualism, love before sexual exploitation, a living environment before profits, peace before war, justice before unjust 'order', and morality before expediency" (Van Deburg, 1997, 142). Changing society meant creating an independent black agenda and an independent black political party to make that agenda a reality. The absence of specific, concrete ways to create the independent black political party meant that while the Declaration created enthusiasm and excitement among its readership, its vision went largely unrealized. This fact, however, does not detract from its significance or the significance of the two other black power meetings in 1967 or 1970. In all three meetings, concerned citizens came together, voiced their grievances, spoke truth to power, and continued a tradition of black political protest that began in the early 1930s.

Black power activism, like civil rights activism, was decentralized and responded to the political circumstances on the ground in any given location. However, unlike civil rights activists who sought the protection of the federal government, black power organizations like the Black Panther Party and other organizations were the victims of the FBI's Counter Intelligence Program. Such repression did not deter the young and the old in urban areas in the Midwest, northeast, and west as well as thousands in the border states from imagining what life would be like without racism and injustice. Legal obstacles had been removed because of Civil

Rights Movement victories, but economic and educational opportunities remained a chimera. Undeterred, a coterie of activists emerged during the classical period of black power to fill a political void that civil rights activism left empty.

References

Allen, Robert. *Black Awakening in Capitalist America* (Trenton: Africa World Press, 1992).

Baraka, Amiri. *The Autobiography of Leroi Jones* (Chicago: Lawrence Hill Books, 1997).

Brown, Elaine. *A Taste of Power: A Black Woman's Story* (New York: Pantheon Books, 1992).

Carmichael, Stokely, and Ekwueme Michael Thelwell. *Ready for Revolution: The Life and Struggles of Stokely Carmichael [Kwame Ture]* (New York: Scribner, 2003).

Churchill, Ward. " 'To Disrupt, Discredit, and Destroy': The FBI's Secret War Against the Black Panther Party," in Kathleen Cleaver and George Katsiaficas, eds., *Liberation, Imagination, and the Black Panther Party* (New York: Routledge, 2001), 79–117.

Jeffries, Judson. *Huey P. Newton: The Radical Theorist* (Jackson: University Press of Mississippi, 2002).

Jones, Charles E., and Judson Jeffries, "Don't Believe the Hype": Debunking the Panther Mythology," in Charles E. Jones, ed., *The Black Panther Party Reconsidered* (Baltimore: Black Classic Press, 1998), 25–55.

Joseph, Peniel. "Revolution in Babylon: Stokely Carmichael and America in the 1960s," in Manning Marable and Elizabeth Kai Kinton, eds., *The New Black History: Revisiting The Second Reconstruction* (New York: Palgrave MacMillan, 2011), 169–193.

Joseph, Peniel. *Waiting 'til the Midnight Hour: A Narrative History of Black Power in America* (New York: Henry Holt and Company, 2006).

Katsiaficas, George. "Organization and Movement: The Case of the Black Panther Party and the Revolutionary People's Constitutional Convention of 1970," in Kathleen Cleaver and George Katsiaficas, eds., *Liberation, Imagination, and the Black Panther Party* (New York: Routledge, 2001), 141–155.

K'Meyer, Tracy E. "Empowerment, Consciousness, Defense: The Diverse Meanings of the Black Power Movement in Louisville, Kentucky," in Peniel Joseph, ed., *Neighborhood Rebels: Black Power at the Local Level* (New York: Palgrave MacMillan, 2010), 149–71.

Lang, Clarence, "Black Power on the Ground: Continuity and Rupture in St. Louis," in Peniel Joseph, ed., *Neighborhood Rebels: Black Power at the Local Level* (New York: Palgrave MacMillan, 2010), 67–89.

Lincoln, C. Eric. *The Black Muslim in America* (Boston: Beacon Press, 1961).

Lomax, Louis. *When the Word is Given* (New York: New American Library, 1963).

Malcolm X, and Alex Haley. *The Autobiography of Malcolm X: As Told to Alex Haley* (New York: Ballantine Books, 1987).

Marable, Manning. *Malcolm X: A Life of Reinvention* (New York: Penguin Group, 2011).

Newton, Huey P. *War Against the Panthers: A Study of Repression in America* (Harlem River Press, 1996).

Seale, Bobby. *Seize the Time: The Story of the Black Panther Party and Huey P. Newton* (New York, Random House, 1970).

Van Deburg, William. *Modern Black Nationalism: From Marcus Garvey to Louis Farrakhan* (New York: New York University Press, 1997).

Williams, Rhonda Y., "The Pursuit of Audacious Power: Rebel Reformers and Neighborhood Politics in Baltimore, 1966–1968," in Peniel Joseph, ed., *Neighborhood Rebels: Black Power at the Local Level* (New York: Palgrave MacMillan, 2010), 215–41.

Wilson, Jamie. "Black Panther Party," in Leslie M. Alexander and Walter C. Rucker, eds., *Encyclopedia of African American History* (Santa Barbara: ABC-CLIO, 2010).

EIGHT

From *Amos 'n' Andy* to *I Spy*: African Americans in Television and Film in the 1960s

DURING THE 1950s, at the birth of television, African Americans were rarely seen and when they were, they played the parts of servants or characters that harkened back to the days of black minstrelsy. Amos Jones, Andrew Hogg Brown, and George "Kingfish" Stevens, the three characters in the television show *Amos 'n' Andy*, are such examples. Civil rights and black power activists' struggles influenced movie companies and television executives who brought new images of African Americans to the large and small screens in the 1960s. The creators and purveyors of popular culture were not always altruistic in their motives and in many ways wanted to capitalize on growing African American markets from which vast sums of money could be made. Their motives were complicated, to say the least, cannot always be discerned, and are not the purview of this chapter. What this chapter attempts to do is to provide the reader with a glimpse of some of the iconic African American actors, figures, characters, television shows, and films who changed white and black Americans' perception of black people. The struggle that changed black political rights was accompanied by a shift in how African Americans were seen in popular culture.

During the 1960s, the majority of television shows that featured black actors and actresses did not employ them in lead roles; instead, most were cast in supporting roles. With a few exceptions, most of the programs did not last long or employed African American actors shortly before the show went off the air. *Cowboy in Africa* lasted for one season, with 26 episodes, and tells the adventures of Jim Clair (played by Chuck Connor), a white, former rodeo cowboy summoned to Kenya to assist a white rancher. The young black actor Gerald Edwards portrays Samson, a local Kenyan boy who adopts Clair. Wayne Grice, the black actor, was partner

Promotional photo from *The Amos 'n' Andy Show*, featuring Tim Moore, top, playing Kingfish, Spencer Williams, lower left, as Andy, and Alvin Childress as Amos. (AP Photo)

to Burt Reynolds, a white actor who depicted a crime-fighting Native American in New York City, in 7 of 16 total episodes of *Hawk*, a television crime drama in 1966. In 1965, *Rawhide*, a western themed show that was televised for eight seasons from 1959 to 1966 and boosted Clint Eastwood's career, employed Raymond St. Jacques as Simon Blake, a cattle driver, for 13 episodes. Simon Blake was the show's only recurring black character. *Peyton Place* aired from 1964 to 1969 as a 30-minute prime time soap opera. Filled with drama, intrigue, betrayal, and romance, it followed the lives of individuals and families in what appears to be an all-white town. In 1968, the first black family, the Miles, arrive. Percy Rodrigues plays Dr. Harry Miles. The award-winning Ruby Dee played his wife, Alma, and the then up-and-coming actor Glynn Turman played Lew Miles, Harry and Alma's son. From the summer of 1968 to the spring of 1969, both Rodrigues and Turman appeared in 33 episodes as compared to Dee's 20. The arrival of the black family in Peyton Place provided the arena to discuss racial issues in ways that had not been discussed before in soap operas, including interracial dating when Lew dates one of the white coeds in town. The last show aired on June 2, 1969.

At least three variety shows either starred or co-starred black performers. Leslie Uggams appeared in 9 of 13 episodes of *Sing Along with Mitch,* which was hosted by the talented singer, Mitch Miller. Sammy Davis Jr., the sole black member of the Rat Pack, who was himself a versatile dancer, singer, and actor, hosted a variety show for a mere three episodes. Davis worked beside Diahann Carroll, who was lead actress in *Julia* from 1968 to1971, and the talented Judy Garland who, among other roles, played Dorothy in *The Wizard of Oz.* In 1969, the short-lived variety show *The Leslie Uggams Show* aired for 10 episodes with Uggams as host, singer, and comedic actor. The show featured a number of famous white and black actors, dancers, and musicians including but not limited to actor and comedian Dick Van Dyke; the rhythm and blues singer Stevie Wonder; the soul and funk band Sly and the Family Stone; the Donald McKayle Dancers, an African American modern dance troupe; Don Knotts, the white comedian, movie star, and television star; singer, comedian, and actor Robert Guillaume. Guillaume would go on to have his own sitcom, *Benson,* in the late 1970s and the early 1980s.

The most influential show in terms of a re-envisioning of black actors was *I Spy.* The show ran for three seasons between 1965 and 1968 and starred Bill Cosby as Alexander Scott and partner of Kelly Robinson (played by Robert Culp). Cosby was the first African American actor to have a lead role in a television drama. Scott's cover is a tennis coach for Robinson, a professional tennis player, but both are spies for the United States and travel the world during the Cold War era to protect American national interests. The pilot episode featured Ivan Dixon, the television and film star and director. He plays Leroye Brown, a black Olympian who becomes an expatriate in China and supports the founding of the Afro-Asian Olympic games. Little to Brown's knowledge, Chinese officials were attempting to use the games as a imperialist foray into the African continent. Scott's and Robinson's primary objective is to travel to Hong Kong to convince Brown to return home. The two run through a shanty town in Hong Kong and over roof tops in an attempt to escape the clutches of political gangsters. In the end, their quick wits and fast thinking are enough to get Brown, who had been poisoned by his Chinese colleagues, to agree to return home. Throughout the episode and series, Cosby is presented as a multilingual, athletic, and clever spy with a patriotic zeal.

I Spy featured several other black actors and actresses throughout its three seasons. In the sixth episode, Eartha Kitt, the black actress and singer, co-stars as a jazz singer and heroin addict. When Scott and Robinson are captured by a drug gang, Angel helps them escape, but when they return to rescue her, she refuses to leave. Kitt was not new to the stage and screen by 1967. In 1958, she performed alongside the jazz singer and pianist Nat King Cole in *St. Louis Blues*, a dramatic story about the life of singer and

Bill Cosby and Leslie Uggums carry an ice-cream cart down the famed Spanish steps in the center of Rome, Italy on July 7, 1966, during shooting of an episode for the NBC-TV series *I Spy*. (AP Photo)

composer W.C. Handy. In 1959, she appeared along with Sammy Davis Jr. in *Anna Lucasta*. Throughout the 1950s and the 1960s, she recorded several singles and albums, worked on stage (on and off Broadway) and screen, becoming one of the most famous black actresses of the era. She also had a re-occurring appearance as Catwoman on the drama *Batman* in the late 1960s.

In the series' 18th episode *Court of the Lion*, Godfrey Cambridge appeared as Cetshyayo, a great grand-nephew of the last Zulu king in South Africa. Cambridge was a popular comedian in the late 1950s through the early 1970s. In the late 1950s and the early 1960s, he toured the country and performed in comedy clubs while landing a role in Ossie Davis' Broadway production of *Purlie Victorious* and Jean Genet's off-Broadway show, *The Blacks*. In 1966, he appeared in *The Dick Van Dyke Show* as an FBI agent. As Cetshyayo, he was taken from his tribe by the South African government and educated in England. Upon returning to South Africa, he worked for a diamond mining company to recruit black workers, a job he surreptitiously used to steal industrial strength diamonds, which he sells to Chinese authorities. The diamonds were traded through a small Japanese fishing village that had been taken as a slave camp by the Chinese authorities. Only after a Zen Buddhist master uses his bow and arrow to defeat several of the government's henchman do villagers rise up to defeat Cetshyayo by raiding his yacht.

The episode is remarkable for two reasons. The first and obvious is that it was a rare opportunity wherein two black comedians (Cambridge and Cosby) make an appearance on prime time drama that takes place in the Chinese Pacific. The second is that despite Cosby's casting in a leading role, networks were still afraid of depicting black men as sensitive, sexual beings. Throughout the episode and series, Alexander Scott is portrayed as sexually impotent, though desirous of a woman's company. Upon entering the fishing village, it is he who communicates with the villagers in their native Japanese. He understands the social and religious customs. He even acts as an interpreter for his partner Kelly Robinson. But it is Robinson, who once again gets the girl. While a Japanese maiden massages Robinson's back after a scuffle with a martial arts expert, Scott says to Robinson "I just don't understand it, man. I get beat up just as much as you do and I never wind up with a beautiful girl. Every time I wake up in some alley sleeping next to a snoring wine-o." At the end of the show, though Scott repeatedly refuses, Robinson begs him to translate while he caresses his maiden.

That Scott does not find suitable sexual partners is not surprising. Jet-setting across the world as government spies often do, one is not likely to find a black woman. Once, while in Italy on assignment, he is seen flirting with and even dancing with an African American woman, but this romance was disrupted when government officials call on him to find a missing atomic bomb. In another episode, while in Paris his flirtation was stalled when another government official blows his cover. His lack of female companionship is best explained by looking at societal norms. Laws in most states and social mores throughout the country forbade black men from cross-racial sexual liaisons, but allowed white men access to the woman of their choice.

Episode 30, "Lori," features Greg Morris and Nancy Wilson, the popular jazz and rhythm and blues singer, who play siblings and victims of extortion by a rogue double agent. Cicely Tyson and Raymond St. Jacques star in episode 34, "Trial by Tree House." Tyson plays Vicki Harmon, an undercover agent who stands in for Scott's wife, who goes undercover as an industrial worker. St. Jacques is Prince Edward, the villain in this installment and wants to cause a power outage in southern California to create chaos. Leslie Uggams appears as an Italian communist, baker, and pastry peddler in the 45th episode. Her mother was a performer with the United Service Organization and after her service with the agency ended transplanted herself and her daughter, Tonia, to Italy. Throughout this chapter of the series, Scott attempts to befriend her to obtain counterintelligence about Italian leftwing activists. In the end, Tonia is double-crossed and is killed by the same leftwing activist group to which she belongs. The 56th episode, "Cops and Robbers," has an almost exclusive black cast. Sans Robert Culp, it includes the National Football League fullback, Jim Brown; Beah Richards who was nominated for an Oscar award for best supporting actress in 1968 for her work in *Guess Who's Coming to Dinner*, as well as Rupert Crosse and Hazel Medina.

Cosby won three Emmy Awards for all three seasons. By the late 1960s and the early 1970s, Cosby had a major network television show, *The Bill Cosby Show*, and recorded an album with the famous record producer Quincy Jones. In the early 1970s, he played a prominent role in *The Electric Company*, a children's educational program (along with the famous black actor Morgan Freeman). He was also a movie star in the 1970s and the 1980s. From the early 1980s to the early 1990s, he played the role of a loving father and obstetrician in the award-winning *The Cosby Show* and was one of the creators and producers of *A Different World*, a spin-off of *The Cosby Show*, which starred Lisa Bonet as Denise Huxtable and followed her through her life as a college student at a historically black college. In early 21st century, Cosby is, among other things, an author and cultural and political commentator. His work in *I Spy* is historic because it set a new template for black actors and actresses to follow. No longer would they have to solely play the roles of a maid or butler.

As the Civil Rights Movement brought about a shift in how black people were depicted on television, the same is true in film. Before the genre of the blaxploitation film of the late 1960s and the early 1970s, black actors and actresses portrayed a variety of characters that challenged them and attempted to show the breadth and depth of the African American experience in the mid-20th century. It should be noted, however, that black women were not presented with leading roles in major motion picture companies. Such an opportunity was only afforded to black men. Sidney Poitier was by far the most important black actor in the 1960s and he set the standard by which other black actors and actresses were measured. Poitier appeared in numerous films in the 1950s, but it was not until the late 1950s that he became well known, following his nomination for best actor at the Academy Awards in 1959. Though he did not win the Oscar that year, he would five years later, in 1964, for his portrayal of Homer Smith in *Lilies of the Field*. From 1960 to 1970, Poitier starred in over a dozen films: *All the Young Men* (1960), *A Raisin in the Sun* (1961), *Paris Blues* (1961), *Pressure Point* (1962), *Lilies of the Field* (1963), *The Long Ships* (1964), *The Greatest Story Ever Told* (1965), *The Bedford Incident* (1965), *A Patch of Blue* (1965), *The Slender Thread* (1965), *Duel at Diablo Toller* (1966), *To Sir, with Love* (1967), *In the Heat of the Night* (1967), *Guess Who's Coming to Dinner* (1967), *For Love of Ivy* (1968), *The Lost Man* (1969), and *They Call Me MISTER Tibbs!* (1970). Of these, *A Raisin in the Sun*, *Lilies of the Field*, and *Guess Who's Coming to Dinner* are often considered his best from the era.

The film *A Raisin in the Sun* (1961) is a screenplay by Lorraine Hansberry based on her earlier Broadway play of the same name. In it, Poitier plays Walter Lee Younger, husband to Ruth Younger (played by Ruby Dee), brother to a precocious college student Beneatha (Diana Sands), son to Lena (Claudia McNeil), father to Travis (Stephen Perry), and working class chauffeur to a rich white financier. The family lives in a crowded tenement apartment in the all-black Southside of Chicago in the 1950s and awaits a $10,000 life insurance check after Big Walter, the family patriarch, dies. As the story develops, the viewer learns that Ruth is pregnant and is considering having an abortion. Walter Lee wants to use a portion of the money to invest in a liquor store. But, after the check arrives and noticing her family falling apart, Lena decides to put a down payment of $3,500 on a house in an all-white Chicago suburb whose residents do not want a black family moving in. She trusts Walter Lee with the remaining $6,500: $3,000 of which is to be placed in a savings account for Beneatha, who seeks to attend medical school, and $3,500 to be put in a checking account for Walter to control as he takes the position of head of the household. Despite Lena's demand not to invest in the liquor store, Walter Lee gives the remainder of his father's life insurance money to a friend to pay off state officials to obtain a liquor license and to invest in the store. His friend absconds with the family's and another investor's money, leaving the Youngers penniless. After considering the all-white neighborhood's offer of buying the Youngers home at a premium, to make up for his poor investment decision, Walter Lee becomes the force behind the family relocating and integrating the all-white Chicago suburb.

The film is particularly important in that it brings to the big screen several intersecting issues. The first is black pan-African sentiments that were present in African American cultural politics during the Civil Rights Movement. Walter Lee and Beneatha look to Africa for cultural and political inspiration. In an important scene, Beneatha opposes African American assimilation and dresses as a Nigerian woman with clothes provided by Joseph Assagai (played by Ivan Dixon), a Nigerian exchange student. Adorned in traditional Nigerian garb, she dances to a song by Olatunji, the West African musician who created what many consider to be the first world music album. As she dances, Walter Lee enters and, as if in a dream state, dramatically repels an enemy African force as he invokes the anti-colonial activity of Jomo Kenyatta of Kenya and African American pan-Africanist ideas of the early 20th century. They are interrupted by George Murchison, played by the famed black actor Louis Gossett Jr. Gossett's character and his interactions with the Younger family represent the second major issue, black inter-class conflict. Murchison is the son of a wealthy black businessman, attends the same college as Beneatha, and is her suitor. When Walter Lee tries to discuss business dealings with Murchison to gain access to the latter's father, he is snubbed, suggesting that the black elite want little to do with the black poor and working classes.

The third important issue the film addresses is intergenerational conflict and a cultural divide that existed between black migrants from the South and their northern-born children, an unintended consequence of the Great Migration. Lena and Big Walter are products of the South, having arrived in Chicago 40 years prior. Though dreaming of a life free from domestic servitude, they both end up working for white families. Walter Lee and Beneatha are the results of northern, urban life and see the world in ways that Lena cannot imagine. To Ruth, her daughter in law, Lena declares that "they frightens me, my children. There is something that come down between them and me that don't let us understand each other anymore." Beneatha attends college and pursues numerous extracurricular activities, including horseback riding, photography, and music. She has her sights on being a black woman physician and does not believe in God, as her mother and father did. Walter Lee dreams of becoming a prosperous black businessman, despite Lena's notions that the members of the Younger family are "just plain working folks." The variety of ways in which the family members attempt to improve themselves and the entire family (Lena through purchasing a home, Beneatha by attending college, and Walter Lee through the acquisition of a liquor store) as well as the highlighting of pan-Africanist sentiments, black inter-class tensions, and intergenerational misunderstandings, show a people who, while in the midst of a struggle for constitutional rights, are considering and dealing with other issues that are particular to black people in the United States.

In *Lilies of the Field* (1963), Poitier plays Homer Smith, a Baptist, itinerant handyman, carpenter, and construction worker who works out of his station wagon which doubles as his home. He lives off his wit and on his own schedule. When his wagon is in need of water, he stumbles across a convent where Mother Superior (played by Lilia Skala) and the nuns, all of Austrian-Hungarian nationality, convince him to build a chapel for a predominantly Chicano population in the American southwest. From the outset, he says to the Mother Superior: "I get up when I feel like getting' up and if I don't want to work then I don't work." Despite his stubbornness and desire to be free from the mundane contrivances of day labor, he is compelled to work for the nuns without pay after realizing that he works for a higher power. He is assisted by the local Chicanos, led by Juan (Stanley Adams), a local restaurateur, who help him build the chapel. The film is a wonderful work of cinematography set against the beautiful, mountainous desert backdrop of Arizona. Poitier's portrayal of Smith earned him an Oscar for best leading man and a British Academy of Film and Television Arts award.

Guess Who's Coming to Dinner (1967) was released the same year as the U.S. Supreme Court decided *Loving vs. Virginia* (1967), which banned anti-miscegenation laws. The setting is a posh San Francisco home and the story opens and resolves in less than 12 hours. In the film, Poitier plays Dr. John Wade Prentiss, a 37-year-old African American man, widower, and world famous physician. While in Hawaii, he meets Joanna Drayton

(Katharine Houghton), a 23-year-old white woman. Over a period of 10 days, the two fall in love and decide to marry. Upon their return to the mainland United States, John and Joanna visit her parents' home in the city of San Francisco to inform them of their intent to marry. Unbeknownst to Joanna, John informs Matt and Christian Drayton (played by Spencer Tracy and Katharine Hepburn) that despite his love for Joanna, he will not marry her if they disapprove. Throughout most of the film, we see the Draytons, especially Matt Drayton, a self-described white liberal, wrestle with their liberalism and latent racism. Toward evening, John's parents arrive from Los Angeles to join the Draytons for dinner. His father, a retired letter carrier for the U.S. Post Office (Roy Glenn) opposes the marriage. His mother, played by Beah Richards, argues that the two families should trust John and Joanna to love each other and make a way for their love. In the end, Matt Drayton recognizes that John and Joanna love each other and gives his blessing to the union. The film is significant because of its discussion of interracial unions, something taboo in film and on television during the 1960s, and resolves in a way that does not depict the union as a tragedy.

Poitier's acting portrayed black men not as gangsters, hooligans, and servants, and his work opened the door for new portrayals of African American men and women in a period when so few opportunities on the large and small screen presented themselves. He was the most famous black artist on the big screen, but he was not the only one. Ivan Dixon worked beside Poitier in *Raisin in the Sun* and *Patch of Blue* and was an important side man on television. He also was the leading man in *Nothing But a Man* (1964).

The film starts with Duff Anderson (played by Dixon) working as a member of a section gang, a group of men who lay train tracks in the rural South, outside of Birmingham, Alabama. He makes $80 per week—a handsome sum for a black man in the South during the early 1960s. After courting Josie Dawson (the singer and actor Abbey Lincoln), a teacher in the local black elementary school and daughter of a local black minister, the two marry despite her father's dislike for Anderson and fear that Josie's relationship with Anderson will ruin the family name. As a married man, Anderson leaves the section gang, known for its rough and tumble crowd, heavy drinking, and womanizing, to find work in a saw mill. There he finds poorly paid black workers suffering constant humiliation by their white peers and encourages them to "stick together." Such a call is soon found out by the mill bosses who fire him accusing him of trying to start a union

From left to right: Sidney Poitier, Katharine Houghton, Katharine Hepburn, and Spencer Tracy in a scene from the film *Guess Who's Coming to Dinner,* 1967. (AP Photo)

and making trouble. Word gets around about him and Anderson is blacklisted and unable to find work around town until his father in-law puts in a good word for him at the local white-owned gas station. There he suffers abuse by white customers who threaten to burn the station down and is let go.

His inability to find work is only one of his many problems. The second is his four-year-old son, James Lee. Anderson has not seen James Lee since he was two years old. During that time, the boy's mother remarried, moved to Detroit, and left him with a caretaker. After making a surprise visit to see him, Anderson is unwilling and unable to care for James Lee himself and decides to send money to the caretaker to raise him. Anderson's other problem is his estranged relationship with his alcoholic father who hardly recognizes him as his son. Finally, like so many men of his generation, he linked his masculinity to his (in)ability to work, and as his frustrations grow, he becomes verbally and physically abusive to Josie, who he eventually deserts. After he buries his father, however, Anderson has renewed hope in the future and gets custody of his son and returns to Josie. In the final scene, the two embrace. With Josie weeping in his arms, Anderson says, "It ain't going to be easy, baby, but it's goin' to be alright."

Nothing But a Man is important because it is one of the earliest films that included a predominantly black cast presented to an integrated viewing audience and told a story of a southern working class black man in all his ugliness and beauty. Duff Anderson is not Dr. John Prentiss in *Guess Who's Coming to Dinner* and far from perfect. He is a father who deserted his son, a fragile son of a man who wants nothing to do with him, a loving husband, an abusive spouse, and a black man trying to make ends meet in a society that sees him only as a boy. The film is also significant due to the presentation of the musical world within which the cast lives. The music for the film comes from Motown Records which, by 1964, was founded and incorporated a few years earlier. Throughout the film, one hears Mary Wells, The Gospel Stars, Martha and the Vandellas, The Miracles, Holland-Dozier, Little Stevie Wonder, and The Marvelettes, as well as gospel tunes and the Negro spirituals that African Americans have sung for generations. Together, the songs give the viewer a sense of the secular and sacrosanct worlds of Duff Anderson, Josie Dawson, and black America in the 1960s.

Ossie Davis and Ruby Dee may not have been as well known among viewers as Poitier on the big screen or as popular as Dixon on television, but they were successful in their own right. Both co-starred in *Purlie Victorious* (1963), the movie adaptation of Davis' Broadway play *Purlie*, a satire about a black preacher who struggles to regain his inheritance from a white plantation owner. While working on *Peyton Place*, Ruby Dee also starred in and helped produce *Uptight!* (1968). *Uptight!* examines black power politics in Cleveland, Ohio, shortly following the assassination of Martin Luther King Jr. and was directed by Jules Dassin, the popular director from the 1940s to the early 1980s, and starred a number of black actors, including Raymond St. Jacques, Ruby Dee, and Frank Silvera. That same year, Davis portrayed the character of Joseph Lee in the western film, *The Scalp Hunters*, which included Burt Lancaster, Telly Savalas, and Shelley Winters, who plays Katie, Howie's girlfriend and a former prostitute. Set in Texas in the early-to-mid-19th century, the movie follows Joe Bass' (Burt Lancaster) attempts to recover his fur pelts stolen by Two Crows (played by Armando Silvestre), the leader of a band of Kiowa Indians. In exchange for pelts, Two Crows gives Bass Joseph Lee, an educated, escaped slave from Louisiana who is seeking safe passage to Mexico where he will be permanently free from bondage. Right before Bass and Lee are about recover the pelts, they are stolen by Jim Howie (Telly Savalas), a criminal and gang leader who, along with his band of renegades, raids the Kiowa, scalps as many as they can, and steals their horses.

Throughout the movie, Lee uses his education and wit to shift his loyalty from Bass, who promises to sell him at a slave market, to Katie and Jim Howie who are going to Mexico, one step ahead of the law. This passage to Mexico is threatened by Bass who continues to follow Howie, threaten his convoy, kill his men, and demand his pelts. When Lee suggests Howie return the pelts to Bass to end Bass' assaults, Howie sends Lee to negotiate. Armed with a bottle of whiskey, Lee goes to speak with Bass. As Bass takes a long drink to slake his thirst, Lee talks him out of continuing his attacks on Howie's convoy. Lee then asks Bass for a drink. Bass replies: "whiskey is a man's drink, and you ain't no man. You ain't no part of a man. You are a mealy-mouth, shuffle-butt slave and you picked yourself a master [ie. Howie]. So don't you go asking to take a drink with a man." This statement is a turning point in the two's relationship. As they go to retrieve Bass's pelts, Bass is attacked by Howie, who is lying in wait. Lee wrestles Howie to the ground, and in the scuffle, Howie is killed. Despite saving Lee's saving his life, Bass still doubts his manhood and the two start to brawl. When the fight is over, Bass comes to see Lee as his equal. He offers him a drink and helps Lee onto his horse and the two ride off together: one white man, one black man, one free, one slave, but both equal.

As African Americans fought for their rights in the streets and the courts during the 1960s, African American actors and actresses tried to portray new images of black people in film and television. Cosby, Davis, Dee, Dixon, and Poitier reflected the changes in blacks' opportunities. Neither the battle for black equality nor the equitable and accurate representations of black people on television or in film was won in the 1960s or in the early 21st century. Black actors continue to challenge black stereotypes embedded in the American consciousness and black activists continue to search for justice for African Americans in every section of the nation.

References

Bogle, Donald. *Toms, Coons, Mulattoes, Mammies, and Bucks: An Interpretive History of Blacks in American Films* (New York: Continuum International, 2001).

Bogle, Donald. *Primetime Blues: African Americans on Network Television* (Darby, Pennsylvania: Diane Publishing Company, 2004).

Cripps, Thomas. *Making Movies Black: The Hollywood Message Movie from World War II to the Civil Rights Era* (New York: Oxford University Press, 1993).

Guerrero, Ed. *Framing Blackness: The African American Image in Film* (Philadelphia: Temple University Press, 1993).

McDonald, J. Fred. *Blacks and White TV: African Americans in Television Since 1948* (Boston: Cengage, 1994).

Conclusion

STUDYING AND UNDERSTANDING the Civil Rights Movement is important for several reasons. First, it exposed discrimination to the nation in stark terms and forced it to grapple with one of its most pressing problems, the color line. Grassroots activists, leaders, and organizations forced the politicians, legislators, and decision makers of this nation to rethink and reconsider some of the most basic democratic principles by which we lived. In addition, the movement brought about a fundamental shift in what equal protection under the law meant. No longer was it codified in law or socially acceptable to discriminate against a person based on the color of their skin. What used to only mean equal protection for certain segments of white Americans was expanded to include African Americans and later other people of color including Native Americans and Asian Americans. Further, in the closing decades of the 20th century and the opening decades of the 21st century, groups including gay, lesbian, bisexual, and transgendered Americans, women, and the disabled use the political arguments of equal protection posed by civil rights attorneys to challenge their mistreatment.

Most importantly, the Civil Rights Movement empowered many individuals who, for most of their lives, believed they had no power. Children, women, and men, the impoverished, those just making ends meet, and the middle-class put their lives, jobs, careers, and livelihoods in jeopardy to try to make life better for themselves and their descendants. One need only look at some of the images of the movement to get a sense of how political participation transformed and inspired participants. In 1968, for example, during the sanitation workers' strike in Memphis, Tennessee, participants wore sandwich board signs which read "I Am a Man. " Of course, they knew they were living, breathing human creatures, but the sign represents an inner strength and courage to announce that fact to the world, anxious maybe, but unafraid.

Finally, the Civil Rights Movement's significance lies in its democratic ethos and highlights that fact that the Black Panther's famous declaration "All Power to the People" was not a cliché. People do have power to challenge their social, cultural, and political institutions and the power to change their world. Activists recognized the importance of local, state, and federal electoral politics. But for them, that was not the end of democracy. They supplemented their voting, attempts to vote, voter mobilization, and voter empowerment with grassroots organizing, lobbying, and street protests that captured the attention of the public and forced the hand of elected officials. Movement people have also shown that those wanting to create a more just and equitable society must be diligent, creative, and patient, but not passive. Massive societal changes do not occur overnight and are not brought about through a singular strategy or by one individual. Societal shifts take years and decades. Sometimes social changes take generations, but they are always brought to fruition through multi-pronged political strategies. W.E.B. Du Bois's life and activism bears this out. Du Bois was an activist and scholar for over half of the 20th century. He experimented with accommodationism, black cooperatives, integrationist causes, boycotts, electoral politics, and leftist political ideologies. He challenged the conventional wisdom of Booker T. Washington, critiqued Marcus Garvey and the Universal Negro Improvement Association, was politically active in both World Wars, and was a victim of 1950s Cold War political backlashes. He eventually died in Ghana on the eve of the March on Washington in 1963. His life, times, and activism reveal that exacting political change takes commitment and time, even when change does not seem possible.

The political struggle that we call the Civil Rights Movement is a continuation of generations of struggles against injustice. The Civil Rights Movement may have ended decades ago, but the fight for black equality has not. Since Barack Obama was elected president in 2008, there has been considerable debate about whether or not we live in a post-racial society, a society in which the color of one's skin is not an issue. The parameters of that debate are beyond the scope of this work, but evidence suggests there are still race-based disparities in wealth, education, health, incarceration, and fair treatment in the legal system. African American workers earn less than their white counterparts. According to the Pew Research Center, in 2009, typical black households had just $5,677 in wealth (assets minus debts), while whites had $113,149. The Department of Justice has recently discovered that during the first decade of the 21st century, Wells Fargo, one of the largest banks in the United States, charged African American and

Latinos higher interest rates for home loans than their white customers. The National Center for Education Statistics has noted major educational achievement gaps between white and black elementary and middle public school students in the areas of math and reading. African Americans continue to have a shorter life expectancy compared to whites. Racial bias has always been, and continues to be, an issue in death penalty cases and large numbers of black men are targeted by the criminal justice system. As of this writing, Texas, Florida, and other states and municipalities are attempting to purge African Americans from voting roles. To be sure, no longer can a group of white vigilantes lynch black men, but today anti-black and racist violence is on the rise throughout the country.

Life chances for African Americans have improved over the years, but racial justice has not been achieved. As new social justice organizations take the place of and their place beside older civil rights organizations, they turn to the organizing strategies, hopes, goals, and visions of civil rights activists from generations past. Like Martin Luther King Jr., Fannie Lou Hamer, Malcolm X, Rosa Parks, Fred Shuttlesworth, Modjeska Simkins, Stokely Carmichael, Ella Baker, and the many heroes that have been written about in these pages, as well as those unknown heroes who quietly resisted dehumanization, many continue to dream and believe in the words of the famous freedom song: "deep in my heart, I do believe, we shall overcome someday."

References

Alexander, Michelle. *The New Jim Crow: Mass Incarceration in the Age of Colorblindness* (New York: The New Press, 2012).

Arias, Elizabeth. "United States Life Tables, 2007," *National Vital Statistics Reports*, Vol. 59, No. 9 (September 28, 2011), 5.

Death Penalty and Race: Race of Homicide Victims in Cases Resulting in an Execution since 1976, http://www.amnestyusa.org/our-work/issues/death-penalty/us-death-penalty-facts/death-penalty-and-race.

National Center for Education Statistics, *Achievement Gaps: How Black and White Students in Public Schools Perform in Mathematics and Reading on the National Assessment of Educational Progress*, Statistical Analysis Report (Washington, D.C., U.S. Department of Education, 2009), 58

"Wealth Gaps Rise to Record Highs between Whites, Blacks, Hispanics", July 26, 2011, http://www.pewsocialtrends.org/2011/07/26/wealth-gaps-rise-to-record-highs-between-whites-blacks-hispanics.

Biographies of Figures

Ralph Abernathy
(1926–1990)

Abernathy was a Baptist preacher, pastor of the West Hunter Street Baptist Church, one of the founding members of the Southern Christian Leadership Conference (SCLC), a close associate of Martin Luther King Jr., and civil rights leader. After King's assassination in 1968, he took over as leader of the SCLC, a position he held until 1977. In 1977, he ran an unsuccessful bid for the House of Representatives. He published his autobiography *And the Wall Came Tumbling Down* in 1989.

Muhammad Ali
(1942–)

Born Cassius Clay in Louisville, Kentucky, Clay gained notoriety as the gold medal winner in the light-heavy weight division at the 1960 Olympics in Rome, Italy. In the early 1960s, after he became a professional boxer, Clay changed his name to Muhammad Ali and joined the Nation of Islam. In 1967, he was drafted by the U.S. Army, but, as an opponent of the Vietnam War, refused to be inducted. As a result, he was stripped of his heavyweight title, his passport, and his ability to box. Ali regained the heavyweight title in 1974 after defeating George Foreman.

Ella Josephine Baker
(1903–1986)

Baker was an activist for human dignity for six decades. She is most known for her work with the Student Nonviolent Coordinating Committee (SNCC). As the organization's ideological godmother and mentor, Baker instilled a group-centered leadership philosophy in the youth group. Using this approach, SNCC's organizers' primary goals were to create leadership among the people they worked with.

James Baldwin
(1924–1987)

Baldwin was a novelist, essayist, social critic, and cultural commentator. During the 1950s and the 1960s, his novels examined urban African American culture and life. In 1963, he published *The Fire Next Time*, which discussed the effects of racial oppression on black communities throughout the nation and urged white policy makers to bring about real and meaningful political change. His essays appeared in a number of popular newspapers and magazines, giving him the ability to explain the Civil Rights Movement's goals and black people's anger to a larger white audience.

Daisy Bates
(1914–1999)

When nine African American students integrated Central High School in Little Rock, Arkansas, in 1957, Daisy Bates acted as an advisor to them and their families. Bates became president of the Little Rock Branch of the National Association for the Advancement of Colored People (NAACP) in 1952 and used her position and the *Arkansas State Press*, a newspaper she and her husband operated, to attack segregation throughout the state. In 1962, she published the award-winning *The Long Shadow of Little Rock*.

Harry Belafonte
(1927–)

Belafonte was one of the most popular black actors and singers in the 1950s. While he is mostly remembered as the King of Calypso for popularizing the "Banana Boat Song," he helped redefine roles played by black actors in Hollywood and used his stardom to garner support for the SCLC. During the 1963 Birmingham campaign, when the SCLC ended segregation in public accommodations, for example, Belafonte personally raised thousands of dollars to keep the movement going. As of this writing, Belafonte continues to support progressive causes as a humanitarian.

James Bevel
(1936–2008)

Bevel was a Baptist preacher, pastor of Chesnutt Grove Baptist Church, and member of the SCLC. In 1961, he helped organize Freedom Rides throughout the South. In 1963, during the SCLC's attempts to desegregate Birmingham, Alabama, he helped mobilize children during the Children's Crusade.

Beyond Vietnam

An April 1967 sermon delivered by Martin Luther King Jr. at Riverside Church in New York City before the group Clergy and Laymen Concerned about Vietnam. In it, he calls for an end to all American bombing on the Vietnamese peninsula, a unilateral ceasefire, and a timetable for American withdrawal from Vietnam. The sermon would be breaking point for him and President Lyndon Johnson, who had consulted with King on poverty and racial matters on numerous occasions.

Black Panther Party (1966–1982)

The Black Panther Party began in Oakland, California, as an armed community police patrol. It was founded by Huey Newton and Bobby Seale. The organization is one of the most well known black power organizations that became a victim of the federal government's Counter Intelligence Program. Throughout the late 1960s and the early 1970s, chapters were organized throughout the country and developed community-based aid programs.

Elaine Brown (1943–)

Brown was a grassroots activist in the state of California during the late 1960s and the early 1970s. In 1967, she joined the southern California chapter of the Black Panther Party. In 1971, she became the Minister of Information for the chapter. In 1974, she became the Chairperson of the National Party, a position she held until 1977. Brown was instrumental in creating a school and continuing the Panthers' survival programs.

H. Rap Brown (1943–)

Born Hubert Gerold Brown, he obtained the moniker "Rap" for his linguistic dexterity. While in college, from 1961 to 1964, he joined SNCC. In 1967, he became chair of the organization. One year later, he joined the Black Panther Party as the Minister of Justice.

Stokely Carmichael
(1941–1998)

Carmichael was a prominent member and chairperson of SNCC in the 1960s. In 1967, he helped popularize the phrase "Black Power." Carmichael, like others of his time, linked black Americans' struggle for political rights with the struggles of other people in the African Diaspora. During the 1970s, he was a prominent member of the All African People's Revolutionary Party and changed his name to Kwame Ture after his two major Pan Africanist influences, Kwame Nkrumah of Ghana and Sekou Toure of Guinea.

Shirley Chisholm
(1924–2005)

Chisholm served in the New York State Assembly as an assemblywoman from 1964 to 1968. In 1968, she became the first African American women to be elected to the U.S. Congress, where she served her constituents for 13 years. In 1972, she unsuccessfully ran for the presidency of the country. Throughout her career as a public servant she was a champion for the rights of African Americans, women, and the poor.

Septima Clark
(1898–1987)

Clark was an activist and educator. Her years teaching African Americans in her home state of South Carolina and throughout the South earned her the title "teacher to a movement." In the 1950s, Clarke worked at the Highlander Folk School in Monteagle, Tennessee, where she taught citizenship classes. Like many other women, Clarke was one of the organizers of the Montgomery Bus Boycott in 1955. In the early 1960s, she joined the SCLC and became the organization's Director of Education and Teaching. At SCLC, she perfected her citizenship workshops and the organization implemented its Citizenship Education Program to teach voter education and literacy to southern African Americans.

Eldridge Cleaver
(1935–1998)

After living a life of crime in the 1950s, Cleaver became one of the most vocal supporters of black power in the late 1960s and the early 1970s. In 1967, he published *Soul on Ice*, a series of articles he published for

Ramparts magazine while in prison. That year he became the Minister of Information for the Black Panther Party in Oakland, California. He lived in exile in Algeria and France in the late 1960s to avoid imprisonment for the killing a police officer. He was expelled from the Black Panther Party in 1971.

Kathleen Cleaver
(1945–)

While a student at Barnard College, Cleaver joined SNCC in New York City. In 1967, she left the organization to become the first woman member of the Black Panther Party for which she served as the communications secretary from 1967 to 1971. She was instrumental in organizing the International Section of the Party while in exile in Algeria with her husband Eldridge Cleaver. In 1971, the Cleavers organized the Revolutionary Peoples Communication Network which dissolved several years later.

Congress of Racial Equality

The organization was founded in Chicago, Illinois, in 1942 by an interracial group of college-age students committed to nonviolent direct action. It became one of the leading civil rights groups in the country. CORE was the primary organizational force behind the 1961 Freedom Rides. From its origins to the early 1960s, CORE was committed to seeking integration in public accommodations and challenging unconstitutional laws that circumscribed the political and economic opportunities of African Americans, including voter registration. By the late 1960s, under the leadership of Floyd McKissick, the group embraced Black Nationalist principles.

Medgar Evers
(1925–1963)

In the 1950s, Evers accepted a Field Secretary position with the NAACP and opened a branch office in Jackson, Mississippi. Throughout the remainder of the 1950s and the early 1960s, he toured the state, speaking with young people, recruiting members, investigating political violence against blacks, and trying, albeit unsuccessfully, to get the federal government involved in desegregating Mississippi. In the early 1960s, Evers organized a boycott of downtown Jackson stores to force them to integrate their workforce and end discriminatory service. When SNCC entered the state in 1961,

Evers assisted them in spreading their ideas in rural areas that had been untouched by other civil rights groups, including the NAACP. In 1962, he supported James Meredith in his attempts to integrate the University of Mississippi. He was assassinated by Byron de la Beckwith in 1963.

Dick Gregory
(1932–)

Gregory is a comedian and civil rights activists. He published his autobiography, *Nigger*, in 1963. By that time, he had released four comedy albums, making him one of the most famous black comedians of the 1960s. Like other black celebrities, he lent his help to the civil rights cause by raising money. In 1965, he participated in the march from Selma to Montgomery. Three years later, in 1968, he ran for president as a candidate for the Peace and Freedom Party.

Fannie Lou Hamer
(1917–1977)

In late August 1962 Hamer, a former sharecropper, became a field secretary for SNCC and combed the Mississippi Delta in an attempt to register African Americans to vote. In 1964, she became one of the founding members of the Mississippi Freedom Democratic Party (MFDP). As co-chair of the organization and one of its delegates, Hamer appeared on national television at the Democratic National Convention in Atlantic City, New Jersey, and told of the threats, intimidation, and violence blacks suffered in Mississippi and how they were prevented from voting.

Fred Hampton
(1948–1969)

Hampton was immersed into political activism as a high school student when he became a member of the Maywood, Illinois, chapter of the NAACP. The chapter was particularly important in that it highlighted the reality that civil rights and the political empowerment of African Americans was as important in the North as it was in the South. Seeking a more direct way to help Chicago's poor black population, he founded and became the leader of the Chicago chapter of the Black Panther Party in 1968. As an eloquent and enthusiastic young leader, he was instrumental in establishing the Panther's survival programs in the city. When the Black Panthers were considered a threat to national security by the Federal Bureau of Investigation in the late 1960s, Hampton was one of the targets of its Counter Intelligence Program. On December 4, 1969, he was shot and killed by the Chicago Police Department while sleeping in his home.

Coretta Scott King
(1927–2006)

King was the wife and widow of Martin Luther King Jr. She studied music at the New England Conservatory in Boston, Massachusetts, and used her talents to raise funds for the SCLC in the late 1950s and the early 1960s. As Martin King's life partner, she raised four children and acted as a sounding board for many of her husband's ideas. During the Poor People's Campaign, she was instrumental in organizing the Mother's Day March in 1968. In the 1970s and 1980s, she was instrumental in raising national awareness of the legacy of Martin Luther King Jr. and lobbied for a national holiday in his honor.

Martin Luther King Jr.
(1929–1968)

King was a Baptist preacher, nonviolent theorist, Nobel Peace Prize winner, and the most well known civil rights activists. In 1955, he became the leader of the Montgomery Bus Boycott, where he and community activists organized a one-day boycott of the city's buses that turned into a successful boycott of 381 days. King and other clergy, mainly from southern states, organized the SCLC in January 1957 in Atlanta, Georgia. In 1963, he delivered his famous "I Have a Dream" speech at the March on Washington. He was assassinated by James Earl Ray on April 4, 1968, in Memphis, Tennessee, where he was supporting a sanitation workers' strike.

Joyce Ladner
(1943–)

Ladner was one of the principal organizers of the NAACP Youth Council in her hometown of Hattiesburg, Mississippi, while still a high school student. In college, she joined SNCC. She earned her doctorate in sociology in 1968, and in 1971, she published *Tomorrow's Tomorrow: The Black Woman*.

James Lawson
(1921–)

Lawson was one of the founders of SNCC and an important member of the Fellowship of Reconciliation. He was a Methodist minister and committed Christian nonviolent theorist. As a practitioner of this approach, he became a member of the Nashville Chapter of the SCLC for which he served as the organization's project director in that city. In this capacity, he inspired hundreds of undergraduates and graduate students at historically black colleges to take up the cudgels of nonviolent political protest and demonstrate in Nashville and throughout the South.

League of Revolutionary Black Workers

The League was founded in 1967 to unite workers and community organizations and to speak to the needs of black workers in the Detroit area auto factories.

Letter from a Birmingham Jail

The letter was written by Martin Luther King Jr. in 1963 while he was imprisoned and is addressed to southern clergymen who criticized King's direct, nonviolent demonstrations. It elucidates King's moral and political compass, outlines King's political platform, and maintains that he answers not to humans with their many frailties, but to God who sides with the oppressed.

John Lewis
(1940–)

Between 1963 and 1966, Lewis was the chairperson of SNCC. Prior to being elected to the position, he helped organize sit-ins in Nashville, Tennessee, while at the American Baptist Theology Seminary in *of Figures* 1960. He also participated in the Freedom Rides in 1961. Lewis was known for his fiery rhetoric and as a youth leader who forced older civil rights leaders into taking more concrete and militant stances on the civil rights issues. Lewis left SNCC in 1966, shortly after Stokely Carmichael was elected Chair. Since the ending of the movement, he has served in elected office in the House of Representatives.

Malcolm X
(1925–1965)

Born Malcolm Little, Malcolm X was a reformed criminal who went on to become the national spokesperson for the Nation of Islam in the late 1950s. He split with the Nation of Islam in 1964, made a pilgrimage to Mecca, converted to Sunni Islam, and changed his name to El Hajj Malik el Shabazz. In 1964, he organized Muslim Mosque Incorporated and the Organization of Afro American Unity. His 1964 speech, "The Ballot or the Bullet," is considered by many to be his most profound contribution to the black freedom struggle of the 1960s. In it, he connects black Americans' struggle with anti-colonial struggles and anti-racist movements by people of color throughout the world, gives his definition of black nationalism, and calls for a united political front comprised of black political organizations. His black nationalist ideologies influenced black power activists in the late 1960s and the early 1970s. *The Autobiography of Malcolm X* was published posthumously in 1965.

Thurgood Marshall
(1908–1993)

Marshall graduated from Howard University Law School in 1933. He devoted his legal career to eliminating racist laws and policies that stripped African Americans of their constitutional rights. In 1938, he began his tenure as the NAACP's chief legal counsel. Two years later, he became the director for the organization's Legal Defense and Educational Fund. Throughout the 1940s and the 1950s, he appeared before the U.S. Supreme Court, seeking to abolish segregation in the public sector. His most famous case, *Brown vs. Board of Education of Topeka* (1954), overturned the 1896 *Plessy vs. Ferguson* ruling, which allowed for segregated publicly funded schooling. In 1967, he was became the first African American to be confirmed to the Supreme Court of the United States.

James Meredith
(1933–)

Having served in the U.S. Air Force for most of the 1950s, Meredith returned to civilian life seeking to challenge segregation laws throughout the South in the 1960s. In 1962, he was the first African American admitted to the University of Mississippi and graduated, despite a hostile learning environment, in 1963 with a degree in political science. In 1966, he embarked on his March Against Fear, a one-man march throughout the South. During his march, he was shot by a sniper. Thousands of protestors continued his march, including Martin Luther King Jr. Dick Gregory, and Stokely Carmichael. The March from Selma to Jackson was one of the defining moments of the Civil Rights Movement.

Mississippi Freedom Democratic Party

The MFDP was created to offer black Mississippians, who had been discriminated against in the local, statewide, and national elections, the opportunity to participate in the electoral process. During the summer of 1964, the MFDP conducted an electoral primary and selected candidates for the U.S. Senate and the House of Representatives. In an attempt to show white Mississippi politicos and the national Democratic Party their willingness to participate in the electoral process if given a chance, the MFDP traveled to the 1964 Democratic Convention in Atlantic City, New Jersey, in an attempt to unseat the all white Mississippi state delegation.

Anne Moody
(1940–)

Moody became an activist in the Civil Rights Movement while studying at Tougaloo College in Mississippi. She worked with several of the major civil rights organizations, including the National Association for the Advancement of Colored People, the Congress of Racial Equality, and the Student Nonviolent Coordinating Committee. As a member of SNCC, she participated in sit-ins at Woolworth's stores. In 1969, she published her critically acclaimed *Coming of Age in Mississippi*.

Robert Moses
(1935–)

Moses grew up in Harlem, New York, and graduated with a master's degree in mathematics from Harvard University. He entered the Civil Rights Movement in 1959 while working with Bayard Rustin on a youth march. In 1960, he joined the SCLC and later SNCC, for which he organized voter registration drives in Mississippi throughout the early 1960s. As a member and leader of SNCC, he emphasized participatory democracy and encouraged the creation of leadership among those who SNCC was working with. Using his organizing experiences, Moses became one of the primary organizers of Freedom Summer in 1964. In 1965, Moses became an active member of the anti-war movement. One year later, he moved to Canada to evade the draft.

Elijah Muhammad
(1897–1975)

Muhammad, née Elijah Poole, was one of the founders of the Lost-Found Nation of Islam in the Wilderness of North America, commonly called the Nation of Islam. He was the leader of the movement from the mid 1940s to 1975 as well as the group's theologian. As the Nation gained popularity in the late 1950s and the early 1960s, Muhammad stressed conservative economic principles and social mores, thrift, racial solidarity, and heterodox Islamic ideas. These ideas attracted thousands of working-class and some middle-class blacks, mainly in urban areas throughout the northeast, Midwest, and western parts of the country.

Diane Nash
(1938–)

Educated and raised in the Chicago area, Nash was compelled to assist southern African Americans in their quest for civil rights while a student at Fisk University in Nashville, Tennessee. At Fisk, she was mentored by James Lawson, who convinced her of the efficacy of nonviolent, direct action. In 1959 she, along with other Fisk students, staged sit-ins in local, Nashville department stores in an attempt to desegregate them. They would attempt to desegregate stores again in 1960, when students throughout the South began their sit-in movement. During that year, she was also a founding member of SNCC. Nash coordinated Freedom Rides from Birmingham, Alabama, to Jackson, Mississippi. Her civil rights activity and commitment to pacifism made her one of the most important African American women activists in the movement.

National Association for the
Advancement of Colored People

The NAACP is one of oldest civil rights organizations in the United States. It was founded in 1909 by white and black progressives to assist African Americans in obtaining their constitutional rights. Throughout its century-long existence, its members have challenged restrictive housing covenants, school segregation, and voting discrimination in federal court. Branches throughout the country were also participants in nonviolent direct political action. The organization is most known for challenging separate but equal educational practices in *Brown vs. Board of Education of Topeka* (1954). The case not only declared separate but equal education unconstitutional, but also laid the legal foundation to challenge segregated accommodations throughout the country.

The Nation of Islam

The Lost Found Nation of Islam in the Wilderness of North America (commonly called the Nation of Islam) is a heterodox American Islamic movement in the United States founded in Detroit, Michigan, during the Great Depression by W. Fard Muhammad, a traveling peddler. Muhammad declared he was the messiah for black people. From the early 1940s to 1975, the organization was led by Elijah Muhammad. In the late 1950s and the early 1960s, Malcolm X served as the organization's national spokesperson. Through his charisma and dedication, the organization became a nationwide movement. Malcolm X's departure in 1964 and subsequent assassination in 1965 brought about a schism within the organization. In 1975, the organization split and Louis Farrakhan assumed leadership of the Nation.

Huey P. Newton
(1942–1989)

Founder, with Bobby Seale, of the Black Panther Party for Self Defense in Oakland, California. During the late 1960s and the early 1970s, Newton served as the organization's Minister of Self Defense and chief political philosopher. He is the author of *War Against the Panthers: A Study of Repression in America.*

Rosa Parks
(1913–2005)

Parks was a local political activist and secretary of the Montgomery, Alabama, chapter of the National Association for the Advancement of Colored People in the 1940s. On December 1, 1955, she was arrested for refusing to obey the segregated seating policy on a Montgomery public bus. Her act of defiance proved to be the spark for the 381-day Montgomery Bus Boycott that ended segregation on public buses in the city.

Poor People's Campaign

In late 1967, the SCLC announced its Poor People's Campaign. In early 1968, King and other clergy toured the country meeting on a fact finding mission with black and white people to ascertain the depth and breadth of poverty throughout the nation and offer specific policy initiatives to the federal government. The pinnacle of the campaign occurred in May and June of 1968, when thousands of demonstrators erected Resurrection City, an encampment on the Mall in Washington, D.C., to call attention to poverty issues around the country.

Adam Clayton Powell Jr.
(1908–1972)

The son of a minister after whom he was named, Powell was the pastor of the Abyssinian Baptist Church in Harlem, New York, one of the most politically important African American churches in the country. His activism lasted from the 1930s to the late 1960s. In the 1930s, he assisted black Harlem residents in securing basic necessities during the Great Depression and fought discriminatory hiring practices among employers. In the 1940s, he continued to pastor at Abyssinia and used his popularity among Harlem residents to be elected to the New York City Council, a position he held until 1945. In 1945, he was elected to the U.S. House of Representatives where, despite legal battles and accusations of misconduct, he remained until 1970.

A. Philip Randolph
(1889–1979)

Randolph had a long, illustrious career as an activist in the black freedom struggle and labor movement and is considered by many to be one of the fathers of the modern Civil Rights Movement. In the 1920s and the 1930s, he was a noted socialist and helped found the Brotherhood of Sleeping Car Porters, an organization he worked with until the late 1960s. In the 1940s, he organized the March on Washington Movement to force the federal government to change discrimination policies in wartime industries. Though the 1940s march never materialized, it became the template for the famous March on Washington For Jobs and Opportunities in August 1963 that featured King's "I Have a Dream" speech.

Gloria Richardson
(1922–)

Richardson was one of the leading activists and organizers of the Cambridge Nonviolent Action Committee in Cambridge, Maryland. She and the

organization sought to address political and economic issues facing black
residents in that city and its environs during the early 1960s.

Jo Ann Robinson
(1912–1992)

Robinson was an educator and major organizing force behind the Montgomery Bus Boycott of 1955. As a member of the Women's Political
Council, a group of professional middle-class women in the city, she
helped organize the one-day boycott of the Montgomery Bus Line after
Rosa Parks was arrested in December 1955. When the boycott continued,
Robinson and others helped organize the Montgomery Improvement Association, an organization for which she served on the executive board
and editor of its newsletter. Her memoir of her participation in the boycott, *The Montgomery Bus Boycott and the Women Who Started It*, was
published in 1987 and argues that women were the backbone of the
movement.

Bayard Rustin
(1912–1987)

By the time the modern Civil Rights Movement emerged in the mid-1950s,
Rustin had been an activist for social justice for over a decade. In the late
1930s, while a student in New York City, he was a member of the Young
Communist League. As a committed pacifist, he worked with the Fellowship of Reconciliation and the Congress for Racial Equality in the early
1940s. His pacifist philosophy led him to serve a prison sentence in the mid-
1940s for refusing to participate in World War II as a conscientious objec-
tor. In the 1950s, he was a member of the War Resisters League and served
as the organization's Executive Director for several years. He is credited
with exposing Martin Luther King Jr. to the philosophical underpinnings of
Gandhian nonviolent theory during the Montgomery Bus Boycott. During
the months leading up to the August 23, 1968, March on Washington for
Jobs and Opportunity, he, along with A. Philip Randolph, was the primary
strategists behind the demonstration.

Bobby Seale
(1936–)

Co-founder and Chairman of the Black Panther Party. In 1973, he ran an
unsuccessful campaign for the mayoralty of Oakland. He is the author of *A*

Lonely Rage: The Autobiography of Bobby Seale and *Seize the Time: The Story of the Black Panther Party.*

Fred Shuttlesworth
(1922–2011)

Shuttlesworth was a Baptist preacher, minister at First Baptist Church in Selma and later Bethel Baptist Church in Birmingham, Alabama. In 1956, he founded the Alabama Christian Movement for Human Rights in Birmingham and was president of the organization until 1969. In 1957, he joined with fellow clergymen to found the SCLC. In 1961, he challenged segregation on interstate buses by participating in the Freedom Rides. In 1963, he sought the assistance of the SCLC, who along with the Shuttlesworth's organization, used direct action and negotiations to desegregate public accommodations in the city of Birmingham.

Southern Christian Leadership Conference

The organization was formed in 1957 to "save the soul of America." Comprised mainly of southern clergymen, it highlights the Civil Rights Movement as both a religious and political undertaking. It sought to use nonviolent political action to end segregation throughout the South. In the late 1950s and the early 1960s, the organization launched several campaigns. In 1957, it sponsored the Prayer Pilgrimage in Washington, D.C. In 1963, the ministers, with the assistance of other civil rights organizations and thousands of participants, desegregated public accommodations in Birmingham, Alabama. Operation Breadbasket was launched in 1962 to act as the economic wing of the organization. This campaign, combined with other political exigencies, led the organization to launch its Poor People's Campaign in 1968. The organization continues social justice and civil rights work in Atlanta, Georgia.

Student Nonviolent Coordinating Committee

Known as SNICK, the Student Nonviolent Coordinating Committee was founded and run by college age students in the spring of 1960. Within months, the organization became one of the most dynamic and important civil rights groups. Its members participated in almost every civil rights campaign in the 1960s. Ella Baker was the ideological mother of the organization and her ideas of participatory democracy informed the political activities of the group. In its early years, SNCC members included white and black college students. In 1964, during a campaign the organization called Freedom Summer, students (mostly white) from prestigious colleges and universities worked in Mississippi to help register African Americans to vote and create freedom schools. In 1966, the organization moved away from its original political goals of integration and embraced black nationalist principles. By the late 1960s, the organization was virtually defunct, but many of its members went on to participate in other political movements in the 1970s and the 1980s.

Emmett Till
(1941–1955)

Till was killed by Roy Bryant and J.W. Milam, for allegedly whistling at Carolyn Bryant, Ron Bryant's wife, while visiting his family on the outskirts of Money, Mississippi, in 1955. Both Bryant and Milam were found innocent by an all white-jury, but later admitted killing Till in *Look* magazine. Till's killing was a call to action and encouraged many African Americans to participate in the Civil Rights Movement.

Robert F. Williams
(1925–1996)

In the mid 1950s, Williams was elected president of the Monroe, North Carolina, chapter of the NAACP. He believed civil rights workers who were brutalized by whites should defend themselves by armed force, if necessary. He published these ideas in *Crusader*, a newsletter that featured his political approaches. His views on self-defense led him to be dismissed by the national NAACP. In 1961, he went into exile in Havana, Cuba, where he produced Radio Dixie, a radio program. In 1965, he sought asylum in Beijing, China. Williams returned to the United States in 1969 and many of his ideas influenced young radicals in the black power movement.

Primary Documents

PLESSY vs. FERGUSON (1896)
MAY 18, 1896

Homer Plessy was a multiracial man who appeared white to the average reasonable person. In Louisiana, Plessy's home state, he was considered an octoroon, someone who has one of eight ancestors who was of African descent. In the early 1890s, he joined the Committee of Citizens to challenge Louisiana's Separate Car Act of 1890. The Act required separate accommodations for blacks and whites on railroad cars and rail stations. In 1892, he sat in the whites-only section of a railcar and refused to relinquish his seat and sit in the all-black section when asked by a railroad employee. As a result, he was arrested and charged a fine of $25. He challenged his arrest and conviction in court, suggesting that the Louisiana Separate Car Act violated the Thirteenth and Fourteenth Amendments to the Constitution of the United States of America. The local court upheld his sentence. During his appeal, the Supreme Court of Louisiana upheld the lower court's decision. Plessy persevered to the U.S. Supreme Court. The Court's majority decision determined who was and who was not black, and decided that discriminating against people of African descent in public accommodations did not violate federal law. Justice John Marshall Harlan, a former slave owner who experienced a conversion as a result of Ku Klux Klan excesses and a champion of black civil rights, wrote a scathing dissent. Harlan went on to say: "But in view of the Constitution, in the eye of the law, there is in this country no superior, dominant, ruling class of citizens. There is no caste here. Our Constitution is color-blind, and neither knows nor tolerates classes among citizens. In respect of civil rights, all citizens are equal before the law." The case provided the legal foundation for the doctrine of separate but equal, the idea that segregation based on racial classification was legal as long as facilities were of equal quality. It opened the floodgates for discrimination against African Americans in all facets of American life. Southern state governments refused to provide blacks with genuinely equal facilities and resources in the years after the *Plessy* decision. The states not only separated races but, in actuality, ensured differences in quality. In January 1897, Homer Plessy pleaded guilty to the violation and paid the $25 fine. That the court would decide that discrimination was constitutional demonstrates the way in which American law was skewed to favor whites and white privilege over a large portion of the country's history. It also demonstrates how notions of equal protection have changed with the times. The court's decision was reversed in 1954 with the *Brown vs. Board of Education* decision.

This case turns upon the constitutionality of an act of the general assembly of the state of Louisiana, passed in 1890, providing for separate railway carriages for the white and colored races.

The first section of the statute enacts 'that all railway companies carrying passengers in their coaches in this state, shall provide equal but separate accommodations for the white, and colored races, by providing two or more passenger coaches for each passenger train, or by dividing the passenger coaches by a partition so as to secure separate accommodations: provided, that this section shall not be construed to apply to street railroads. No person or persons shall be permitted to occupy seats in coaches, other than the ones assigned to them, on account of the race they belong to.'

By the second section it was enacted 'that the officers of such passenger trains shall have power and are hereby required to assign each passenger to the coach or compartment used for the race to which such passenger belongs; any passenger insisting on going into a coach or compartment to which by race he does not belong, shall be liable to a fine of twenty-five dollars, or in lieu thereof to imprisonment for a period of not more than twenty days in the parish prison, and any officer of any railroad insisting on assigning a passenger to a coach or compartment other than the one set aside for the race to which said passenger belongs, shall be liable to a fine of twenty-five dollars, or in lieu thereof to imprisonment for a period of not more than twenty days in the parish prison; and should any passenger refuse to occupy the coach or compartment to which he or she is assigned by the officer of such railway, said officer shall have power to refuse to carry such passenger on his train, and for such refusal neither he nor the railway company which he represents shall be liable for damages in any of the courts of this state.'

The third section provides penalties for the refusal or neglect of the officers, directors, conductors, and employees of railway companies to comply with the act, with a proviso that 'nothing in this act shall be construed as applying to nurses attending children of the other race.' The fourth section is immaterial.

The information filed in the criminal district court charged, in substance, that Plessy, being a passenger between two stations within the state of Louisiana, was assigned by officers of the company to the coach used for the race to which he belonged, but he insisted upon going into a coach used by the race to which he did not belong. Neither in the information nor plea was his particular race or color averred.

The petition for the writ of prohibition averred that petitioner was seven-eighths Caucasian and one-eighth African blood; that the mixture of colored blood was not discernible in him; and that he was entitled to every right, privilege, and immunity secured to citizens of the United States of the white race; and that, upon such theory, he took possession of a vacant seat in a coach where passengers of the white race were accommodated, and was ordered by the conductor to vacate said coach, and take a seat in another, assigned to persons of the colored race, and, having refused to comply with such demand, he was forcibly ejected, with the aid of a police officer, and imprisoned in the parish jail to answer a charge of having violated the above act.

The constitutionality of this act is attacked upon the ground that it conflicts both with the thirteenth amendment of the constitution, abolishing slavery, and the fourteenth amendment, which prohibits certain restrictive legislation on the part of the states.

1. That it does not conflict with the thirteenth amendment, which abolished slavery and involuntary servitude, except a punishment for crime, is too clear for argument. Slavery implies involuntary servitude,-a state of bondage; the ownership of mankind as a chattel, or, at least, the control of the labor and services of one man for the benefit of another, and the absence of a legal right to the disposal of his own person, property, and services. This amendment was said in the Slaughter-House Cases, to have been intended primarily to abolish slavery, as it had been previously known in this country, and that it equally forbade Mexican peonage or the Chinese coolie trade, when they amounted to slavery or involuntary servitude, and that the use of the word 'servitude' was intended to prohibit the use of all forms of involuntary slavery, of whatever class or name. It was intimated, however, in that case, that this amendment was regarded by the statesmen of that day as insufficient to protect the colored race from certain laws which had been enacted in the Southern states, imposing upon the colored race onerous disabilities and burdens, and curtailing their rights in the pursuit of life, liberty, and property to such an extent that their freedom was of little value; and that the fourteenth amendment was devised to meet this exigency.

So, too, in the Civil Rights Cases, it was said that the act of a mere individual, the owner of an inn, a public conveyance or place of amusement, refusing accommodations to colored people, cannot be justly regarded as imposing any badge of slavery or servitude upon the applicant, but only as involving an ordinary civil injury, properly cognizable by the laws of the state, and presumably subject to redress by those laws until the contrary appears. 'It would be running the slavery question into the ground,' said Mr. Justice Bradley, 'to make it apply to every act of discrimination which a person may see fit to make as to the guests he will entertain, or as to the people he will take into his coach or cab or car, or admit to his concert or theater, or deal with in other matters of intercourse or business.'

A statute which implies merely a legal distinction between the white and colored races-a distinction which is founded in the color of the two races, and which must always exist so long as white men are distinguished from the other race by color-has no tendency to destroy the legal equality of the two races, or re-establish a state of involuntary servitude. Indeed, we do not understand that the thirteenth amendment is strenuously relied upon by the plaintiff in error in this connection.

2. By the fourteenth amendment, all persons born or naturalized in the United States, and subject to the jurisdiction thereof, are made citizens of the United States and of the state wherein they reside; and the states are forbidden from making or enforcing any law which shall abridge the privileges or immunities of citizens of the United States, or shall deprive any person of life, liberty, or property without due process of law, or deny to any person within their jurisdiction the equal protection of the laws.

The proper construction of this amendment was first called to the attention of this court in the Slaughter-House Cases, which involved, however, not a question of race, but one of exclusive privileges. The case did not call for any expression of opinion as to the exact rights it was intended to secure to the colored race, but it was said generally that its main purpose was to establish the citizenship of the negro, to give definitions of citizenship of the United States and of the states, and to protect from the hostile legislation of the states the privileges and immunities of citizens of the United States, as distinguished from those of citizens of the states. The object of the amendment was undoubtedly to enforce the absolute equality of the two races before the law, but, in the nature of things, it could not have been intended to abolish distinctions based upon color, or to enforce social, as distinguished from political, equality, or a commingling of the two races upon terms unsatisfactory to either. Laws permitting, and even requiring, their separation, in places where they are liable to be brought into contact, do not necessarily imply the inferiority of either race to the other, and have been generally, if not universally, recognized as within the competency of the state legislatures in the exercise of their police power. The most common instance of this is connected with the establishment of separate schools for white and colored children, which have been held to be a valid exercise of the legislative power even by courts of states where the political rights of the colored race have been longest and most earnestly enforced.

One of the earliest of these cases is that of *Roberts v. City of Boston,* in which the supreme judicial court of Massachusetts held that the general school committee of Boston had power to make provision for the instruction of colored children in separate schools established exclusively for them, and to prohibit their attendance upon the other schools. 'The great principle,' said Chief Justice Shaw, 'advanced by the learned and eloquent advocate for the plaintiff [Mr. Charles Sumner], is that, by the constitution and laws of Massachusetts, all persons, without distinction of age or sex, birth or color, origin or condition, are equal before the law. . . . But, when this great principle comes to be applied to the actual and various conditions of persons in society, it will not warrant the assertion that men and women are legally clothed with the same civil and political powers, and that children and adults are legally to have the same functions and be subject to the same treatment; but only that the rights of all, as they are settled and regulated by law, are equally entitled to the paternal consideration and protection of the law for their maintenance and security.' It was held that the powers of the committee extended to the establishment of separate schools for children of different ages, sexes and colors, and that they might also establish special schools for poor and neglected children, who have become too old to attend the primary school, and yet have not acquired the rudiments of learning, to enable them to enter the ordinary schools. Similar laws have been enacted by congress under its general power of legislation over the District of Columbia, as well as by the legislatures of many of the states, and have been generally, if not uniformly, sustained by the courts.

Laws forbidding the intermarriage of the two races may be said in a technical sense to interfere with the freedom of contract, and yet have been universally recognized as within the police power of the state.

The distinction between laws interfering with the political equality of the negro and those requiring the separation of the two races in schools, theaters, and railway carriages has been frequently drawn by this court. Thus, in *Strauder v. West Virginia*, it was held that a law of West Virginia limiting to white male persons 21 years of age, and citizens of the state, the right to sit upon juries, was a discrimination which implied a legal inferiority in civil society, which lessened the security of the right of the colored race, and was a step towards reducing them to a condition of servility. Indeed, the right of a colored man that, in the selection of jurors to pass upon his life, liberty, and property, there shall be no exclusion of his race, and no discrimination against them because of color, has been asserted in a number of cases. So, where the laws of a particular locality or the charter of a particular railway corporation has provided that no person shall be excluded from the cars on account of color, we have held that this meant that persons of color should travel in the same car as white ones, and that the enactment was not satisfied by the company providing cars assigned exclusively to people of color, though they were as good as those which they assigned exclusively to white persons.

Upon the other hand, where a statute of Louisiana required those engaged in the transportation of passengers among the states to give to all persons traveling within that state, upon vessels employed in that business, equal rights and privileges in all parts of the vessel, without distinction on account of race or color, and subjected to an action for damages the owner of such a vessel who excluded colored passengers on account of their color from the cabin set aside by him for the use of whites, it was held to be, so far as it applied to interstate commerce, unconstitutional and void. The court in this case, however, expressly disclaimed that it had anything whatever to do with the statute as a regulation of internal commerce, or affecting anything else than commerce among the states.

In the Civil Rights Cases, it was held that an act of congress entitling all persons within the jurisdiction of the United States to the full and equal enjoyment of the accommodations, advantages, facilities, and privileges of inns, public conveyances, on land or water, theaters, and other places of public amusement, and made applicable to citizens of every race and color, regardless of any previous condition of servitude, was unconstitutional and void, upon the ground that the fourteenth amendment was prohibitory upon the states only, and the legislation authorized to be adopted by congress for enforcing it was not direct legislation on matters respecting which the states were prohibited from making or enforcing certain laws, or doing certain acts, but was corrective legislation, such as might be necessary or proper for counter-acting and redressing the effect of such laws or acts. In delivering the opinion of the court, Mr. Justice Bradley observed that the fourteenth amendment 'does not invest congress with power to legislate upon subjects that are within the domain of state legislation, but to provide modes of relief against state legislation or state action of the kind referred to. It does not authorize congress to create a code of municipal law for the regulation of private rights, but to provide modes of redress against the operation of state laws, and the action of state officers, executive or judicial, when these are subversive of the fundamental rights specified in the amendment. Positive rights and privileges are undoubtedly secured by the fourteenth amendment; but they are secured by way of prohibition against state laws and state proceedings affecting those rights and privileges, and by power given to congress to legislate for the purpose of carrying such prohibition into effect; and such legislation must necessarily be predicated upon such supposed state laws or state proceedings, and be directed to the correction of their operation and effect.'

Much nearer, and, indeed, almost directly in point, is the case of the Louisville, *N. O. & T. Ry. Co. v. State,* wherein the railway company was indicted for a violation of a statute of Mississippi, enacting that all railroads carrying passengers should provide equal, but separate, accommodations for the white and colored races, by providing two or more passenger cars for each passenger train, or by dividing the passenger cars by a partition, so as to secure separate accommodations. The case was presented in a different aspect from the one under consideration, inasmuch as it was an indictment against the railway company for failing to provide the separate accommodations, but the question considered was the constitutionality of the law. In that case, the supreme court of Mississippi had held that the statute applied solely to commerce within the state, and, that being the construction of the state statute by its highest court, was accepted as conclusive. 'If it be a matter,' said the court, 'respecting commerce wholly within a state, and not interfering with commerce between the states, then, obviously, there is no violation of the commerce clause of the federal constitution.' No question arises under this section as to the power of the state to separate in different compartments interstate passengers, or affect, in any manner, the privileges and rights of such passengers. All that we can consider is whether the state has the power to require that railroad trains within her limits shall have separate accommodations for the two races. That affecting only commerce within the state is no invasion of the power given to congress by the commerce clause.'

A like course of reasoning applies to the case under consideration, since the supreme court of Louisiana, in the case of *State v. Judge,* held that the statute in question did not apply to interstate passengers, but was confined in its application to passengers traveling exclusively within the borders of the state. The case was decided largely upon the authority of *Louisville, N. O. & T. Ry. Co. v. State* and affirmed by this court. In the present case no question of interference with interstate commerce can possibly arise, since the East Louisiana Railway appears to have been purely a local line, with both its termini within the state of Louisiana. Similar statutes for the separation of the two races upon public conveyances were held to be constitutional in *Railroad v. Miles, Day v. Owen, Railway Co. v. Williams, Railroad Co. v. Wells, Railroad Co. v. Benson, Logwood v. Railroad Co., McGuinn v. Forbes, People v. King, Houck v. Railway Co.*, [and] *Heard v. Railroad Co.*

While we think the enforced separation of the races, as applied to the internal commerce of the state, neither abridges the privileges or immunities of the colored man, deprives him of his property without due process of law, nor denies him the equal protection of the laws, within the meaning of the fourteenth amendment, we are not prepared to say that the conductor, in assigning passengers to the coaches according to their race, does not act at his peril, or that the provision of the second section of the act that denies to the passenger compensation in damages for a refusal to receive him into the coach in which he properly belongs is a valid exercise of the legislative power. Indeed, we understand it to be conceded by the state's attorney that such part of the act as exempts from liability the railway company and its officers is unconstitutional. The power to assign to a particular coach obviously implies the power to determine to which race the passenger belongs, as well as the power to determine who, under the laws of the particular state, is to be deemed a white, and who a colored, person. This question, though indicated in the brief of the plaintiff in error, does not properly arise upon the record in this case, since the only issue made is as to the unconstitutionality of the act, so far as it requires the railway to provide separate accommodations, and the conductor to assign passengers according to their race.

It is claimed by the plaintiff in error that, in an mixed community, the reputation of belonging to the dominant race, in this instance the white race, is 'property,' in the same sense that a right of action or of inheritance is property. Conceding this to be so, for the purposes of this case, we are unable to see how this statute deprives him of, or in any way affects his right to, such property. If he be a white man, and assigned to a colored coach, he may have his action for damages against the company for being deprived of his so-called 'property.' Upon the other hand, if he be a colored man, and be so assigned, he has been deprived of no property, since he is not lawfully entitled to the reputation of being a white man.

In this connection, it is also suggested by the learned counsel for the plaintiff in error that the same argument that will justify the state legislature in requiring railways to provide separate accommodations for the two races will also authorize them to require separate cars to be provided for people whose hair is of a certain color, or who are aliens, or who belong to certain nationalities, or to enact laws requiring colored people to walk upon one side of the street, and white people upon the other, or requiring white men's houses to be painted white, and colored men's black, or their vehicles or business signs to be of different colors, upon the theory that one side of the street is as good as the other, or that a house or vehicle of one color is as good as one of another color. The reply to all this is that every exercise of the police power must be reasonable, and extend only to such laws as are enacted in good faith for the promotion of the public good, and not for the annoyance or oppression of a particular class. Thus, in *Yick Wo v. Hopkins*, it was held by this court that a municipal ordinance of the city of San Francisco, to regulate the carrying on of public laundries within the limits of the municipality, violated the provisions of the constitution of the United States, if it conferred upon the municipal authorities arbitrary power, at their own will, and without regard to discretion, in the legal sense of the term, to give or withhold consent as to persons or places, without regard to the competency of the persons applying or the propriety of the places selected for the carrying on of the business. It was held to be a covert attempt on the part of the municipality to make an arbitrary and unjust discrimination against the Chinese race. While this was the case of a municipal ordinance, a like principle has been held to apply to acts of a state legislature passed in the exercise of the police power.

So far, then, as a conflict with the fourteenth amendment is concerned, the case reduces itself to the question whether the statute of Louisiana is a reasonable regulation, and with respect to this there must necessarily be a large discretion on the part of the legislature. In determining the question of reasonableness, it is at liberty to act with reference to the established usages, customs, and traditions of the people, and with a view to the promotion of their comfort, and the preservation of the public peace and good order. Gauged by this standard, we cannot say that a law which authorizes or even requires the separation of the two races in public conveyances is unreasonable, or more obnoxious to the fourteenth amendment than the acts of congress requiring separate schools for colored children in the District of Columbia, the constitutionality of which does not seem to have been questioned, or the corresponding acts of state legislatures.

We consider the underlying fallacy of the plaintiff's argument to consist in the assumption that the enforced separation of the two races stamps the colored race with a badge of inferiority. If this be so, it is not by reason of anything found in the act, but solely because the colored race chooses to put that construction upon it. The argument necessarily assumes that if, as has been more than once the case, and is not unlikely to be so again, the colored race should become the dominant power in the state legislature, and should enact a law in precisely similar terms, it would thereby relegate the white race to an inferior position. We imagine that the white race, at least, would not acquiesce in this assumption. The argument also assumes that social prejudices may be overcome by legislation, and that equal rights cannot be secured to the negro except by an enforced commingling of the two races. We cannot accept this proposition. If the two races are to meet upon terms of social equality, it must be the result of natural affinities, a mutual appreciation of each other's merits, and a voluntary consent of individuals. As was said by the court of appeals of New York in *People v. Gallagher:* 'This end can neither be accomplished nor promoted by laws which conflict with the general sentiment of the community upon whom they are designed to operate. When the government, therefore, has secured to each of its citizens equal rights before the law, and equal opportunities for improvement and progress, it has accomplished the end for which it was organized, and performed all of the functions respecting social advantages with which it is endowed.' Legislation is powerless to eradicate racial instincts, or to abolish distinctions based upon physical differences, and the attempt to do so can only result in accentuating the difficulties of the present situation. If the civil and political rights of both races be equal, one cannot be inferior to the other civilly or politically. If one race be inferior to the other socially, the constitution of the United States cannot put them upon the same plane.

It is true that the question of the proportion of colored blood necessary to constitute a colored person, as distinguished from a white person, is one upon which there is a difference of opinion in the different states; some holding that any visible admixture of black blood stamps the person as belonging to the colored; others, that it depends upon the preponderance of blood, and still others, that the predominance of white blood must only be in the proportion of three-fourths. But these are questions to be determined under the laws of each state, and are not properly put in issue in this case. Under the allegations of his petition, it may undoubtedly become a question of importance whether, under the laws of Louisiana, the petitioner belongs to the white or colored race.

The judgment of the court below is therefore affirmed.

Source: *Plessy v. Ferguson*, 163 U.S. 537 (1896).

BROWN vs. BOARD OF EDUCATION (1954)

The *Brown vs. Board of Education* (1954) decision came on the heels of other court cases tried by the National Association for the Advancement of Colored People (NAACP). In *Sweat vs. Painter* (1950) and *McLaurin v. Oklahoma State Regents* (1950), they challenged segregation in postsecondary education. *Brown* was argued before the U.S. Supreme Court by Thurgood Marshall, Robert Carter, and Jack Greenberg, lawyers for the NAACP, and was the culmination of class action lawsuits brought by African Americans in Delaware, Kansas, South Carolina, and Virginia. As part of their argument, they argued that separate but equal schools were inherently unequal and compromised African American children's self worth. In his decision, Chief Justice Warren argued that segregated schools "deprive the children of the minority group of equal educational opportunities," and by doing so, the court unanimously overturned *Plessy v. Ferguson* (1896), which 58 years earlier, decided that federally and publicly funded institutions could be segregated. The *Brown* decision was a ray of hope for African American families whose children had suffered under educational segregation. It was proof to some that the federal government was ready to confront the American racial dilemma head on. For others, it was a chink in the armor of Jim Crow. But despite the progressive nature of the ruling, it contained no provisions for enforcement and integration remained a chimera for most black families. In 1955, in what is commonly called *Brown II*, the court reconsidered the case. To force states to comply with the 1954 decision, it ordered that the process of school desegregation be carried out by district courts. Even with the 1955 ruling, however, largely white municipalities resisted integration and African Americans in urban slums had no recourse. De facto segregation persisted and no government agency or court could legislate or rule housing patterns. In response, complicated school transportation plans and bussing schemes were created, but even they were abandoned throughout the country. With school segregation persisting in urban areas and suburban districts remaining predominantly white, *Brown* remains both largely unenforceable and a dream of racial equality.

Supreme Court of the United States

Brown v. Board of Education

Syllabus

Segregation of white and Negro children in the public schools of a State solely on the basis of race, pursuant to state laws permitting or requiring such segregation, denies to Negro children the equal protection of the laws guaranteed by the Fourteenth Amendment—even though the physical facilities and other "tangible" factors of white and Negro schools may be equal.

(a) The history of the Fourteenth Amendment is inconclusive as to its intended effect on public education.

(b) The question presented in these cases must be determined not on the basis of conditions existing when the Fourteenth Amendment was adopted, but in the light of the full development of public education and its present place in American life throughout the Nation.

(c) Where a State has undertaken to provide an opportunity for an education in its public schools, such an opportunity is a right which must be made available to all on equal terms.

(d) Segregation of children in public schools solely on the basis of race deprives children of the minority group of equal educational opportunities, even though the physical facilities and other "tangible" factors may be equal.

(e) The "separate but equal" doctrine adopted in Plessy v. Ferguson, has no place in the field of public education.

(f) The cases are restored to the docket for further argument on specified questions relating to the forms of the decrees.

Opinion

MR. CHIEF JUSTICE WARREN delivered the opinion of the Court.

These cases come to us from the States of Kansas, South Carolina, Virginia, and Delaware. They are premised on different facts and different local conditions, but a common legal question justifies their consideration together in this consolidated opinion.

In each of the cases, minors of the Negro race, through their legal representatives, seek the aid of the courts in obtaining admission to the public schools of their community on a nonsegregated basis. In each instance, they had been denied admission to schools attended by white children under laws requiring or permitting segregation according to race. This segregation was alleged to deprive the plaintiffs of the equal protection of the laws under the Fourteenth Amendment. In each of the cases other than the Delaware case, a three-judge federal district court denied relief to the plaintiffs on the so-called "separate but equal" doctrine announced by this Court in *Plessy v. Ferguson.* Under that doctrine, equality of treatment is accorded when the races are provided substantially equal facilities, even though these facilities be separate. In the Delaware case, the Supreme Court of Delaware adhered to that doctrine, but ordered that the plaintiffs be admitted to the white schools because of their superiority to the Negro schools.

The plaintiffs contend that segregated public schools are not "equal" and cannot be made "equal," and that hence they are deprived of the equal protection of the laws. Because of the obvious importance of the question presented, the Court took jurisdiction. Argument was heard in the 1952 Term, and reargument was heard this Term on certain questions propounded by the Court.

Reargument was largely devoted to the circumstances surrounding the adoption of the Fourteenth Amendment in 1868. It covered exhaustively consideration of the Amendment in Congress, ratification by the states, then-existing practices in racial segregation, and the views of proponents and opponents of the Amendment. This discussion and our own investigation convince us that, although these sources cast some light, it is not enough to resolve the problem with which we are faced. At best, they are inconclusive. The most avid proponents of the post-War Amendments undoubtedly intended them to remove all legal distinctions among "all persons born or naturalized in the United States." Their opponents, just as certainly, were antagonistic to both the letter and the spirit of the Amendments and wished them to have the most limited effect. What others in Congress and the state legislatures had in mind cannot be determined with any degree of certainty.

An additional reason for the inconclusive nature of the Amendment's history with respect to segregated schools is the status of public education at that time. In the South, the movement toward free common schools, supported by general taxation, had not yet taken hold. Education of white children was largely in the hands of private groups. Education of Negroes was almost nonexistent, and practically all of the race were illiterate. In fact, any education of Negroes was forbidden by law in some states. Today, in contrast, many Negroes have achieved outstanding success in the arts and sciences, as well as in the business and professional world. It is true that public school education at the time of the Amendment had advanced further in the North, but the effect of the Amendment on Northern States was generally ignored in the congressional debates. Even in the North, the conditions of public education did not approximate those existing today. The curriculum was usually rudimentary; ungraded schools were common in rural areas; the school term was but three months a year in many states, and compulsory school attendance was virtually unknown. As a consequence, it is not surprising that there should be so little in the history of the Fourteenth Amendment relating to its intended effect on public education.

In the first cases in this Court construing the Fourteenth Amendment, decided shortly after its adoption, the Court interpreted it as proscribing all state-imposed discriminations against the Negro race. The doctrine of "separate but equal" did not make its appearance in this Court until 1896 in the case of *Plessy v. Ferguson*, involving not education but transportation. American courts have since labored with the doctrine for over half a century. In this Court, there have been six cases involving the "separate but equal" doctrine in the field of public education. In *Cumming v. County Board of Education* and *Gong Lum v. Rice* the validity of the doctrine itself was not challenged. In more recent cases, all on the graduate school level, inequality was found in that specific benefits enjoyed by white students were denied to Negro students of the same educational qualifications. In none of these cases was it necessary to reexamine the doctrine to grant relief to the Negro plaintiff. And in *Sweatt v. Painter*, the Court expressly reserved decision on the question whether *Plessy v. Ferguson* should be held inapplicable to public education.

In the instant cases, that question is directly presented. Here, unlike *Sweatt v. Painter*, there are findings below that the Negro and white schools involved have been equalized, or are being equalized, with respect to buildings, curricula, qualifications and salaries of teachers, and other "tangible" factors. Our decision, therefore, cannot turn on merely a comparison of these tangible factors in the Negro and white schools involved in each of the cases. We must look instead to the effect of segregation itself on public education.

In approaching this problem, we cannot turn the clock back to 1868, when the Amendment was adopted, or even to 1896, when *Plessy v. Ferguson* was written. We must consider public education in the light of its full development and its present place in American life throughout the Nation. Only in this way can it be determined if segregation in public schools deprives these plaintiffs of the equal protection of the laws.

Today, education is perhaps the most important function of state and local governments. Compulsory school attendance laws and the great expenditures for education both demonstrate our recognition of the importance of education to our democratic society. It is required in the performance of our most basic public responsibilities, even service in the armed forces. It is the very foundation of good citizenship. Today it is a principal instrument in awakening the child to cultural values, in preparing him for later professional training, and in helping him to adjust normally to his environment. In these days, it is doubtful that any child may reasonably be expected to succeed in life if he is denied the opportunity of an education. Such an opportunity, where the state has undertaken to provide it, is a right which must be made available to all on equal terms.

We come then to the question presented: Does segregation of children in public schools solely on the basis of race, even though the physical facilities and other "tangible" factors may be equal, deprive the children of the minority group of equal educational opportunities? We believe that it does.

In *Sweatt v. Painter*, in finding that a segregated law school for Negroes could not provide them equal educational opportunities, this Court relied in large part on "those qualities which are incapable of objective measurement but which make for greatness in a law school." In *McLaurin v. Oklahoma State Regents*, the Court, in requiring that a Negro admitted to a white graduate school be treated like all other students, again resorted to intangible considerations: " . . . his ability to study, to engage in discussions and exchange views with other students, and, in general, to learn his profession." Such considerations apply with added force to children in grade and high schools. To separate them from others of similar age and qualifications solely because of their race generates a feeling of inferiority as to their status in the community that may affect their hearts and minds in a way unlikely ever to be undone. The effect of this separation on their educational opportunities was well stated by a finding in the Kansas case by a court which nevertheless felt compelled to rule against the Negro plaintiffs:

Segregation of white and colored children in public schools has a detrimental effect upon the colored children. The impact is greater when it has the sanction of the law, for the policy of separating the races is usually interpreted as denoting the inferiority of the negro group. A sense of inferiority affects the motivation of a child to learn. Segregation with the sanction of law, therefore, has a tendency to [retard] the educational and mental development of negro children and to deprive them of some of the benefits they would receive in a racial[ly] integrated school system.

Whatever may have been the extent of psychological knowledge at the time of *Plessy v. Ferguson*, this finding is amply supported by modern authority. Any language in *Plessy v. Ferguson* contrary to this finding is rejected.

We conclude that, in the field of public education, the doctrine of "separate but equal" has no place. Separate educational facilities are inherently unequal. Therefore, we hold that the plaintiffs and others similarly situated for whom the actions have been brought are, by reason of the segregation complained of, deprived of the equal protection of the laws guaranteed by the Fourteenth Amendment. This disposition makes unnecessary any discussion whether such segregation also violates the Due Process Clause of the Fourteenth Amendment.

Because these are class actions, because of the wide applicability of this decision, and because of the great variety of local conditions, the formulation of decrees in these cases presents problems of considerable complexity. On reargument, the consideration of appropriate relief was necessarily subordinated to the primary question—the constitutionality of segregation in public education. We have now announced that such segregation is a denial of the equal protection of the laws. In order that we may have the full assistance of the parties in formulating decrees, the cases will be restored to the docket, and the parties are requested to present further argument on Questions 4 and 5 previously propounded by the Court for the reargument this Term The Attorney General of the United States is again invited to participate. The Attorneys General of the states requiring or permitting segregation in public education will also be permitted to appear as amici curiae upon request to do so by September 15, 1954, and submission of briefs by October 1, 1954.

It is so ordered.

Source: *Brown v. Board of Education*, 347 U.S. 483 (1954).

MARCH TO FREEDOM FLIER

The Civil Rights Movement was as much a religious movement as a political one. Though Reverend Dr. Martin Luther King, Jr. was the most popular leader, many of its leaders, like Reverend James Hinton, were clergymen. The ministers' salaries were paid by congregation members. Consequently, they did not suffer from the same kinds of economic reprisals and pressures that sharecroppers, blue collar workers, and even black professionals suffered for participation in the movement. In addition, the black church was one of the few institutions that African Americans owned in Jim Crow America. While they were routinely bombed and targeted by white vigilantes, they still had a political independence to do the will of the people and the will of their God. Of those who were not in the ministry, many had experiences in the African American church as members of a congregation. Like the Montgomery Bus Boycott in Montgomery, Alabama, in Charleston, South, Carolina, and other places, the church was often the meeting spaces for community mass meetings where critical decisions were made regarding movement strategies. It was also a place where different political organizations, like the NAACP, could meet as demonstrated in the flier below. Sundays afternoons were popular times for political meetings in many communities situated as it was after morning service and before Sunday dinner. And while many working class and working poor people had to work on Sunday, large numbers of community members rested and had time to attend such gatherings. The flier gives the reader the sense that the boundary between the secular and the sacrosanct was permeable and informed each other so that "soul-stirring" could occur during a religious service or at a political meeting. Gospel and freedom songs were sung, people testified, and encouraged each other to participate. The flier also shows how movement people were simultaneously concerned with a variety of issues including education, public transportation, and access to public facilities and situated African American's search for equality and dignity among universal rights for every American.

Citation: March to Freedom Flier, Exhibit D-A from Etta Clark, et al. vs. C.H. Flory, State Forester, et al., *1955–1055;* Etta Clark, et al., vs. C. H. Flory, State Forester, et. al., Civil 5082, *1955–1956;* Civil Cases Files, *compiled 09/1938–10/27/1965;* Records of District Courts of the United States, *1685–2004;* NARA's Southeast Region (Atlanta) (NRCA), 5780 Jonesboro Road, Morrow, GA, 30260 Online version available through the Archival Research Catalog (ARC Identifier 279310) at www.archives.gov, January 4, 2012.

CALLING ALL CITIZENS!   CALLING ALL CITIZENS!

The Charleston South Carolina, Branch Of N. A. A. C. P.
Requests Your Presence At Its

MARCH TO FREEDOM

MASS MEETING

WITH

Rev. James M. Hinton

President, S. C. Conference of N. A. A. C. P.

GUEST SPEAKER

. . . If you are interested in the future education of your children . . .

. . . If you are interested in knowing why you should not have to pay first class fares to ride as second class citizens . . .

. . . If you are interested in having the right to have your family enjoy the beach facilities that your tax money supports . . .

. . . Then you cannot afford to miss this meeting when all of these topics will be discussed by our guest speaker who believes in the American way of life, with freedom and justice for all people, regardless of race, creed or color.

You owe it to yourself and unborn generations whose world you are molding to hear this soul-stirring, dynamic, courageous American citizen and leader in the fight for the human rights of all people.

— At —

MORRIS BROWN A.M.E. CHURCH

Sunday Afternoon, August 28, 1955

— 4:00 P. M. —

REV. J. C. QUARLES, Pastor   J. ARTHUR BROWN, President

March to Freedom

JACKIE ROBINSON'S LETTER TO
ROBERT F. KENNEDY, MAY 25, 1961

Jackie Robinson is most known for integrating major league baseball when he joined the Brooklyn Dodgers in 1947. But when his tenure as a baseball player ended, Robinson used his notoriety for a variety of political causes and to venture into the business world. In 1957, Robinson joined Chock Full o' Nuts Coffee Company as its Director of Personnel, and by 1961, he was promoted to vice president of the company. During the early 1960s, Robinson had the political clout to carry on letter communications with Robert F. Kennedy, then Attorney General of the United States. In early May 1961, Robert Kennedy expressed his willingness to tackle the issue of African American civil rights at a speech at the University of Georgia Law School. Below is the second letter that Robinson sent to Kennedy that month regarding Kennedy's developing stance on civil rights. In it, he expresses his dismay about the political activity and/or political apathy of unknown segments of the African American population. He also applauds Kennedy for his service even while recognizing that he had been in the office for just a short time (Kennedy was confirmed in January 1961). The real purpose of the letter is manifold. The first is to keep Robinson in the good graces of the administration. He had publicly endorsed Richard Nixon during the 1960 presidential race. The second purpose of the letter is to keep him at least on the margins of federal initiatives on civil rights issues. By 1961, other black leaders and popular black celebrities had eclipsed Robinson's influence. Finally, the letter shows the extent to which African Americans of all political persuasions put their faith in the Kennedy administration to remedy the problems of civil rights in the country.

Chock full o' Nuts
425 Lexington Avenue
New York 17, N.Y.

May 25, 1961

The Honorable Robert Kennedy
Attorney General of the United States
Washington, D.C.

My dear Mr. Attorney General:
Many thanks to you for your very kind answer to my letter of May 8th. While I did not anticipate that my previous letter would get the attention it received, I am pleased that my present position is known to all who read it.

You are doing a capital job, and we applaud you.

Because I have no personal ax to grind, I can express my true feelings. I feel that until more Negroes are willing to sacrifice ease and comfort, we will continue to suffer. You can depend upon my expressing my views. I do not pretend to be an expert, but my views will be voiced.

As you know, I had complete confidence in your predecessor. However, your few months in office have been a real source of inspiration. I can only hope that you are allowed to continue your drive for equality among Americans. There can be no denying that your definite action is responsible for world-wide approval. Everywhere, at home and abroad, your department, under you [sic] dynamic leadership, shows that it means business.

You have earned our respect. We are proud of the job you are doing.

With kindest personal regards I am

Yours most sincerely,
Jackie Robinson

Citation: Jackie Robinson, Jackie Robinson Letter to Robert F. Kennedy May 29, 1961; Robert F. Kennedy Papers: Attorney General Papers: General Correspondence: Robins–Robling, *01/20/1961–08/1964;* Robert F. Kennedy Papers: Attorney General Papers: General Correspondence, *compiled 1961–1964* John F. Kennedy Library (NLJFK), Columbia Point, Boston, MA, 02125 [online version available through the Archival Research Catalog (ARC Identifier 193948) at www.archives.gov, January 4, 2012].

LINCOLN MEMORIAL PROGRAM MARCH ON WASHINGTON FOR JOBS AND FREEDOM, AUGUST 28, 1963

The August 28, 1963, March on Washington for Jobs and Freedom is perhaps the most well known event, during the Civil Rights Movement. The idea for the demonstration has its origins in the 1940s with Brotherhood of Sleeping Car Porters' president A. Philip Randolph, who wanted to call attention to discrimination in the defense industry. In 1962, members from a variety of civil rights organizations discussed the idea of staging such a demonstration to encourage President Kennedy and congress to pass civil rights legislation that would offer further protections for African Americans' constitutional rights. However, not everyone in the federal government or among African American political activists approved of the March on Washington. The Kennedy Administration went to great lengths to prevent the march. President Kennedy, himself, met with civil rights leaders to ask them to call it off. James Farmer of the Congress of

Racial Equality thought the march was too tame and did not apply enough pressure on the government. Malcolm X, who had been on the margins of direct, nonviolent political activity, called the demonstration a "Farce on Washington." Initially, planners only expected 100,000 people. On the day of the march, however, over 250,000 people arrived. The lineup of speakers for the event shows the inextricable link between the religious and secular aspects of the movement. Speakers representing different labor interests and civil rights agencies were integral to the demonstration as were speakers from different religious traditions. Interestingly, Marian Anderson, Mahalia Jackson, and Eva Jessye's choir provided the music for the event, but the majority of the speakers were men. This is surprising, considering that all of the women honored in the "Negro Women Fighters for Freedom" tribute were alive and still fighting injustices at that time. The relative absence of women from the speakers' rostrum demonstrates latent sexism in the movement. The march's crescendo was Martin Luther King's "I Have a Dream" speech. The March on Washington showed the country and the federal government that civil rights activism was growing in popularity, had the support of tens of thousands of black and white Americans, and would not go way without sweeping legislative changes. Along with backdoor politicking, the march succeeded in adding pressure to congress. In 1964, participants of the march celebrated the passage of the 1964 Civil Rights Act, legislation that their activism brought into being.

1. The National Anthem
   Led by Marian Anderson.
2. Invocation
   The Very Rev. Patrick O'Boyle, *Archbishop of Washington.*
3. Opening Remarks
   A.Philip Randolph, *Director March on Washington for Jobs and Freedom.*
4. Remarks
   Dr. Eugene Carson Blake, Stated Clerk, United Presbyterian Church of the U.S.A.; Vice Chairman, Commission on Race Relations of the National Council of Churches of Christ in America.
5. Tribute to Negro Women Fighters for Freedom
   Daisy Bates
   Diane Nash Bevel
   Mrs. Medgar Evers

Mrs. Herbert Lee
Rosa Parks
Gloria Richardson

6. Remarks
   John Lewis, National Chairman, Student Nonviolent Coordinating Committee.

7. Remarks
   Walter Reuther, President, United Automobile, Aerospace and Agricultural Implement Workers of America, AFL-CIO; Chairman, Industrial Union Department, AFL-CIO.

8. Remarks
   James Farmer, National Director, Congress of Racial Equality.

9. Selection
   Eva Jessye Choir.

10. Prayer
    Rabbi Uri Miller, President Synagogue Council of America.

11. Remarks
    Whitney M. Young, Jr., Executive Director, National Urban League.

12. Remarks
    Matthew Ahmann, Executive Director, National Catholic Conference for Interracial Justice.

13. Remarks
    Roy Wilkins, Executive Secretary, National Association for the Advancement of Colored People.

14. Selection
    Miss Mahalia Jackson

15. Remarks
    Rabbi Joachim Prinz, President American Jewish Congress.

16. Remarks
    The Rev. Dr. Martin Luther King, Jr., President, Southern Christian Leadership Conference.

17. The Pledge
    A. Philip Randolph

18. Benediction
    Dr. Benjamin E. Mays, President, Morehouse College.
    "WE SHALL OVERCOME"

Citation: March on Washington (Program), August 28, 1963, Bayard Rustin Papers; John F. Kennedy Library; National Archives and Records Administration.

EXCERPTS FROM FEDERAL CONSTITUTIONAL
AMENDMENTS WHICH FURTHERED THE CAUSE
OF THE CIVIL RIGHTS MOVEMENT

A civil right is a benefit that allows one to bring a lawsuit against another who interfered with that privilege. Oppression occurs when the civil rights of an individual are denied or interfered with because of one's group membership. Attorneys with the National Association for the Advancement of Colored People and other civil rights organizations challenged laws that sanctioned racial discrimination as violations of the U.S. Constitution. The Due Process Clause and the Equal Protection Clause, two separate provisions in the Fourteenth Amendment, were the basis for many Supreme Court decisions that struck down state laws which treated black and white Americans differently. As discussed in Chapter five, lawsuits challenging deprivation of black Americans' civil rights were ultimately successful because of the Fourteenth Amendment. The Supreme Court played a crucial role in interpreting the extent of the civil rights guaranteed by the Constitution because a Court ruling can alter the recognition of a right throughout the country. The cases resulted in the removal of government-sanctioned restrictions against blacks in jury selection, public school and university admission, interracial marriage, public accommodations, and voting. They also eliminated legal discrimination in purchasing, selling, and leasing private property. The Fifteenth Amendment guaranteed African American men the right to vote without facing legalized discrimination. African American activists and civil rights organization often cited this amendment when organizing voter registration drives or attempting to register to vote as private citizens. In an attempt to protect all Americans' right to vote, the Twenty-fourth Amendment was added to the federal Constitution in 1964. It further guaranteed the right to vote for all Americans by eliminating taxes often assessed throughout the South to overcome any obstacles to participation in federal elections.

Fourteenth Amendment

Section 1

All persons born or naturalized in the United States, and subject to the jurisdiction thereof, are citizens of the United States and of the state wherein they reside. No state shall make or enforce any law which shall abridge the privileges or immunities of citizens of the United States; nor shall any state deprive any person of life, liberty, or property, without due process of law; nor deny to any person within its jurisdiction the equal protection of the laws

Fifteenth Amendment

Section 1

The right of citizens of the United States to vote shall not be denied or abridged by the United States or by any state on account of race, color, or previous condition of servitude.

Twenty-Fourth Amendment

Section 1

The right of citizens of the United States to vote in any primary or other election for President or Vice President, for electors for President or Vice President, or for Senator or Representative in Congress, shall not be denied or abridged by the United States or any state by reason of failure to pay any poll tax or other tax.

Source: The House Joint Resolution proposing the 14th amendment to the Constitution, June 16, 1866, 15th amendment to the Constitution, December 7, 1868, and 24th amendment to the Constitution, January 23, 1964; Enrolled Acts and Resolutions of Congress, 1789–1999; General Records of the United States Government; Record Group 11; National Archives.

KEY SECTIONS OF THE CIVIL RIGHTS ACT OF 1964

The Civil Rights Act of 1964 was enacted on July 4, 1964, after lobbying and nonviolent political demonstrations by civil rights activists. Prior to its passing, Presidents Truman, Eisenhower, and Kennedy and congress had passed acts and signed into law executive orders. However, none effectively stemmed the tide of continued racial discrimination. The 1964 Act amended and strengthened provisos of the 1957 Civil Rights Act and included clauses to further strengthen laws protecting African Americans. The act included several key provisions. Title I addressed discriminatory voting practices. It made it illegal for an individual or state to use literacy tests to disqualify someone from voting. Title II and III outlawed discrimination in public accommodations and federally funded facilities. Title IV addresses the continued racial segregation of public schools and provides recourse for African American families who are forced to send their children to segregated black schools. Title V makes clearer the role and duties of the Civil Rights Commission. Title VI halts discrimination in any institution receiving federal subsidies. Title VII establishes the Equal Opportunity Commission and makes it illegal to discriminate in the hiring practices on the basis of race, color, religion, sex or national origin. The Civil Rights Act of 1964 was a cause for great rejoicing in the United States especially among African Americans. Ultimately however, like the *Brown* decision, the Civil Rights Act of 1964 did not end racial segregation and the country would continue to search for remedies to centuries-long discrimination against its black citizens. But the legislation created a benchmark against which America could measure itself vis-à-vis its goals and constitutional standards.

An Act

To enforce the constitutional right to vote, to confer jurisdiction upon the district courts of the United States to provide injunctive relief against discrimination in public accommodations, to authorize the Attorney General to institute suits to protect constitutional rights in public facilities and public education, to extend the Commission on Civil Rights, to prevent discrimination in federally assisted programs, to establish a Commission on Equal Employment Opportunity, and for other purposes.

Title I—Voting Rights

SEC. 101.

"(2) No person acting under color of law shall—

"(A) in determining whether any individual is qualified under State law or laws to vote in any Federal election, apply any standard, practice, or procedure different from the standards, practices, or procedures applied under such law or laws to other individuals within the same county, parish, or similar political subdivision who have been found by State officials to be qualified to vote;

"(B) deny the right of any individual to vote in any Federal election because of an error or omission on any record or paper relating to any application, registration, or other act requisite to voting, if such error or omission is not material in determining whether such individual is qualified under State law to vote in such election; or

"(C) employ any literacy test as a qualification for voting in any Federal election unless (i) such test is administered to each individual and is conducted wholly in writing, and (ii) a certified copy of the test and of the answers given by the individual is furnished to him within twenty-five days of the submission of his request made within the period of time during which records and papers are required to be retained and preserved pursuant to title III of the Civil Rights Act of 1960.

Title II—Injunctive Relief against Discrimination in Places of Public Accommodation

SEC. 201. (a) All persons shall be entitled to the full and equal enjoyment of the goods, services, facilities, and privileges, advantages, and accommodations of any place of public accommodation, as defined in this section, without discrimination or segregation on the ground of race, color, religion, or national origin.

(b) Each of the following establishments which serves the public is a place of public accommodation within the meaning of this title if its operations affect commerce, or if discrimination or segregation by it is supported by State action:

(1) any inn, hotel, motel, or other establishment which provides lodging to transient guests, other than an establishment located within a building which contains not more than five rooms for rent or hire and which is actually occupied by the proprietor of such establishment as his residence;

(2) any restaurant, cafeteria, lunchroom, lunch counter, soda fountain, or other facility principally engaged in selling food for consumption on the premises, including, but not limited to, any such facility located on the premises of any retail establishment; or any gasoline station;

(3) any motion picture house, theater, concert hall, sports arena, stadium or other place of exhibition or entertainment; and

(4) any establishment (A)(i) which is physically located within the premises of any establishment otherwise covered by this subsection, or (ii) within the premises of which is physically located any such covered establishment, and (B) which holds itself out as serving patrons of such covered establishment.

SEC. 202. All persons shall be entitled to be free, at any establishment or place, from discrimination or segregation of any kind on the ground of race, color, religion, or national origin, if such discrimination or segregation is or purports to be required by any law, statute, ordinance, regulation, rule, or order of a State or any agency or political subdivision thereof.

SEC. 203. No person shall (a) withhold, deny, or attempt to withhold or deny, or deprive or attempt to deprive, any person of any right or privilege secured by section 201 or 202, or (b) intimidate, threaten, or coerce, or attempt to intimidate, threaten, or coerce any person with the purpose of interfering with any right or privilege secured by section 201 or 202, or (c) punish or attempt to punish any person for exercising or attempting to exercise any right or privilege secured by section 201 or 202.

Title IV—Desegregation of Public Education

Definitions

SEC. 401. As used in this title—

(a) "Commissioner" means the Commissioner of Education.

(b) "Desegregation" means the assignment of students to public schools and within such schools without regard to their race, color, religion, or national origin, but "desegregation" shall not mean the assignment of students to public schools in order to overcome racial imbalance.

(c) "Public school" means any elementary or secondary educational institution, and "public college" means any institution of higher education or any technical or vocational school above the secondary school level, provided that such public school or public college is operated by a State, subdivision of a State, or governmental agency within a State, or operated wholly or predominantly from or through the use of governmental funds or property, or funds or property derived from a governmental source.

(d) "School board" means any agency or agencies which administer a system of one or more public schools and any other agency which is responsible for the assignment of students to or within such system.

Title V—Commission on Civil Rights

"SEC. 104. (a) The Commission shall—

"(1) investigate allegations in writing under oath or affirmation that certain citizens of the United States are being deprived of their right to vote and have that vote counted by reason of their color, race, religion, or national origin; which writing, under oath or affirmation, shall set forth the facts upon which such belief or beliefs are based;

"(2) study and collect information concerning legal developments constituting a denial of equal protection of the laws under the Constitution because of race, color, religion or national origin or in the administration of justice;

"(3) appraise the laws and policies of the Federal Government with respect to denials of equal protection of the laws under the Constitution because of race, color, religion or national origin or in the administration of justice;

"(4) serve as a national clearinghouse for information in respect to denials of equal protection of the laws because of race, color, religion or national origin, including but not limited to the fields of voting, education, housing, employment, the use of public facilities, and transportation, or in the administration of justice;

"(5) investigate allegations, made in writing and under oath or affirmation, that citizens of the United States are unlawfully being accorded or denied the right to vote, or to have their votes properly counted, in any election of presidential electors, Members of the United States Senate, or of the House of Representatives, as a result of any patterns or practice of fraud or discrimination in the conduct of such election; and

Title VI—Nondiscrimination in Federally Assisted Programs

SEC. 601. No person in the United States shall, on the ground of race, color, or national origin, be excluded from participation in, be denied the benefits of, or be subjected to discrimination under any program or activity receiving Federal financial assistance.

Title VII—Equal Employment Opportunity

SEC. 703. (a) It shall be an unlawful employment practice for an employer—

(1) to fail or refuse to hire or to discharge any individual, or otherwise to discriminate against any individual with respect to his compensation, terms, conditions, or privileges of employment, because of such individual's race, color, religion, sex, or national origin; or

(2) to limit, segregate, or classify his employees in any way which would deprive or tend to deprive any individual of employment opportunities or otherwise adversely affect his status as an employee, because of such individual's race, color, religion, sex, or national origin.

(b) It shall be an unlawful employment practice for an employment agency to fail or refuse to refer for employment, or otherwise to discriminate against, any individual because of his race, color, religion, sex, or national origin, or to classify or refer for employment any individual on the basis of his race, color, religion, sex, or national origin.

(c) It shall be an unlawful employment practice for a labor organization—

(1) to exclude or to expel from its membership, or otherwise to discriminate against, any individual because of his race, color, religion, sex, or national origin;

(2) to limit, segregate, or classify its membership, or to classify or fail or refuse to refer for employment any individual, in any way which would deprive or tend to deprive any individual of employment opportunities, or would limit such employment opportunities or otherwise adversely affect his status as an employee or as an applicant for employment, because of such individual's race, color, religion, sex, or national origin; or

(3) to cause or attempt to cause an employer to discriminate against an individual in violation of this section.

(d) It shall be an unlawful employment practice for any employer, labor organization, or joint labor-management committee controlling apprenticeship or other training or retraining, including on-the-job training programs to discriminate against any individual because of his race, color, religion, sex, or national origin in admission to, or employment in, any program established to provide apprenticeship or other training.

Other Unlawful Employment Practices

SEC. 704. (a) It shall be an unlawful employment practice for an employer to discriminate against any of his employees or applicants for employment, for an employment agency to discriminate against any individual, or for a labor organization to discriminate against any member thereof or applicant for membership, because he has opposed, any practice made an unlawful employment practice by this title, or because he has made a charge, testified, assisted, or participated in any manner in an investigation, proceeding, or hearing under this title.

(b) It shall be an unlawful employment practice for an employer, labor organization, or employment agency to print or publish or cause to be printed or published any notice or advertisement relating to employment by such an employer or membership in or any classification or referral for employment by such a labor organization, or relating to any classification or referral for employment by such an employment agency, indicating any preference, limitation, specification, or discrimination, based on race, color, religion, sex, or national origin, except that such a notice or advertisement may indicate a preference, limitation, specification, or discrimination based on religion, sex, or national origin when religion, sex, or national origin is a bona fide occupational qualification for employment.

Equal Employment Opportunity Commission

SEC. 705. (a) There is hereby created a Commission to be known as the Equal Employment Opportunity Commission, which shall be composed of five members, not more than three of whom shall be members of the same political party, who shall be appointed by the President by and with the advice and consent of the Senate. One of the original members shall be appointed for a term of one year, one for a term of two years, one for a term of three years, one for a term of four years, and one for a term of five years, beginning from the date of enactment of this title, but their successors shall be appointed for terms of five years each, except that any individual chosen to fill a vacancy shall be appointed only for the unexpired term of the member whom he shall succeed. The President shall designate one member to serve as Chairman of the Commission, and one member to serve as Vice Chairman. The Chairman shall be responsible on behalf of the Commission for the administrative operations of the Commission, and shall appoint, in accordance with the civil service laws, such officers, agents, attorneys, and employees as it deems necessary to assist it in the performance of its functions and to fix their compensation in accordance with the Classification Act of 1949, as amended. The Vice Chairman shall act as Chairman in the absence or disability of the Chairman or in the event of a vacancy in that office.

(b) A vacancy in the Commission shall not impair the right of the remaining members to exercise all the powers of the Commission and three members thereof shall constitute a quorum.

(g) The Commission shall have power—

(1) to cooperate with and, with their consent, utilize regional, State, local, and other agencies, both public and private, and individuals;

(2) to pay to witnesses whose depositions are taken or who are summoned before the Commission or any of its agents the same witness and mileage fees as are paid to witnesses in the courts of the United States;

(3) to furnish to persons subject to this title such technical assistance as they may request to further their compliance with this title or an order issued thereunder;

(4) upon the request of (i) any employer, whose employees or some of them, or (ii) any labor organization, whose members or some of them, refuse or threaten to refuse to cooperate in effectuating the provisions of this title, to assist in such effectuation by conciliation or such other remedial action as is provided by this title;

(5) to make such technical studies as are appropriate to effectuate the purposes and policies of this title and to make the results of such studies available to the public;

(6) to refer matters to the Attorney General with recommendations for intervention in a civil action brought by an aggrieved party under section 706, or for the institution of a civil action by the Attorney General under section 707, and to advise, consult, and assist the Attorney General on such matters.

(h) Attorneys appointed under this section may, at the direction of the Commission, appear for and represent the Commission in any case in court.

(i) The Commission shall, in any of its educational or promotional activities, cooperate with other departments and agencies in the performance of such educational and promotional activities.

Prevention of Unlawful Employment Practices

SEC. 706. (a) Whenever it is charged in writing under oath by a person claiming to be aggrieved, or a written charge has been filed by a member of the Commission where he has reasonable cause to believe a violation of this title has occurred (and such charge sets forth the facts upon which it is based) that an employer, employment agency, or labor organization has engaged in an unlawful employment practice, the Commission shall furnish such employer, employment agency, or labor organization (hereinafter referred to as the "respondent") with a copy of such charge and shall make an investigation of such charge, provided that such charge shall not be made public by the Commission. If the Commission shall determine, after such investigation, that there is reasonable cause to believe that the charge is true, the Commission shall endeavor to eliminate any such alleged unlawful employment practice by informal methods of conference, conciliation, and persuasion. Nothing said or done during and as a part of such endeavors may be made public by the Commission without the written consent of the parties, or used as evidence in a subsequent proceeding. Any officer or employee of the Commission, who shall make public in any manner whatever any information in violation of this subsection shall be deemed guilty of a misdemeanor and upon conviction thereof shall be fined not more than $1,000 or imprisoned not more than one year.

(b) In the case of an alleged unlawful employment practice occurring in a State, or political subdivision of a State, which has a State or local law prohibiting the unlawful employment practice alleged and establishing or authorizing a State or local authority to grant or seek relief from such practice or to institute criminal proceedings with respect thereto upon receiving notice thereof, no charge may be filed under subsection (a) by the person aggrieved before the expiration of sixty days after proceedings have been commenced under the State or local law, unless such proceedings have been earlier terminated, provided that such sixty-day period shall be extended to one hundred and twenty days during the first year after the effective date of such State or local law. If any requirement for the commencement of such proceedings is imposed by a State or local authority other than a requirement of the filing of a written and signed statement of the facts upon which the proceeding is based, the proceeding shall be deemed to have been commenced for the purposes of this subsection at the time such statement is sent by registered mail to the appropriate State or local authority.

(c) In the case of any charge filed by a member of the Commission alleging an unlawful employment practice occurring in a State or political subdivision of a State, which has a State or local law prohibiting the practice alleged and establishing or authorizing a State or local authority to grant or seek relief from such practice or to institute criminal proceedings with respect thereto upon receiving notice thereof, the Commission shall, before taking any action with respect to such charge, notify the appropriate State or local officials and, upon request, afford them a reasonable time, but not less than sixty days (provided that such sixty-day period shall be extended to one hundred and twenty days during the first year after the effective day of such State or local law), unless a shorter period is requested, to act under such State or local law to remedy the practice alleged.

(d) A charge under subsection (a) shall be filed within ninety days after the alleged unlawful employment practice occurred, except that in the case of an unlawful employment practice with respect to which the person aggrieved has followed the procedure set out in subsection (b), such charge shall be filed by the person aggrieved within two hundred and ten days after the alleged unlawful employment practice occurred, or within thirty days after receiving notice that the State or local agency has terminated the proceedings under the State or local, law, whichever is earlier, and a copy of such charge shall be filed by the Commission with the State or local agency.

(e) If within thirty days after a charge is filed with the Commission or within thirty days after expiration of any period of reference under subsection (c) (except that in either case such period may be extended to not more than sixty days upon a determination by the Commission that further efforts to secure voluntary compliance are warranted), the Commission has been unable to obtain voluntary compliance with this title, the Commission shall so notify the person aggrieved and a civil action may, within thirty days thereafter, be brought against the respondent named in the charge (1) by the person claiming to be aggrieved, or (2) if such charge was filed by a member of the Commission, by any person whom the charge alleges was aggrieved by the alleged unlawful employment practice. Upon application by the complainant and in such circumstances as the court may deem just, the court may appoint an attorney for such complainant and may authorize the commencement of the action without the payment of fees, costs, or security. Upon timely application, the court may, in its discretion, permit the Attorney General to intervene in such civil action if he certifies that the case is of general public importance. Upon request, the court may, in its discretion, stay further proceedings for not more than sixty days pending the termination of State or local proceedings described in subsection (b) or the efforts of the Commission to obtain voluntary compliance.

(f) Each United States district court and each United States court of a place subject to the jurisdiction of the United States shall have jurisdiction of actions brought under this title. Such an action may be brought in any judicial district in the State in which the unlawful employment practice is alleged to have been committed, in the judicial district in which the employment records relevant to such practice are maintained and administered, or in the judicial district in which the plaintiff would have worked but for the alleged unlawful employment practice, but if the respondent is not found within any such district, such an action may be brought within the judicial district in which the respondent has his principal office. For purposes of sections 1404 and 1406 of title 28 of the United States Code, the judicial district in which the respondent has his principal office shall in all cases be considered a district in which the action might have been brought.

(g) If the court finds that the respondent has intentionally engaged in or is intentionally engaging in an unlawful employment practice charged in the complaint, the court may enjoin the respondent from engaging in such unlawful employment practice, and order such affirmative action as may be appropriate, which may include reinstatement or hiring of employees, with or without back pay (payable by the employer, employment agency, or labor organization, as the case may be, responsible for the unlawful employment practice). Interim earnings or amounts earnable with reasonable diligence by the person or persons discriminated against shall operate to reduce the back pay otherwise allowable. No order of the court shall require the admission or reinstatement of an individual as a member of a union or the hiring, reinstatement, or promotion of an individual as an employee, or the payment to him of any back pay, if such individual was refused admission, suspended, or expelled or was refused employment or advancement or was suspended or discharged for any reason other than discrimination on account of race, color,

SEC. 707. (a) Whenever the Attorney General has reasonable cause to believe that any person or group of persons is engaged in a pattern or practice of resistance to the full enjoyment of any of the rights secured by this title, and that the pattern or practice is of such a nature and is intended to deny the full exercise of the rights herein described, the Attorney General may bring a civil action in the appropriate district court of the United States by filing with it a complaint (1) signed by him (or in his absence the Acting Attorney General), (2) setting forth facts pertaining to such pattern or practice, and (3) requesting such relief, including an application for a permanent or temporary injunction, restraining order or other order against the person or persons responsible for such pattern or practice, as he deems necessary to insure the full enjoyment of the rights herein described.

(b) The district courts of the United States shall have and shall exercise jurisdiction of proceedings instituted pursuant to this section, and in any such proceeding the Attorney General may file with the clerk of such court a request that a court of three judges be convened to hear and determine the case. Such request by the Attorney General shall be accompanied by a certificate that, in his opinion, the case is of general public importance. A copy of the certificate and request for a three-judge court shall be immediately furnished by such clerk to the chief judge of the circuit (or in his absence, the presiding circuit judge of the circuit) in which the case is pending. Upon receipt of such request it shall be the duty of the chief judge of the circuit or the presiding circuit judge, as the case may be, to designate immediately three judges in such circuit, of whom at least one shall be a circuit judge and another of whom shall be a district judge of the court in which the proceeding was instituted, to hear and determine such case, and it shall be the duty of the judges so designated to assign the case for hearing at the earliest practicable date, to participate in the hearing and determination thereof, and to cause the case to be in every way expedited. An appeal from the final judgment of such court will lie to the Supreme Court.

In the event the Attorney General fails to file such a request in any such proceeding, it shall be the duty of the chief judge of the district (or in his absence, the acting chief judge) in which the case is pending immediately to designate a judge in such district to hear and determine the case. In the event that no judge in the district is available to hear and determine the case, the chief judge of the district, or the acting chief judge, as the case may be, shall certify this fact to the chief judge of the circuit (or in his absence, the acting chief judge) who shall then designate a district or circuit judge of the circuit to hear and determine the case.

It shall be the duty of the judge designated pursuant to this section to assign the case for hearing at the earliest practicable date and to cause the case to be in every way expedited.

Investigations, Inspections, Records, State Agencies

SEC. 709. (a) In connection with any investigation of a charge filed under section 706, the Commission or its designated representative shall at all reasonable times have access to, for the purposes of examination, and the right to copy any evidence of any person being investigated or proceeded against that relates to unlawful employment practices covered by this title and is relevant to the charge under investigation.

(b) The Commission may cooperate with State and local agencies charged with the administration of State fair employment practices laws and, with the consent of such agencies, may for the purpose of carrying out its functions and duties under this title and within the limitation of funds appropriated specifically for such purpose, utilize the services of such agencies and their employees and, notwithstanding any other provision of law, may reimburse such agencies and their employees for services rendered to assist the Commission in carrying out this title. In furtherance of such cooperative efforts, the Commission may enter into written agreements with such State or local agencies and such agreements may include provisions under which the Commission shall refrain from processing a charge in any cases or class of cases specified in such agreements and under which no person may bring a civil action under section 706 in any cases or class of cases so specified, or under which the Commission shall relieve any person or class of persons in such State or locality from requirements imposed under this section. The Commission shall rescind any such agreement whenever it determines that the agreement no longer serves the interest of effective enforcement of this title.

(c) Except as provided in subsection (d), every employer, employment agency, and labor organization subject to this title shall (1) make and keep such records relevant to the determinations of whether unlawful employment practices have been or are being committed, (2) preserve such records for such periods, and (3) make such reports therefrom, as the Commission shall prescribe by regulation or order, after public hearing, as reasonable, necessary, or appropriate for the enforcement of this title or the regulations or orders thereunder. The Commission shall, by regulation, require each employer, labor organization, and joint labor-management committee subject to this title which controls an apprenticeship or other training program to maintain such records as are reasonably necessary to carry out the purpose of this title, including, but not limited to, a list of applicants who wish to participate in such program, including the chronological order in which such applications were received, and shall furnish to the Commission, upon request, a detailed description of the manner in which persons are selected to participate in the apprenticeship or other training program. Any employer, employment agency, labor organization, or joint labor-management committee which believes that the application to it of any regulation or order issued under this section would result in undue hardship may (1) apply to the Commission for an exemption from the application of such regulation or order, or (2) bring a civil action in the United States district court for the district where such records are kept. If the Commission or the court, as the case may be, finds that the application of the regulation or order to the employer, employment agency, or labor organization in question would impose an undue hardship, the Commission or the court, as the case may be, may grant appropriate relief.

(d) The provisions of subsection (c) shall not apply to any employer, employment agency, labor organization, or joint labor-management committee with respect to matters occurring in any State or political subdivision thereof which has a fair employment practice law during any period in which such employer, employment agency, labor organization, or joint labor-management committee is subject to such law, except that the Commission may require such notations on records which such employer, employment agency, labor organization, or joint labor-management committee keeps or is required to keep as are necessary because of differences in coverage or methods of enforcement between the State or local law and the provisions of this title. Where an employer is required by Executive Order

10925, issued March 6, 1961, or by any other Executive order prescribing fair employment practices for Government contractors and subcontractors, or by rules or regulations issued thereunder, to file reports relating to his employment practices with any Federal agency or committee, and he is substantially in compliance with such requirements, the Commission shall not require him to file additional reports pursuant to subsection (c) of this section.

(e) It shall be unlawful for any officer or employee of the Commission to make public in any manner whatever any information obtained by the Commission pursuant to its authority under this section prior to the institution of any proceeding under this title involving such information. Any officer or employee of the Commission who shall make public in any manner whatever any information in violation of this subsection shall be guilty of a misdemeanor and upon conviction thereof, shall be fined not more than $1,000, or imprisoned not more than one year.

Investigatory Powers

SEC. 710. (a) For the purposes of any investigation of a charge filed under the authority contained in section 706, the Commission shall have authority to examine witnesses under oath and to require the production of documentary evidence relevant or material to the charge under investigation.

SEC. 711. (a) Every employer, employment agency, and labor organization, as the case may be, shall post and keep posted in conspicuous places upon its premises where notices to employees, applicants for employment, and members are customarily posted a notice to be prepared or approved by the Commission setting forth excerpts from or, summaries of, the pertinent provisions of this title and information pertinent to the filing of a complaint.

(b) A willful violation of this section shall be punishable by a fine of not more than $100 for each separate offense.

Source: Citation: An act to enforce the constitutional right to vote, to confer jurisdiction upon the district courts of the United States, to provide injunctive relief against discrimination in public accommodations, to authorize the Attorney General to institute suits to protect constitutional rights in public facilities and public education, to extend the Commission on Civil Rights, to prevent discrimination in federally assisted programs, to establish a Commission on Equal Employment Opportunity, and for other purposes, July 2, 1964; Enrolled Acts and Resolutions of Congress, 1789–; General Records of the United States Government; Record Group 11; National Archives.

A LETTER FROM MRS. E. JACKSON TO THE
HOUSE JUDICIARY COMMITTEE, MARCH 8, 1965

In 1965, the modern Civil Rights Movement was over a decade old. Despite outside calls for civil rights organizations to cease demanding change, movement people and groups continued their unrelenting struggle to secure constitutional rights for African Americans. White clergymen and college-age white students participated as foot soldiers in the struggle as seen in the 1964 Freedom Summer and the 1965 Selma to Montgomery March. Most white Americans, however, though outraged by blatant and televised abuse of black demonstrators by white southerners did not have the ability, inclination, or wherewithal to participate in civil rights demonstrations. Of those who did not, many sent letters to Congress like the letter below. The letter is dated March 8. 1965, a day after Bloody Sunday, the day black and white protestors attempted to continue a peaceful march across the Edmund Pettus Bridge in Selma, Alabama, but were met with wanton brutality at the hands of the police. By this time, nightly news programs were airing civil rights protests and civil rights organizations used the medium to expose the injustices throughout the South. The brutality meted out that day was on the evening news, so citizens around country had the opportunity to view the violence against fellow American citizens. Though short, the letter reveals the outrage felt by thousands of white Americans. It suggests that the ubiquitous "we" had spent some time sitting idly by while blacks were denied basic constitutional rights, but the events of March 7 jolted them into support of blacks and efforts to effect change. The reader should note the letter is addressed to the House Judiciary Committee, a congressional committee whose purview includes, among other things, constitutional amendments and civil liberties. The letter also alludes to the Vietnam War indicating a growing anti-war sentiment, which in 1965, was a smoldering ember about to ignite into a full fledge anti-war movement.

1460 Sterling Place #1G
Brooklyn 13, N.Y.

March 8, 1965

Dear Sir:

For God sakes help those poor innocent people in Selma Alabama. If your voice or vote can be of service now is the time to use it. We can't sit by any longer and watch the shocking events in Ala. Send troops there not overseas and protect those people right to *vote*. It's sicken [sic] and as a mother of *four sons* I can't stand it any longer. To think that one day my sons could lose their lives protecting those ignorant people down there is unbelievable.

Sincerely,
Mrs. E. Jackson

Citation: Letter from Mrs. E. Jackson in Favor of Voting Rights, *03/08/1964;* Bill Files, *compiled 1903–1968;* Records of the U.S. House of Representatives, *1789–2011;* Center for Legislative Archives (NWL), National Archives Building, Room 8E, 7th and Pennsylvania Avenue NW, Washington, DC, 20408 [online version available through the Archival Research Catalog (ARC Identifier 2173239) at www.archives.gov, January 4, 2012].

LYNDON B. JOHNSON, *WE SHALL OVERCOME*, MARCH 15, 1965

The speech lays the foundation for the Voting Rights Act passed in August 1965 and Johnson's attempts at creating social welfare programs of the late 1960s. The speech is titled "We Shall Overcome" because Johnson invokes the popular black freedom song of the same name in his speech. It was given shortly after the events of Sunday, March 7, 1965, called Bloody Sunday, when black and white demonstrators tried to cross the Edmund Pettus Bridge in Selma, Alabama, in an attempt to continue a peaceful march to Montgomery, Alabama. Johnson declares that the problems facing African Americans are national problems and uses moral persuasion to convince congress to have political courage and end voting discrimination. He recognizes that legal and extralegal tactics continued to be used throughout the South to prevent blacks from voting because the Civil Rights Act of 1964 did not go far enough in addressing voting discrepancies. Insuring the right to vote of all citizens and enabling citizens to become active participants in the democracy, he admits, is a difficult task, because of persistent racism and racial discrimination throughout the nation and because southern politicians were unwilling or unable to honor their oath of office. He places African Americans' struggle for voting rights within a century-long national narrative, deems their struggle as one for human rights, and says that voting rights are, and should be, guaranteed by the Constitution and obtained by all citizens. Surprising for the times, because of the country's growing weariness with the Civil Rights Movement, Johnson also calls for the protection of civil rights demonstrators by authorities and a protection of black citizens' right to freedom of assembly. He ends with a call for bipartisanship in congress to work to secure basic rights for its citizens.

I speak tonight for the dignity of man and the destiny of Democracy. I urge every member of both parties, Americans of all religions and of all colors, from every section of this country, to join me in that cause.

At times, history and fate meet at a single time in a single place to shape a turning point in man's unending search for freedom. So it was at Lexington and Concord. So it was a century ago at Appomattox. So it was last week in Selma, Alabama. There, long suffering men and women peacefully protested the denial of their rights as Americans. Many of them were brutally assaulted. One good man—a man of God—was killed.

There is no cause for pride in what has happened in Selma. There is no cause for self-satisfaction in the long denial of equal rights of millions of Americans. But there is cause for hope and for faith in our Democracy in what is happening here tonight. For the cries of pain and the hymns and protests of oppressed people have summoned into convocation all the majesty of this great government—the government of the greatest nation on earth. Our mission is at once the oldest and the most basic of this country— to right wrong, to do justice, to serve man. In our time we have come to live with the moments of great crises. Our lives have been marked with debate about great issues, issues of war and peace, issues of prosperity and depression.

But rarely in any time does an issue lay bare the secret heart of America itself. Rarely are we met with a challenge, not to our growth or abundance, or our welfare or our security, but rather to the values and the purposes and the meaning of our beloved nation. The issue of equal rights for American Negroes is such an issue. And should we defeat every enemy, and should we double our wealth and conquer the stars, and still be unequal to this issue, then we will have failed as a people and as a nation. For, with a country as with a person, "what is a man profited if he shall gain the whole world, and lose his own soul?"

There is no Negro problem. There is no Southern problem. There is no Northern problem. There is only an American problem.

And we are met here tonight as Americans—not as Democrats or Republicans; we're met here as Americans to solve that problem. This was the first nation in the history of the world to be founded with a purpose.

The great phrases of that purpose still sound in every American heart, North and South: "All men are created equal." "Government by consent of the governed." "Give me liberty or give me death." And those are not just clever words, and those are not just empty theories. In their name Americans have fought and died for two centuries and tonight around the world they stand there as guardians of our liberty risking their lives. Those words are promised to every citizen that he shall share in the dignity of man. This dignity cannot be found in a man's possessions. It cannot be found in his power or in his position. It really rests on his right to be treated as a man equal in opportunity to all others. It says that he shall share in freedom. He shall choose his leaders, educate his children, provide for his family according to his ability and his merits as a human being.

To apply any other test, to deny a man his hopes because of his color or race or his religion or the place of his birth is not only to do injustice, it is to deny Americans and to dishonor the dead who gave their lives for American freedom. Our fathers believed that if this noble view of the rights of man was to flourish it must be rooted in democracy. This most basic right of all was the right to choose your own leaders. The history of this country in large measure is the history of expansion of the right to all of our people.

Many of the issues of civil rights are very complex and most difficult. But about this there can and should be no argument: every American citizen must have an equal right to vote. There is no reason which can excuse the denial of that right. There is no duty which weighs more heavily on us than the duty we have to insure that right. Yet the harsh fact is that in many places in this country men and women are kept from voting simply because they are Negroes.

Every device of which human ingenuity is capable, has been used to deny this right. The Negro citizen may go to register only to be told that the day is wrong, or the hour is late, or the official in charge is absent. And if he persists and, if he manages to present himself to the registrar, he may be disqualified because he did not spell out his middle name, or because he abbreviated a word on the application. And if he manages to fill out an application, he is given a test. The registrar is the sole judge of whether he passes this test. He may be asked to recite the entire Constitution, or explain the most complex provisions of state law.

And even a college degree cannot be used to prove that he can read and write. For the fact is that the only way to pass these barriers is to show a white skin. Experience has clearly shown that the existing process of law cannot overcome systematic and ingenious discrimination. No law that we now have on the books, and I have helped to put three of them there, can insure the right to vote when local officials are determined to deny it. In such a case, our duty must be clear to all of us. The Constitution says that no person shall be kept from voting because of his race or his color.

We have all sworn an oath before God to support and to defend that Constitution. We must now act in obedience to that oath. Wednesday, I will send to Congress a law designed to eliminate illegal barriers to the right to vote. The broad principles of that bill will be in the hands of the Democratic and Republican leaders tomorrow. After they have reviewed it, it will come here formally as a bill. I am grateful for this opportunity to come here tonight at the invitation of the leadership to reason with my friends, to give them my views and to visit with my former colleagues.

I have had prepared a more comprehensive analysis of the legislation which I had intended to transmit to the clerk tomorrow, but which I will submit to the clerks tonight. But I want to really discuss the main proposals of this legislation. This bill will strike down restrictions to voting in all elections, federal, state and local, which have been used to deny Negroes the right to vote.

This bill will establish a simple, uniform standard which cannot be used, however ingenious the effort, to flout our Constitution. It will provide for citizens to be registered by officials of the United States Government, if the state officials refuse to register them. It will eliminate tedious, unnecessary lawsuits which delay the right to vote. Finally, this legislation will insure that properly registered individuals are not prohibited from voting. I will welcome the suggestions from all the members of Congress—I have no doubt that I will get some—on ways and means to strengthen this law and to make it effective.

But experience has plainly shown that this is the only path to carry out the command of the Constitution. To those who seek to avoid action by their national government in their home communities, who want to and who seek to maintain purely local control over elections, the answer is simple: open your polling places to all your people. Allow men and women to register and vote whatever the color of their skin. Extend the rights of citizenship to every citizen of this land. There is no Constitutional issue here. The command of the Constitution is plain. There is no moral issue. It is wrong—deadly wrong—to deny any of your fellow Americans the right to vote in this country.

There is no issue of state's rights or national rights. There is only the struggle for human rights. I have not the slightest doubt what will be your answer. But the last time a President sent a civil rights bill to the Congress it contained a provision to protect voting rights in Federal elections. That civil rights bill was passed after eight long months of debate. And when that bill came to my desk from the Congress for signature, the heart of the voting provision had been eliminated.

This time, on this issue, there must be no delay, or no hesitation, or no compromise with our purpose. We cannot, we must not, refuse to protect the right of every American to vote in every election that he may desire to participate in.

And we ought not, and we cannot, and we must not wait another eight months before we get a bill. We have already waited 100 years and more and the time for waiting is gone. So I ask you to join me in working long hours and nights and weekends, if necessary, to pass this bill. And I don't make that request lightly, for, from the window where I sit, with the problems of our country, I recognize that from outside this chamber is the outraged conscience of a nation, the grave concern of many nations and the harsh judgment of history on our acts.

But even if we pass this bill the battle will not be over. What happened in Selma is part of a far larger movement which reaches into every section and state of America. It is the effort of American Negroes to secure for themselves the full blessings of American life. Their cause must be our cause too. Because it's not just Negroes, but really it's all of us, who must overcome the crippling legacy of bigotry and injustice.

And we shall overcome.

As a man whose roots go deeply into Southern soil, I know how agonizing racial feelings are. I know how difficult it is to reshape the attitudes and the structure of our society. But a century has passed—more than 100 years—since the Negro was freed. And he is not fully free tonight. It was more than 100 years ago that Abraham Lincoln—a great President of another party—signed the Emancipation Proclamation. But emancipation is a proclamation and not a fact.

A century has passed—more than 100 years—since equality was promised, and yet the Negro is not equal. A century has passed since the day of promise, and the promise is unkept. The time of justice has now come, and I tell you that I believe sincerely that no force can hold it back. It is right in the eyes of man and God that it should come, and when it does, I think that day will brighten the lives of every American. For Negroes are not the only victims. How many white children have gone uneducated? How many white families have lived in stark poverty? How many white lives have been scarred by fear, because we wasted energy and our substance to maintain the barriers of hatred and terror?

And so I say to all of you here and to all in the nation tonight that those who appeal to you to hold on to the past do so at the cost of denying you your future. This great rich, restless country can offer opportunity and education and hope to all—all, black and white, North and South, sharecropper and city dweller. These are the enemies: poverty, ignorance, disease. They are our enemies, not our fellow man, not our neighbor.

And these enemies too—poverty, disease and ignorance—we shall overcome.

Now let none of us in any section look with prideful righteousness on the troubles in another section or the problems of our neighbors. There is really no part of America where the promise of equality has been fully kept. In Buffalo as well as in Birmingham, in Philadelphia as well as Selma, Americans are struggling for the fruits of freedom.

This is one nation. What happens in Selma and Cincinnati is a matter of legitimate concern to every American. But let each of us look within our own hearts and our own communities and let each of us put our shoulder to the wheel to root out injustice wherever it exists. As we meet here in this peaceful historic chamber tonight, men from the South, some of whom were at Iwo Jima, men from the North who have carried Old Glory to the far corners of the world and who brought it back without a stain on it, men from the east and from the west are all fighting together without regard to religion or color or region in Vietnam.

Men from every region fought for us across the world 20 years ago. And now in these common dangers, in these common sacrifices, the South made its contribution of honor and gallantry no less than any other region in the great republic.

And in some instances, a great many of them, more. And I have not the slightest doubt that good men from everywhere in this country, from the Great Lakes to the Gulf of Mexico, from the Golden Gate to the harbors along the Atlantic, will rally now together in this cause to vindicate the freedom of all Americans. For all of us owe this duty and I believe that all of us will respond to it.

Your president makes that request of every American.

The real hero of this struggle is the American Negro. His actions and protests, his courage to risk safety, and even to risk his life, have awakened the conscience of this nation. His demonstrations have been designed to call attention to injustice, designed to provoke change; designed to stir reform. He has been called upon to make good the promise of America.

And who among us can say that we would have made the same progress were it not for his persistent bravery and his faith in American democracy? For at the real heart of the battle for equality is a deep-seated belief in the democratic process. Equality depends, not on the force of arms or tear gas, but depends upon the force of moral right—not on recourse to violence, but on respect for law and order.

There have been many pressures upon your President and there will be others as the days come and go. But I pledge to you tonight that we intend to fight this battle where it should be fought—in the courts, and in the Congress, and the hearts of men. We must preserve the right of free speech and the right of free assembly. But the right of free speech does not carry with it—as has been said—the right to holler fire in a crowded theatre.

We must preserve the right to free assembly. But free assembly does not carry with it the right to block public thoroughfares to traffic. We do have a right to protest. And a right to march under conditions that do not infringe the Constitutional rights of our neighbors. And I intend to protect all those rights as long as I am permitted to serve in this office.

We will guard against violence, knowing it strikes from our hands the very weapons which we seek—progress, obedience to law, and belief in American values. In Selma, as elsewhere, we seek and pray for peace. We seek order, we seek unity, but we will not accept the peace of stifled rights or the order imposed by fear, or the unity that stifles protest—for peace cannot be purchased at the cost of liberty.

In Selma tonight—and we had a good day there—as in every city we are working for a just and peaceful settlement. We must all remember after this speech I'm making tonight, after the police and the F.B.I. and the Marshals have all gone, and after you have promptly passed this bill, the people of Selma and the other cities of the nation must still live and work together.

And when the attention of the nation has gone elsewhere they must try to heal the wounds and to build a new community. This cannot be easily done on a battleground of violence as the history of the South itself shows. It is in recognition of this that men of both races have shown such an outstandingly impressive responsibility in recent days—last Tuesday and again today.

The bill I am presenting to you will be known as a civil rights bill. But in a larger sense, most of the program I am recommending is a civil rights program. Its object is to open the city of hope to all people of all races, because all Americans just must have the right to vote, and we are going to give them that right.

All Americans must have the privileges of citizenship, regardless of race, and they are going to have those privileges of citizenship regardless of race.

But I would like to caution you and remind you that to exercise these privileges takes much more than just legal rights. It requires a trained mind and a healthy body. It requires a decent home and the chance to find a job and the opportunity to escape from the clutches of poverty.

Of course people cannot contribute to the nation if they are never taught to read or write; if their bodies are stunted from hunger; if their sickness goes untended; if their life is spent in hopeless poverty, just drawing a welfare check.

So we want to open the gates to opportunity. But we're also going to give all our people, black and white, the help that they need to walk through those gates. My first job after college was as a teacher in Cotulla, Texas, in a small Mexican-American school. Few of them could speak English and I couldn't speak much Spanish. My students were poor and they often came to class without breakfast and hungry. And they knew even in their youth the pain of prejudice. They never seemed to know why people disliked them, but they knew it was so because I saw it in their eyes.

I often walked home late in the afternoon after the classes were finished wishing there was more that I could do. But all I knew was to teach them the little that I knew, hoping that I might help them against the hardships that lay ahead. And somehow you never forget what poverty and hatred can do when you see its scars on the hopeful face of a young child.

I never thought then, in 1928, that I would be standing here in 1965. It never even occurred to me in my fondest dreams that I might have the chance to help the sons and daughters of those students, and to help people like them all over this country. But now I do have that chance.

And I'll let you in on a secret—I mean to use it. And I hope that you will use it with me.

This is the richest, most powerful country which ever occupied this globe. The might of past empires is little compared to ours. But I do not want to be the president who built empires, or sought grandeur, or extended dominion.

I want to be the president who educated young children to the wonders of their world. I want to be the President who helped to feed the hungry and to prepare them to be taxpayers instead of tax eaters. I want to be the President who helped the poor to find their own way and who protected the right of every citizen to vote in every election. I want to be the President who helped to end hatred among his fellow men and who promoted love among the people of all races, all regions and all parties. I want to be the President who helped to end war among the brothers of this earth.

And so, at the request of your beloved Speaker and the Senator from Montana, the Majority Leader, the Senator from Illinois, the Minority Leader, Mr. McCullock and other members of both parties, I came here tonight, not as President Roosevelt came down one time in person to veto a bonus bill; not as President Truman came down one time to urge passage of a railroad bill, but I came down here to ask you to share this task with me. And to share it with the people that we both work for.

I want this to be the Congress—Republicans and Democrats alike—which did all these things for all these people. Beyond this great chamber—out yonder—in fifty states are the people that we serve. Who can tell what deep and unspoken hopes are in their hearts tonight as they sit there and listen? We all can guess, from our own lives, how difficult they often find their own pursuit of happiness, how many problems each little family has. They look most of all to themselves for their future, but I think that they also look to each of us.

Above the pyramid on the Great Seal of the United States it says in latin, "God has favored our undertaking." God will not favor everything that we do. It is rather our duty to divine His will. But I cannot help but believe that He truly understands and that He really favors the undertaking that we begin here tonight.

Source: President Lyndon B. Johnson. "We Shall Overcome," Public Speech. March 15, 1965.

KEY SECTIONS OF THE VOTING RIGHTS ACT OF 1965, AUGUST 6, 1965

The Voting Rights Act of 1965 bolsters the Fifteenth Amendment to the Constitution and Title I of the Civil Rights Act of 1964. The Fifteenth Amendment was passed in 1870 and forbade the federal or states' governments to deny men the right to vote based on "race, color, or previous condition of servitude." The Civil Rights Act of 1964 inadvertently allowed the denial of voting rights by permitting the use of literacy tests when they were given to all seeking to register to vote and if they were given entirely in writing rather than orally. Despite the stipulation that everyone was to take a literacy test if such tests were given, the literacy tests continued to be selectively given to African Americans, making a new and more robust law necessary. The Voting Rights Act explicitly prohibits states and municipalities from setting prerequisites of any type (literacy tests, character tests, or educational attainment) for voting in federal elections. Section Five of the Act makes it mandatory for states, mostly in the Deep South, to obtain approval from the U.S. Department of Justice before they change electoral procedures in their states. Section Twelve stipulates penalties for individuals who impede another's right to vote. At the time of its passing, the law was primarily intended to protect African Americans, but in subsequent years, as the citizenry of the country became more racially diverse and racial groups obtained more political power, its effect were broadened to include other racialized groups including Native Americans, Asian Americans, Spanish-speaking populations, and Alaskan Natives. The document is a living entity. Provisions to it have been added and renewed since its initial passage, most recently in 2006.

AN ACT To enforce the fifteenth amendment to the Constitution of the United States, and for other purposes.

Be it enacted by the Senate and House of Representatives of the United States of America in Congress assembled, That this Act shall be known as the "Voting Rights Act of 1965."

SEC. 2. No voting qualification or prerequisite to voting, or standard, practice, or procedure shall be imposed or applied by any State or political subdivision to deny or abridge the right of any citizen of the United States to vote on account of race or color.

SEC. 4. (a) To assure that the right of citizens of the United States to vote is not denied or abridged on account of race or color, no citizen shall be denied the right to vote in any Federal, State, or local election because of his failure to comply with any test or device in any State with respect to which the determinations have been made under subsection (b) or in any political subdivision with respect to which such determinations have been made as a separate unit, unless the United States District Court for the District of Columbia in an action for a declaratory judgment brought by such State or subdivision against the United States has determined that no such test or device has been used during the five years preceding the filing of the action for the purpose or with the effect of denying or abridging the right to vote on account of race or color: Provided, That no such declaratory judgment shall issue with respect to any plaintiff for a period of five years after the entry of a final judgment of any court of the United States, other than the denial of a declaratory judgment under this section, whether entered prior to or after the enactment of this Act, determining that denials or abridgments of the right to vote on account of race or color through the use of such tests or devices have occurred anywhere in the territory of such plaintiff. An action pursuant to this subsection shall be heard and determined by a court of three judges in accordance with the provisions of section 2284 of title 28 of the United States Code and any appeal shall lie to the Supreme Court. The court shall retain jurisdiction of any action pursuant to this subsection for five years after judgment and shall reopen the action upon motion of the Attorney General alleging that a test or device has been used for the purpose or with the effect of denying or abridging the right to vote on account of race or color.

(c) The phrase "test or device" shall mean any requirement that a person as a prerequisite for voting or registration for voting (1) demonstrate the ability to read, write, understand, or interpret any matter, (2) demonstrate any educational achievement or his knowledge of any particular subject, (3) possess good moral character, or (4) prove his qualifications by the voucher of registered voters or members of any other class.

(e)(1) Congress hereby declares that to secure the rights under the fourteenth amendment of persons educated in American-flag schools in which the predominant classroom language was other than English, it is necessary to prohibit the States from conditioning the right to vote of such persons on ability to read, write, understand, or interpret any matter in the English language.(2) No person who demonstrates that he has successfully completed the sixth primary grade in a public school in, or a private school accredited by, any State or territory, the District of Columbia, or the Commonwealth of Puerto Rico in which the predominant classroom language was other than English, shall be denied the right to vote in any Federal, State, or local election because of his inability to read, write, understand, or interpret any matter in the English language, except that, in States in which State law provides that a different level of education is presumptive of literacy, he shall demonstrate that he has successfully completed an equivalent level of education in a public school in, or a private school accredited by, any State or territory, the District of Columbia, or the Commonwealth of Puerto Rico in which the predominant classroom language was other than English.

SEC. 10. (a) The Congress finds that the requirement of the payment of a poll tax as a precondition to voting (i) precludes persons of limited means from voting or imposes unreasonable financial hardship upon such persons as a precondition to their exercise of the franchise, (ii) does not bear a reasonable relationship to any legitimate State interest in the conduct of elections, and (iii) in some areas has the purpose or effect of denying persons the right to vote because of race or color. Upon the basis of these findings, Congress declares that the constitutional right of citizens to vote is denied or abridged in some areas by the requirement of the payment of a poll tax as a precondition to voting.

(b) In the exercise of the powers of Congress under section 5 of the fourteenth amendment and section 2 of the fifteenth amendment, the Attorney General is authorized and directed to institute forthwith in the name of the United States such actions, including actions against States or political subdivisions, for declaratory judgment or injunctive relief against the enforcement of any requirement of the payment of a poll tax as a precondition to voting, or substitute therefore enacted after November 1, 1964, as will be necessary to implement the declaration of subsection (a) and the purposes of this section.

SEC. 11. (a) No person acting under color of law shall fail or refuse to permit any person to vote who is entitled to vote under any provision of this Act or is otherwise qualified to vote, or willfully fail or refuse to tabulate, count, and report such person's vote.

(b) No person, whether acting under color of law or otherwise, shall intimidate, threaten, or coerce, or attempt to intimidate, threaten, or coerce any person for voting or attempting to vote, or intimidate, threaten, or coerce, or attempt to intimidate, threaten, or coerce any person for urging or aiding any person to vote or attempt to vote, or intimidate, threaten, or coerce any person for exercising any powers or duties under section 3(a), 6, 8, 9, 10, or 12(e).

SEC. 12. (a) Whoever shall deprive or attempt to deprive any person of any right secured by section 2, 3, 4, 5, 7, or 10 or shall violate section 11(a) or (b), shall be fined not more than $5,000, or imprisoned not more than five years, or both.

(b) Whoever, within a year following an election in a political subdivision in which an examiner has been appointed (1) destroys, defaces, mutilates, or otherwise alters the marking of a paper ballot which has been cast in such election, or (2) alters any official record of voting in such election tabulated from a voting machine or otherwise, shall be fined not more than $5,000, or imprisoned not more than five years, or both

(c) Whoever conspires to violate the provisions of subsection (a) or (b) of this section, or interferes with any right secured by section 2, 3 4, 5, 7, 10, or 11(a) or (b) shall be fined not more than $5,000, or imprisoned not more than five years, or both.

SEC. 14. (a) All cases of criminal contempt arising under the provisions of this Act shall be governed by section 151 of the Civil Rights Act of 1957 (42 U.S.C.1995).

(c)(1) The terms "vote" or "voting" shall include all action necessary to make a vote effective in any primary, special, or general election, including, but not limited to, registration, listing pursuant to this Act, or other action required by law prerequisite to voting, casting a ballot, and having such ballot counted properly and included in the appropriate totals of votes cast with respect to candidates for public or party office and propositions for which votes are received in an election.(2) The term "political subdivision" shall mean any county or parish, except that, where registration for voting is not conducted under the supervision of a county or parish, the term shall include any other subdivision of a State which conducts registration for voting.

SEC. 17. Nothing in this Act shall be construed to deny, impair, or otherwise adversely affect the right to vote of any person registered to vote under the law of any State or political subdivision.

Approved August 6, 1965.

Source: An act to enforce the fifteenth amendment to the Constitution of the United States and for other purposes, August 6, 1965; Enrolled Acts and Resolutions of Congress, 1789–; General Records of the United States Government; Record Group 11; National Archives.

COMMUNITY ON THE MOVE FOR EQUALITY, *HAVE SANITATION WORKERS A FUTURE?* SPRING 1968

The flier below was created by the Community On the Move for Equality (COME) in support of striking black sanitation workers in Memphis, Tennessee. Throughout the late winter and spring of 1968, black Memphis workers and residents staged a series of demonstrations and boycotts in the city to voice their concern about continued unequal treatment meted out by the city and to attempt to have a local black union of sanitation workers recognized. The organizations brought the Southern Christian Leadership Conference to the city to help it bring about racial justice and highlight discriminatory work conditions in city employment. By 1968, Civil Rights Movement organizations like SCLC, who had started its Poor People's Campaign, expanded their programs and concerns to include issues of discrimination in employment and poverty-related issues. The flier details movement strategies, gives black city residents ways to participate, and attempts to build support for the strike. One of the most important tactics in movement peoples' arsenal was the boycott. It had been a peaceful weapon for change since the early days of the 20th century and continued to be effective into the 1960s. During the Easter season of 1968, black Memphis residents participated in a boycott of downtown stores. Such a boycott, organizers planned, would undoubtedly hurt stores as that holiday season was known to bring about a surge in shopping by blacks and whites in the city. While all of the ten points are interesting, perhaps the most intriguing

Have Sanitation Workers A Future?

Yes, If You Will Help To Build It!

How? That's Simple—

WE NEED YOU!

1. Do not shop downtown, or with the downtown branch stores anywhere in the city or any enterprise named Loeb.

2. Stop your subscriptions to the daily newspapers. Get news about the Movement from the radio or television or by joining the mass meetings. Be sure to pay your newspaper carrier his commission.

3. Do not buy new things for Easter. Let our Lent be one of sacrifices. What better way to remember Jesus' work for us and the world?

4. Support the workers with letters and telegrams to the Mayor and the City Council.

5. Join us in the daily marches downtown.

6. Call others each day and remind them of the movement.

7. Attend the nightly mass meetings Monday through Friday.

8. Do not place your garbage at the curb. Handle it the best way you can without helping the city and the Mayor's effort to break the strike.

9. Whenever you associate with white people, let them know what the issues are and why you support this cause.

10. Support the relief efforts for the workers and their families with gifts of money and food. Checks can be made out to "C.O.M.E." and food taken to Clayborn Temple A.M.E. Church, 280 Hernando.

- -

Community On the Move for Equality
WORK CARD

Name _____ Phone _____
Address_____
I will march _____ I will picket _____
I can answer phone or do clerical work _____
I can serve on a committee:
      Work Committee   _____
      Telephone Committee   _____
      Transportation Committee   _____
Hours I can best serve:
  9:00am-11:00am_____   11:00am- 1:00pm_____
  1:00pm- 3:00pm_____   3:00pm- 6:00pm_____
  6:00pm- 8:00pm_____   8:00pn-10:00pm_____
  10:00pm-12:00pm_____

Signature _____

Have Sanitation Workers a Future?

is point number nine, where the organizers tell community members to tell white Memphis residents what the issues are and that they support the cause. Such a statement demonstrates that segregation policies in the city did not create situations wherein white and blacks had no interaction. In fact, the opposite was true, blacks and whites had a host of daily interactions and segregation policies were geared to monitor and limit these interactions. Point number nine also shows a new sense of empowerment by black activists. They may have discussed their grievances and strategized next steps in the frequent mass meets to which point number seven alludes, but now they were emboldened to discuss their issues in front of and even with white residents. It was in Memphis at the Lorraine Hotel that Martin Luther King Jr. was assassinated on May 4, 1968. After King's assassination, the Johnson Administration intervened into the sanitation worker-city dispute and the city met African Americans' demands.

Citation: Exhibit 2 in City of Memphis vs. Martin Luther King Jr *1968–1968;* City of Memphis vs. Martin Luther King Jr. et al., Civil C-68–80, *1968–1968;* Civil Cases, *compiled 01/ 1965–12/1975;* Records of District Courts of the United States, *1685–2004;* NARA's Southeast Region (Atlanta) (NRCA), 5780 Jonesboro Road, Morrow, GA, 30260 [online version available through the Archival Research Catalog (ARC Identifier 279326) at www.archives.gov, January 4, 2012].

Glossary

Black Nationalism: At its most basic definition, black nationalism is the belief that African Americans have a common history of racial oppression, language, and culture that make them a distinct ethnic, cultural, and political group or nation. As such, they have a right to political self-determination. The political aspirations of black nationalists vary. Separatists argue that black people have no political future in the United States of America and should, consequently, create a separate territory within the geopolitical boundaries of the United States, create a separate nation-state outside of the country, or settle on the African continent. The Nation of Islam is an example of a separatist organization, while Marcus Garvey's Universal Negro Improvement Association of the 1920s is an example of an organization who wanted blacks to settle in Liberia, West Africa. Cultural nationalists, like Ron Karenga, suggested that blacks appropriate neo-traditional, African values and behaviors. Other nationalists, like Malcolm X and the Black Panther Party (during its earliest iteration), maintained that American political and social life segregated African Americans in all-black or predominantly black neighborhoods and communities. Since blacks were not likely to leave these neighborhoods and communities, they should control the political, educational, and economic tools of these areas. Some, but very few, black nationalists argued black superiority or the subjugation of white Americans.

Black Power: A term that gained popularity in the late 1960s, used to express African Americans' experimentation with democratic processes to bring about social, cultural, and political self-determination for the communities they lived in and served. At times, this experimentation involved community police patrol, electoral politics, creation of economic cooperatives, and the institutionalization of black studies curriculums on college and university campuses. Black Power also represented a general sentiment of African American pride in African American history and culture.

border states: Slave states which did not secede from the United States in the 1860s. By virtue of their location between the northern states and southern states, they have been deemed border states. In the late 19th century and early 20th century, these states including Delaware, Kentucky, Maryland, and Missouri enforced segregation laws. These states had and continue to have large African American populations. Consequently, the states were stages for civil rights and black power organizing.

de jure segregation: The term denotes the social, political, educational and economic separation of white and black Americans in southern states, as dictated by local, state, or federal law. De jure is Latin for "of the law." Such laws were commonly called Jim Crow Laws.

de facto segregation: De facto is a Latin term that means in reality. The term denotes the social, political, educational, and economic separation of white and black Americans by custom. Such separation is not mandated by law and was practiced and continues to be the reality of most whites and blacks throughout the United States. It emerges from a variety of factors, including housing patterns, social preferences, and bigotry.

disfranchisement: The policies and processes of legally and illegally depriving another citizen of the right to vote. During the early-to-mid 20th century, Africans Americans throughout the South and in some northern locations were prevented from voting by means of poll taxes, literacy tests, understanding clauses, and threats of violence.

Great Migration: The largest domestic migration of American citizens in U.S. history. The migration began in the second decade of the 20th century and did not end until the early 1970s. African Americans left the constant threat of legal and extra-legal violence, disfranchisement, segregated and inferior education, and codified segregation in search of economic and educational opportunities, political rights, and personal freedom. In the early decades of the migration, the majority of the migrants moved to Midwestern and northern cities, like Chicago, New York, Pittsburgh, and Philadelphia. During World War II, their destinations expanded to include locations farther west in California. Throughout the over-six-decade period, African Americans also moved from the Deep South to Upper South cities and locations in border states.

Liberationist Theology: A school of Christian theological thought whose proponents argue that God or the ultimate life force of the universe is concerned with the lives of oppressed people, has an intimate concern with those who suffer, and actively works in the daily lives of human creatures to effect positive social and political change and bring about social justice. Members of the Southern Christian Leadership Conference subscribed to this theology.

lynching: The extra legal killing of an American citizen. While most lynchings were carried out by a mob and resulted in hangings and or burnings, bombings and shootings performed or carried by a smaller group of people or by an individual can also be considered a lynching. Lynchings were attempts to maintain the racial order and segregation in the South. During the early 20th century, most victims of lynchings were African American men, though black women and men of other ethnic groups were victims.

restrictive covenants: Private agreements between whites that expressly excluded blacks from owning or occupying property in certain predominantly white locations.

Satyagraha: With reference to the Civil Rights Movement, "satyagraha" refers to nonviolent, direct political action. The idea originated with Mahatma Gandhi during India's fight against British imperialism on the Indian subcontinent. Its use against state-sanctioned segregation during the 1950s and the 1960s demonstrates that African American civil rights activists were open to a variety of political strategies in their attempts to achieve justice.

Sharecropping: An exploitative agricultural and economic system wherein one large cultivatable tract of cotton producing land is divided into smaller plots. Black and white landless families occupied the divided tracts and worked for the landlord for a share of the crop after the autumn harvest. The system was exploitative because many landlords kept families in debt and tied to the land by adding hidden costs to cotton production and refused families their fair share of the cotton profits at the end of the season.

South, the: States which had large slave populations and seceded from the United States in the 1860s. These include Alabama, Arkansas,

Florida, Georgia, Louisiana, Mississippi, North Carolina, South Carolina, Tennessee, Texas, and Virginia. In the late 19th and early 20th century, these states instituted segregation laws that separated white and black life. In the early 21st century, they continue to have large populations of African Americans.

Annotated Bibliography

Websites

Center for Documentary Studies, Behind the Veil Oral History Project, *Remembering Jim Crow*, http://americanradioworks.publicradio.org/features/remembering/index.html.

Remembering Jim Crow offers oral interviews with African Americans and white Americans to consider the rise of racial segregation commonly called Jim Crow. It also highlights African Americans' attempt to negotiate, circumvent, and resist the system during the early-to-mid 20th century. Students can download podcasts or listen to them through the website. The site also provides slide shows with black and white images from different geographic regions and decades and a one-hour documentary, *Radio Fights Jim Crow*, which aired on National Public Radio. Finally, it includes transcripts of the interviews, a bibliography of important historical works about Jim Crow, and links to websites in the field of African American history that include, but is not limited to, Jim Crow. The website has limited search capacity, but students interested in the subject will find browsing easy and accessible. It is a good place to begin one's search or enhance one's research about institutions, practices, and laws that the Civil Rights Movement attempted to change and eliminate.

The Center for National Archives Experience, Foundations for the National Archives, Second Story, *Docs Teach*, http://docsteach.org/documents.

Docs Teach houses thousands of digitized copies of primary documents in U.S. history from the founding of the Republic to the present. Researchers can browse or search for written documents, images, maps, charts, graphs, and audio and video materials. Items relevant to the Civil Rights Movement include, but are not limited to, fliers and handbills for key events, civil rights legislation, photographs, and videos. These materials are found in two sections on the site: Postwar United States, 1945–1968, and Contemporary United States,

1968-present. The search options only allows for basic searches and results are not organized chronologically within the section, but the site offers students of the movement valuable information about the people and events that made the movement successful.

The Civil Rights Digital Library, http://crdl.usg.edu/

The Civil Rights Digital Library is the result of collaboration between libraries, web gurus, archives, historians of the movement, government agencies, and book publishers. It is a clearinghouse for information, sources, and websites about the Civil Rights Movement and is one of the most comprehensive on the web. All aspects of the movement are covered and one has access to sources that include, but are not limited to, sound recordings, pamphlets, visual works, and government records from almost every state that had civil rights activity. When the actual historical artifact is not available, the site contains information on how to access it. Despite the large amount of sources, the site is easily navigated. Researchers can perform a basic or advanced search and browse by event, place, people, topics, archival and historical collections, and media types. The content of this site, however, depends on the maintenance of other sites and this is a major drawback. One obtains frequent error messages or blocked content when servers from outside sources are down, or the original link is changed.

Civil Rights Movement Veterans, crmvet.org/index.htm.

Civil Rights Movement Veterans examines the Civil Rights Movement from 1951 to 1968 from the viewpoint of lesser known but important civil rights activists. It is still growing as submissions continue to be posted on the website. At the time of this writing, the most salient features include a history and timeline of the movement in the South, photos, personal stories, and interview transcripts from those active in the movement during the 1950s and the 1960s. It also includes links to other reputable and not so reputable Civil Rights Movement websites and primary documents from the era. Two of the most astonishing parts of this website are the "Letters and Reports from the Field" and "Documents of the Southern Freedom Movement, 1951–1968." As the name suggests, "Letters and Reports from the Field" includes letters, memos, position papers, field reports, and diary entries written by civil rights workers. The Documents section includes copies of documents from a host of Civil Rights Movement groups including the Student Nonviolent Coordinating Committee, Southern Christian Leadership Conference, the National Association for the Advancement of Colored People, Mississippi Freedom Democratic Party, Congress of

Racial Equality, the Southern Student Organizing Committee, a predominantly white political organization, and several others. Researchers can even read monthly publications from several organizations to get a sense of how specific campaigns unfolded over time. Together, the website demonstrates the decentralized nature of the Civil Rights Movement across the country and the commitment of many people, young and old, in changing the status quo in race relations. In so doing, it compliments sites solely focused on the big names of the movement. The site is a bit cumbersome to navigate as it only has a simple search engine that only searches keyword phrases and it lacks the bells and whistles of other sites. However, if students take the time to peruse its many documents and stories, they will be rewarded with interesting primary documents and perspectives from movement participants in their own words.

The Martin Luther King, Jr., Research and Education Institute, http://mlk-kpp01.stanford.edu/index.php.

The website for the Martin Luther King, Jr. Research and Education Institute presents a well rounded presentation of the life and times of Martin Luther King Jr. It offers scholarly works written by the staff at the King Papers, information about scholarly works written about King by scholars across the world, and features primary source document information about major developments in the Civil Rights Movement. Two of the most important features on the site are a searchable online version of the *The Martin Luther King, Jr., Encyclopedia*, which features biographies of organizations, events, ideas, other key civil rights leaders, and the Online King Records Access Database, which provides access to materials written by King including letters, speeches, and sermons. Searches can be performed using author's name, dates, organizations, places and other search options.

National Association for the Advancement of Colored People, http://www.naacp.org.

The website for the National Association for the Advancement of Colored People is a good stop for those interested in researching the oldest civil rights organization in the country. By clicking on the "history" tab, students can access a clever and interactive timeline of the organization, from 1909 to 2010. It features the actor Laurence Fishburne, hundreds of biographies of famous African Americans, and information about other people of color, including Cesar Chavez, and white Americans who fought for the betterment of society and equal rights for all. A multimedia gallery highlights historical developments, interviews with movement people, and discussions by individuals whose lives have been affected by the NAACP's work. A photo gallery displays iconic images of the Civil Rights Movement to allow students a visual approach to understanding the life and times of the organization. The site also includes access to primary documents and links to the Smithsonian National Museum of American History. When one is finished considering the history of the organization, they may also peruse the organization's recent work and their continued effort at bringing about racial justice in the United States.

Documentaries

The Black Power Mixtape 1967–1975. **Directed by Göran Olsson. New York: Louverture Films, 2011. DVD.**

This 2011 documentary was filmed by Swedish reporters in the late 1960s to the mid-1970s and offers a discussion of the social, political, and cultural situations facing African Americans in urban areas. It provides first-hand details of events and interviews with individuals popular in the black power movement including Stokely Carmichael, Huey Newton, and Angela Davis. Commentary for the film is provided by scholars, activists who participated in contemporary events, and present-day cultural artists. The story is told in nine chapters, each corresponding to a year between 1967 and 1975. While all nine are interesting, several stand out as particularly important because of their length and content. 1967 follows Stokely Carmichael during his European tour in which he discussed the black freedom movement and searched for new strategies to confront racism. The chapter about 1968 details the growing anti-war sentiments of Martin Luther King Jr. and the subsequent urban violence following his assassination. 1969 features an expose about the Oakland-based Black Panther Party. Angela Davis' imprisonment and trial for murder is discussed in the chapter about 1972. 1974 features a young Louis Farrakhan, who was then the minister at Temple No. 7 in Harlem, New York, and the national spokesperson for the Nation of Islam. With rare footage, the 90-minute documentary reveals a side of the black freedom struggle often ignored and argues that the political gains of the 1960s did not immediately bring about a change in the lives of everyday black Americans in the nation's cities.

Eyes on the Prize. **Directed by James DeVinney and Orlando Bagwell. Boston: Blackside Production Inc with WGBH, 1987. DVD.**

The *Eyes on the Prize* series, produced by Blackside, has been and continues to be the quintessential audio-visual narrative source for those interested in the Civil Rights Movement. It has won numerous awards including six Emmys and the George Foster Peabody Award. The series contains 12 episodes that document the movement from 1954 to 1985 and shows the economic, political, social, and cultural aspects of the era. Well known and lesser known aspects and individuals of the movement are included and *Eyes on the Prize* does a marvelous job of fitting local political activities into a larger political movement. For years, the series was only available in VHS format, but it has recently become available in DVD format (and more affordable) for institutions and individuals interested in purchasing it.

FBI's War on Black America. Directed by Denis Mueller and Deb Ellis. Maljack Productions, 1989. DVD.

This 1989 documentary examines the Counter Intelligence Program of the Federal Bureau of Investigation in the 1960s and 1970s. It contains fascinating video footage and interviews with important historical figures. It argues, which has since been proven by government documents, that the federal government knowingly had an unconstitutional and unwarranted program against black and white progressive and radical organizations, which led to organizational dissolution and fragmentation. Black historical figures are featured including Kathleen Cleaver and Fred Hampton of the Black Panther Party, Malcolm X, Martin Luther King Jr., Geronimo Pratt, and Stokely Carmichael. The documentary re-imagines and historicizes the Black Panther Party and rethinks the organization's position as an important political organization. The documentary is not particularly cinematographically pleasing, but it is informative.

The Murder of Emmett Till. Directed by Stanley Nelson. Boston: WGBH, 2003. DVD.

The Murder of Emmett Till features family members' accounts and archival footage to tell the story of the lynching of Emmett Till, a 14-year-old teenager from Chicago, Illinois, who was murdered in Money, Mississippi, in August 1955. Like scores of other black Americans, he was murdered for crossing the southern color line. J.W. Milam and Roy Bryant, two Mississippi residents, beat and killed Till in August 1955. For many, Till's death was the motivating factor for their participation in the Civil Rights Movement of the late 1950s and the early 1960s.

Roads to Memphis. Directed by Stephen Ives. Boston: WGBH, 2010. DVD.

The documentary tells the story of the 15 months leading to the arrest of James Earl Ray for the murder of Martin Luther King Jr. on May 4, 1968. Audio-visual footage of King's last year is presented and the viewer gets a cursory sense of his attempts to broaden his political position to include anti-Vietnam War stances and anti-poverty issues, especially with the Southern Christian Leadership Conference's Poor People's Campaign. The film also includes substantial portions of King's final sermon delivered on May 3, 1968 and first-hand, eye-witness accounts from those closest to King. A large portion of the work is dramatization and a speculative recreation of Ray's planning of the murder. It makes the case that Ray was a part of a white rightwing, anti-King culture, which included segregationists, members of the Ku Klux Klan, Alabama Governor and presidential candidate George Wallace, and J. Edgar Hoover of the Federal Bureau of Investigation. The film concludes, however, that Ray was a sociopathic criminal who acted alone to murder King in hopes of gaining fame. Despite claims of innocence after initially pleading guilty, Ray died in prison in April 1998.

Scandalize My Name: Stories from the Blacklist. Directed by Alexandra Isles. New York: Urban Works, 1998. DVD.

Scandalize My Name examines black performing artists of the late 1940s and early 1950s who suffered repression and blacklisting for fighting to improve the opportunities and life chances of African Americans during the early years of the Cold War. This documentary demonstrates the connections between black cultural and performing artists and black activism. It also shows that African Americans' quest for equal opportunity predated what is commonly called the Civil Rights Movement. Rosetta Lenoir, Dick Campbell, Ossie Davis, and Harry Belafonte are prominently featured as participants and victims of the mid-20th century Red Scare. Paul Robeson's roll as a mentor to black actors/activists is also discussed as well as that of Dick Campbell, the prominent black actor, director, and activist. The documentary is particularly important as it shows how black activists had international sensibilities that were hamstrung by federal government intervention. It was this intervention and limitations that would determine the political and domestic restraints of the Civil Rights Movement and led the way for Martin Luther King Jr.

Soundtrack for a Revolution. Directed by Bill Guttentag and Dan Sturman. New York: Louverture Films, 2009. DVD.

Soundtrack for a Revolution features video footage, interviews, commentary, and testimony by well known and lesser known activists in the Civil Rights Movement as well as songs of freedom from the movement performed by popular soul, gospel, hip-hop, and folk singers of the early 21st century. The basic premise of the documentary is that music, in the form of songs based on old

Negro spirituals, was integral to the movement. These songs nourished weary souls during protests, reinforced a commitment to struggle, provided hope for change, and instilled courage in movement people. The documentary provides a summary, albeit a short one, of the major campaigns of the movement, including the Montgomery Bus Boycott, the Sit-in Movement, Freedom Rides, the Children's Crusade of the Birmingham, Alabama, movement, the March on Washington, the 1964 Freedom Summer, Bloody Sunday and the March from Selma to Montgomery, the Selma Campaign, and the 1968 Sanitation Workers Strike of the spring of 1968. The documentary is entertaining, educational, and soul-stirring. The images and video footage, combined with song, gives the viewer an exhilarating visual and aural understanding of what the movement meant to those who participated in it. Freedom songs in the video include, but are not limited to: *Ain't Gonna Let Nobody Turn Me 'Round, Eye on the Prize, We Shall Not Be Moved, Let the Circle Be Unbroken,* and *Wade in the Water.*

Books

Branch, Taylor. *Parting the Waters: America in the King Years, 1954–1963.* New York: Simon and Schuster, 1989; *Pillar of Fire: America in the King Years, 1963–65.* New York: Simon and Schuster, 1999; *At Canaan's Edge: America in the King Years, 1965–1968.* New York: Simon and Schuster, 2006.

Branch's trilogy offers a well researched and deftly written biography of Martin Luther King Jr. from his political beginnings during the Montgomery Bus Boycott to his assassination. The books' comprehensive nature also introduces readers to other civil rights leaders and groups. Together, the trilogy is over 3,000 pages in length. Unless one is writing solely about King, the indices of the books are helpful to pinpoint particular political, campaigns, individuals, and organizations.

Carson, Clayborne, David Garrow, Gerald Gill, Vincent Harding, Darlene Clarke Hine, eds., *Eyes on the Prize Reader: Documents, Speeches, and Firsthand Accounts from the Black Freedom Struggle.* New York: Penguin Books, 1991.

The edited collection contains primary source material for students and is a textual companion to the *Eyes on the Prize* documentary produced by Blackside Productions, Inc. The book is organized chronologically and each of the 14 chapters opens with an introduction by one of the general editors and noted historians, which paints a picture of the larger setting for the documents. The sources demonstrate the breadth and depth of the Civil Rights Movement, the variety of political strategies and types of activism employed to force political change, and the large number of people who participated across the country.

Crawford, Vicki L., Rouse, Jacqueline Ann, Woods, Barbara, eds. *Women in the Civil Rights Movement: Trailblazers and Torchbearers, 1941–1965.* **Bloomington: Indiana University Press, 1993.**

This edited collection contains 17 essays that highlight the roles that women played in the Civil Rights Movement. Well known and lesser known women are discussed including, but not limited to, Septima Clarke, Modjeska Simkins, and Gloria Richardson. Together, the essays argue that even though African American men were spokespersons for political organizations, received the majority of media attention during the 1950s and 1960s, and have been the subjects of historical works about the Civil Rights Movement, black women played major roles as leaders of local political groups and held key positions in national organizations like the National Association for the Advancement of Colored People and the Student Nonviolent Coordinating Committee. *Women in the Civil Rights Movement* corrects historical narratives that have ignored women's political participation and compliments studies that examine issues of race, class, and gender within African American communities.

Early, Gerald L. *This is Where I Came In: Black American in the 1960s.* Lincoln, Nebraska: University of Nebraska Press, 2003.

Early provides a relatively short, but interesting book that discusses the connection between African American cultural production, sports, and African American political activity in the 1960s. The book is a compilation of three essays he delivered in 2000. In the first essay about Muhammad Ali, he places the heavyweight boxer at the intersection of national racial politics, the growth of the Nation of Islam, and politics and culture on the African continent. Ali, he argues, was much more than a boxer; instead, he was a Third World hero. The second essay discusses the life and contributions of Sammy Davis Jr. In it, Early shows Davis as a multitalented performer whose work fused politics and music and as someone who defied conventional roles for black celebrity. The third essay examines Cecil B. Moore, the head of the Philadelphia, Pennsylvania, chapter of the National Association for the Advancement of Colored People in the mid-to-late 1960s. It shows that Philadelphia had a Civil Rights Movement and Moore was at the forefront of it as a political strategist. Moore successfully challenged institutional racism in city government, organized a grassroots effort to integrate Girard College, an all-white school in a predominantly black section of Philadelphia, and protested the racist tradition of whites parading in black-face during the traditional New Year's Day Mummer's Parade.

Higginbotham, Evelyn Brooks, Leon Litwack, Darlene Clark Hine, Randall Burkett. *The Harvard Guide to African-American History.* **Cambridge, MA: Harvard University Press, 2001.**

Higginbotham et al. have produced a comprehensive bibliography of African American historical scholarship published before the year 2000. For those interested in the Civil Rights Movement, chapter 23, edited by historian Clayborne Carson, will be of particular interest. The chapter presents bibliographic information for books discussing black and white race relations, black and ethnic relations, segregation, civil rights activities, and the black power movement. The *Guide* is essential for those interested in any aspect of African American history. It also comes with a searchable disc to assist with research.

Joseph, Peniel. *Neighborhood Rebels: Black Power at the Local Level.* **New York: Palgrave MacMillan, 2010.**

Peniel Joseph has assembled 10 different articles written by scholars in the emerging field of Black Power Studies. The primary argument of the work, like his *Waiting 'til the Midnight Hour*, is that the black power movement paralleled the Civil Rights Movement. Black power is defined as political attempts by African Americans to achieve "radical self determination" (11) in urban areas throughout the United States. Essays address political activities in St. Louis, Missouri; Harlem, New York; Milwaukee, Wisconsin; Oakland and Los Angeles, California; Louisville, Kentucky; Atlanta, Georgia; New Orleans, Louisiana; and Baltimore, Maryland, to demonstrate that black power politics responded to local political, economic, and cultural realities. The book is useful in expanding one's understanding of different aspects of the movement.

Joseph, Peniel. *Waiting 'til the Midnight Hour: A Narrative History of Black Power in America.* **New York: Henry Holt and Company, 2006.**

Joseph provides a narrative synthesis of the black power movement and argues that it paralleled the Civil Rights Movement. Malcolm X, Stokely Carmichael, and the Black Panther Party are prominently featured in the work. The work shows that African Americans' quest for political and economic equality was not limited to the southern states. He shows how northern and urban political hierarchies and constraints shaped blacks' opportunities and strategies to effect political change. The work is well researched and well written and offers student researchers insights into another side of the freedom struggle. Students should consult the bibliography section for further readings and sources.

Kelley, Robin D.G. *Freedom Dreams: The Black Radical Imagination.* Boston: Beacon Press, 2002.

Kelley examines African Americans' political struggles in the 20th century. He argues that African American have and continue to dream of being free. In using the word "dream," he leads the reader to consider and rethink their own ideas about the ubiquitous and often unrealized American Dream. Black people's freedom dreams, he asserts, have not always coincided with the dreams of politicians and corporations. Instead, their dreams had and have a variety of forms and led to political activity that challenged racism, classism, nationalism, militarism, and sexism. The work is skillfully written and ties together threads of conventional civil rights scholarship and that of more militant, forgotten, and obscured movements like the black feminist movement and the movement to obtain economic reparations from the United States.

Marable, Manning. *Malcolm X: A Life of Reinvention.* New York: Penguin Group, 2011.

Marable examines the life of Malcolm X from his childhood to his assassination in 1965 and argues that Malcolm X's life was a series of personal transformations and reinventions. Unlike other biographies of the slain black Muslim and black nationalist, Marable moves beyond a surface reading of speeches and Malcolm X's *Autobiography* and does not paint the Nation of Islam as a curious group. Instead, he offers a depth and breadth of analysis and consults a variety of sources to offer a complicated narrative about Malcolm X's personal and political life. Readers should consult the notes section of the book as it offers important bibliographic and archival material.

Marable, Manning and Kai Hinton, *The New Black History: Revisiting the Second Reconstruction.* New York: Palgrave MacMillan, 2011.

Marable and Hinton provide 16 cutting-edge essays by historians of the African American experience to reconceptualize the Civil Rights Movement. The title is a bit misleading. The histories presented are not new to those individuals and communities who lived them. They are, however, fresh perspectives on issues and events that shaped black political discontent in the mid-20th century.

Essays examine local, national, and international developments, political groups, and activists who made the movement dynamic. Together, they show that the black freedom struggle during the 1950s and the 1960s included both those who sought integration and used nonviolent direct action as well as those who used militant strategies and called for black power.

Marable, Manning. *Race, Reform, and Rebellion: The Second Reconstruction in Black America, 1945–1990.* **Jackson: University of Mississippi Press, 1991.**

Marable examines the causes, political activity, and consequences of the Civil Rights Movement from WWII to the end of the 20th century. Like the Reconstruction Era from 1865 to 1877, the Civil Rights Movement was an experiment in race relations and American democracy. As the first Reconstruction's goals were undermined and progressive attempts at integrating African Americans into the social, political, and economic fabric failed, Marable argues that the second Reconstruction's liberal and progressive policies failed to reach and improve the life chances of much of the African American population. Only a third, radical Reconstruction, he declares, can offer real economic and political empowerment to African Americans and other people of color. *Race, Reform, and Rebellion* does an excellent job of combining an examination of larger structural forces, like institutionalized racism, with political activity and social history to offer a nuanced narrative.

Martin Luther King Jr. *I Have A Dream: Writings and Speeches That Changed The World.* **Edited by James M. Washington. New York: Harper San Francisco, 1992.**

This edited collection contains 20 of the most important speeches and writings delivered and authored by Martin Luther King Jr. from 1956 to 1968. They demonstrate both King's widening political views and his commitment to the most marginalized segments of American society. Some of his more famous speeches like the August 1963 "I Have a Dream" are included, along with others that may not be familiar to students, like the 1963 eulogy for four African American girls who died in a Birmingham church bombing and his 1967 "A Time to Break Silence" speech in which he publicly opposed the Vietnam War and links militarism with racism and poverty on the domestic front. The work also includes a preface by Coretta Scott King, the slain leader's wife, as well as an informative introduction to the book about the life and contributions of King written by James M. Washington. The book is an important one as it helps students frame King's political discourse.

Malcolm X (as told to Alex Haley). *Autobiography of Malcolm X.* **New York: Ballantine Books, 1992.**

The *Autobiography of Malcolm X* stands as one of the most read books about civil rights leaders and any student writing about the Civil Rights Movement must consider it in their research. The book documents the life of Malcolm X from his childhood to his life as a Muslim minister with the Nation of Islam, and then later as the leader of Muslim Mosque, Inc., the religious organization he founded after his departure from the Nation of Islam. In it, Malcolm X emerges as the voice for the voiceless of black urban residents who wanted changes in their life situation, similar to African Americans in the American South.

Malcolm X, *Speeches at Harvard.* **Edited by Archie Shepp. New York: Paragon Books, 1991.**

The book is divided into two parts. Part One, "The Paradoxes of Malcolm X," provides an interesting and informative discussion of the life, historical parallels, and social and political contexts that informed Malcolm X as an African American, Black Muslim, and political theorist. The second part of the book, "The Harvard Speeches," includes several speeches Malcolm X delivered at Harvard University. It includes his addresses at the Harvard Law School on March 24, 1961 and December 16, 1964. It also includes the "The Leverett House Forum of March 18, 1964." The speeches lift Malcolm X from his station as a rabble rousing black nationalist (as he was often considered) to the realm of a legitimate political theorist. The three speeches are also important as they show his growth from an adherent of Elijah Muhammad to an independent, religious leader, and civil rights leader.

Sitkoff, Harvard. *The Struggle for Black Equality, 1954–1980.* **New York: Hill and Wang, 1993.**

Sitkoff provides a meaningful and informative introduction to the Civil Rights Movement. He does not provide a finer level of detail like other books on the subject; rather, he uses broad historical strokes to introduce the reader to major political campaigns and movement people. The most important feature of the book is the 13-page bibliographic essay, which provides a discussion of the historical scholarship of the movement that may be of use to researchers. *The Struggle for Black Equality* is an excellent supplemental text for students interested in filling in the historical gaps in their research.

Von Eschen, Penny M. *Race against Empire: Black Americans and Anticolonialism, 1937–1957.* **Ithaca, New York: Cornell University Press, 1997.**

Von Eschen argues that the stage of the black freedom struggle that immediately preceded the Civil Rights Movement was marked by an internationalist anti-colonial discourse. This discourse linked African Americans struggles within the United States with the struggles of African nations and people of African descent throughout the world. The global perspective, however, was challenged by Cold War ideologies within the federal government and anticommunist sentiments throughout the nation. These challenges, in turn, determined the character of the Civil Rights Movement and led movement leaders to recast the black freedom struggle in domestic terms and define racism as not one rooted in American and western slavery and economic systems, but as an American anomaly. Von Eschen's work is dense, and students should take time to read and ponder her ideas. *Race Against Empire* is a needed revision and chronologic re-envisioning of how and why African Americans organized themselves politically.

West, Thomas and James Mooney. *To Redeem a Nation: A History and Anthology of the Civil Rights Movement.* **St. James, New York: Brandywine Press, 1993.**

West and Mooney offer a compilation of primary source materials from the Civil Rights Movement era. The book is thematically organized into five chapters and address different facets of the movement. Part One, "Precursors," offers documents from the early days of Reconstruction to the 1920s. Part Two, "Integration," contains documents that show how movement thinkers understood, organized around, and espoused integration, especially throughout the South. Part Three, "Nonviolence," features material discussing how nonviolent direct action was used as a political strategy. "Liberals," chapter four of the book, gives voice to white participants in the movement and highlights that the Civil Rights Movement was, indeed, an interracial one. The last chapter, "Power," contains documents related to the black power movement. A range of voices and perspectives are found in the book and include names students may be familiar with and some they may not.

Index

About the Author

JAMIE J. WILSON is an Associate Professor of Modern United States and African American History at Salem State University in Salem, Massachusetts. His work has appeared in *The History Teacher, International Social Science Review, African Americans in New York Life and History, The Western Journal of Black Studies*, and *The Journal of African American History*. He is also the author of *Building a Healthy Black Harlem: Health Politics in Harlem, New York, from the Jazz Age to the Great Depression*. Wilson holds a doctorate from New York University.